SAGE was founded in 1965 by Sara Miller McCune to support the dissemination of usable knowledge by publishing innovative and high-quality research and teaching content. Today, we publish more than 750 journals, including those of more than 300 learned societies, more than 800 new books per year, and a growing range of library products including archives, data, case studies, reports, conference highlights, and video. SAGE remains majority-owned by our founder, and on her passing will become owned by a charitable trust that secures our continued independence.

Los Angeles | London | Washington DC | New Delhi | Singapore

Diversity, Special Needs and Inclusion in Early Years Education

Diversity, Special Needs and Inclusion in Early Years Education

Edited by
Sophia Dimitriadi

SAGE   www.sagepublications.com
Los Angeles • London • New Delhi • Singapore • Washington DC

First published in 2015 by

 SAGE Publications India Pvt Ltd
B1/I-1 Mohan Cooperative Industrial Area
Mathura Road, New Delhi 110 044, India
www.sagepub.in

SAGE Publications Inc
2455 Teller Road
Thousand Oaks, California 91320, USA

SAGE Publications Ltd
1 Oliver's Yard, 55 City Road
London EC1Y 1SP, United Kingdom

SAGE Publications Asia-Pacific Pte Ltd
3 Church Street
#10-04 Samsung Hub
Singapore 049483

Published by Vivek Mehra for SAGE Publications India Pvt Ltd, Phototypeset in 10/13 pts Times New Roman by RECTO Graphics, Delhi, and printed at Chaman Enterprises, New Delhi.

Library of Congress Cataloging-in-Publication Data Available

ISBN: 978-93-515-0029-2 (HB)

The SAGE Team: Supriya Das, Vandana Gupta, Rajib Chatterjee and Rajinder Kaur

To Sotiris,
for his constant support and encouragement ....

To my children, Jason and Kimon,
for their patience and understanding ....

Thank you for choosing a SAGE product! If you have any comment, observation or feedback, I would like to personally hear from you. Please write to me at <u>contactceo@sagepub.in</u>

—Vivek Mehra, Managing Director and CEO,
SAGE Publications India Pvt Ltd, New Delhi

Bulk Sales

SAGE India offers special discounts for purchase of books in bulk. We also make available special imprints and excerpts from our books on demand.

For orders and enquiries, write to us at

Marketing Department
SAGE Publications India Pvt Ltd
B1/I-1, Mohan Cooperative Industrial Area
Mathura Road, Post Bag 7
New Delhi 110044, India
E-mail us at <u>marketing@sagepub.in</u>

Get to know more about SAGE, be invited to SAGE events, get on our mailing list. Write today to <u>marketing@sagepub.in</u>

This book is also available as an e-book.

Contents

List of Abbreviations

A.B.C.	Anti-Bias Curriculum
ABI	Activity-based Instruction
ASD	Autism Spectrum Disorder
ATWS	All Third World Studies
CBA	Curriculum-based Assessment
CEC	Council for Exceptional Children
CECDE	Centre for Early Childhood Development and Education
CIE	Centre for the Educational Integration of Children and Students
CP	Community Practitioner
DCDD	Dutch Coalition on Disability and Development
DEC	Division of Early Childhood
DES	Department of Education and Science
DFA	Draft Framework for Action
DHC	Department of Health and Children
DIET	District Institutes of Education and Training
EBD	Emotional and Behaviour Disorder
ECCE	Early Childhood Care and Education
ECD	Early Childhood Development
ECE	Early Childhood Education
ECPRP	Early Childhood Policy Review Project
ECSE	Early Childhood Special Education
EGYMI	Egységes Gyógypedagógiai Módszertani Központ (Centre for a Single Methodology in Special Education)
EIT	Early Intervention Team
EPSEN	Education for Persons with Special Education Needs
EQI	Education Queensland International
ETA	Education and Training Act
EU	European Union

EYTARN	Early Years Trainers Anti-Racist Network
FETAC	Further Education and Training Awards Council
GDP	Gross Domestic Product
GERA	Global Education Research Association
GOI	Government of India
ICDS	Integrated Child Development Services
ICIDH	International Classification of Functioning, Disability and Health
ICT	Information and Communication Technology
IEDC	Integrated Education for the Disabled Children
IDP	Individual Development Plan
IEP	Individual Education Plan
IFSP	Individualised Family Services Plan
IGNOU	Indira Gandhi National Open University
KIM	Kenya Institute of Management
MCWL	My Child without Limits
MISC	Mediational Intervention for Sensitising Caregivers
MoCYS	Ministry of Children and Youth Services
MOEST	Ministry of Education Science and Technology
MoWCD	Ministry of Women and Child Development
MP	Metamorphosis Project
MUM	Multicultural Umbrella Model
NCCA	National Council for Curriculum and Assessment
NCERT	National Council of Educational Research and Training
NFQ	National Framework of Qualifications
NGO	Non-Governmental Organisation
NIMH	National Institute for the Mentally Handicapped
NPE	National Policy on Education
OECD	Organisation for Economic Cooperation and Development
OMI	Observing Mediational Interaction
PBS	Positive Behaviour Supports
PDCA	Plan–Do–Check–Act
PP	Private Practitioner
PPT	PowerPoint
PSNA	Preschool Special Needs Assistant
PWPBS	Programme-wide Positive Behaviour Support
SEN	Special Educational Needs

SES	Socioeconomic Status
SNA	Special Needs Assistants
SPSS	Statistical Package for Social Science
SSA	Sarva Shiksha Abhiyan
SQC	Student's Quality Circles
TQ	Total Quality
TQE	Total Quality in Education
TQP	Total Quality Person
UDL	Universal Design for Learning
UEE	Universalisation of Elementary Education
UN	United Nations
UNCRC	United Nations Convention on the Rights of the Child
UNESCO	United Nations Educational Scientific and Cultural Organisation
UNICEF	United Nations International Children's Emergency Fund
UNISA	University of Salerno
WCTQEE	World Council for Total Quality and Excellence in Education
WHO	World Health Organisation

Foreword

In this book, the authors discuss issues of diversity, inclusion and equality. They need to be congratulated because these issues are often swept under the carpet. To ensure that they are more widely addressed, I believe that an anti-discriminatory approach needs to be adopted. It is a professional requirement that includes identifying and breaking down barriers to participation, belonging and achievement. It is an approach embodied in the UN Convention on the Rights of the Child (1989) of which Article 29 is the most relevant. It states that the education of the child shall be directed to:

1. Giving the pupil the possibility to develop in his or her own way and according to his or her ability
2. Teaching respect for human rights and freedoms
3. Developing respect for the pupil's cultural identity, language and values and for cultures different from his or her own
4. Preparing the pupil for a responsible life as an adult in a free society in a spirit of understanding, peace, tolerance, equality of the sexes and friendship among all peoples

Article 24 of the UN Convention on the Rights of People with Disabilities (2006) requires countries to ensure that disabled children 'can access an inclusive, quality, primary and secondary education on an equal basis with others in the communities in which they live'.

We can make a difference to children's lives by:

1. Developing their ability to empathise, and empowering them so that they can stand up when they experience or witness discrimination.
2. Building on their understanding of fairness and unfairness so that they can appreciate that name calling, teasing, exclusion from play

and treating other people unfairly causes pain and unhappiness, just as hitting, kicking and other physical responses do.

3. Encouraging them to unlearn any prejudices and discriminatory behaviour they may have absorbed from the world around them, we can help them grow up to respect and accept people different from themselves.

A tall order but achievable if the curriculum is based on anti-discriminatory principles and implemented by sensitive, empathetic people.

According to an old Chinese proverb:

> People will forget what you said ...
> People will forget what you did ...
> But people will never forget how you made them feel.

The Shadow

A lonely shadow enters.
   He produces a ball.
   'Anyone want to play?'
   They turn away,
   He is different.
'My father told me to stay clear of them sort'
He moves towards the playground wall
He knows each red brick almost by name
The wall is his friend.
He scratches his curly black head
   'Go back to where you came from'
   The daily chant begins
   He closes his ears and moves on.

School finishes
At the back of the queue he stands
   desolate and alone

His expressionless face
disguises the day's deep damage like a veil.
He climbs the stairs to his humble flat,
 the lift is out of order
 He reaches for his key and enters
He greets his mother and his sister
 goes quickly to his room.
 He covers his black face with his hands
 and cries softly into the pillow
 that knows his tears so well.

—written anonymously by a 14-year-old

Children can become active, enthusiastic and independent learners if, as their educators, we value their cultures, personality and unique abilities and understand how social inequalities influence their lives, if we hold high expectations of all children, not limited by stereotyped views about class, cultural background, gender or special educational needs.

Babette Brown
Writer on race and diversity issues in the United Kingdom.
She has won the Guardian Jerwood Award for her work with Early
Years Trainers Anti-Racist Network in 1997. Since 2001 she
has been the Co-ordinator of the Charity, Persona Doll Training.

Preface

The inner need and passion for working towards quality and equality in education has always guided and influenced my choices. Constantly seeking contemporary developments and working on communicating them to the academic community as well as to all parties involved in an educational process (practitioners, parents, school management, policy makers, etc.) had become my prime concern and interest during my professional course of work. The idea of a book on diversity and inclusion in education was inspired when I was fortunate enough to meet people committed and dedicated to education, from almost all parts of the world.

The present book is the result of the joint forces of these people, experienced and renowned in their own fields of work. The diverse expertise backgrounds of the authors as well as the countries of origin and countries of work have been a strong asset to the present collection of chapters. As the book is concerned with inclusionary education, every author contribution to theories, issues, research projects, ideas and practices provides a strong insight into the way diversity and inclusion in education is perceived and worked on in different parts of the world.

We had a strong belief in our minds and hearts while creating this book, that diversity and inclusion are important issues which should be addressed in education and most importantly, in early years education. We feel that this is the key factor which makes this edited volume unique, and that is the emphasis on early childhood education. At the same time, we feel privileged that all the work collected for this book comes from countries that may differ in policies, practices, legislation and culture, yet it has a common goal: promoting respect for the individual.

The 10 chapters that constitute this book reflect issues, trends, experiences, theories, practices, processes and perspectives, as well as their interrelated nature that transcend regions and nations. It has been accomplished to gather work from countries across almost all continents:

India, Turkey, Greece, Hungary, Ireland, United States, Kenya and New Zealand. All 16 contributors involved in this project are experienced professionals and researchers, the majority of whom have spent years teaching in both schools and higher education. It has been an honour to work with these fine and respected people who have gained high levels of academic recognition in their fields of expertise. Admittedly, the attempt of working towards such an endeavour with people from different countries, cultures, languages, academic backgrounds and career paths, and with different personal schedules, timetables, even holiday vacation periods, has been a great challenge and a true example that diversity is a strength which offers rich opportunities to gain knowledge and broaden our spectrum.

Sophia Dimitriadi

Acknowledgements

I would like to express my sincere appreciation to all the authors involved in this book, for working with me and entrusting me with their work. I feel privileged that I had the opportunity to collaborate with so many fine academics and researchers from different parts of the world and learn from them. It has been an enjoyable and creative journey.

I would also like to express my gratitude to SAGE, our publisher, for believing in us and our work, as well as to the entire publishing team engaged in this project. My special thanks is due to our Associate Commissioning Editor Supriya Das and Associate Production Editor Vandana Gupta for being always responsive and deeply professional, thus enabling this book to come to fruition.

Thank you to all the people I have heard or read and who inspired me all these years. A big acknowledgement is also owed to the many students whom I have taught and learned from.

A special thanks to Babette Brown for being an inspiration to my work.

Finally, my deepest love and appreciation to my parents and my family for their moral support, encouragement and valuable comments and for sharing my ups and downs along this journey.

Sophia Dimitriadi

Introduction

Sophia Dimitriadi

Once you have a commitment to inclusiveness,
you'll simply find a way around barriers.

Kevin Taylor
Professor, Cal Poly (California)

How many more writings will be needed so that issues of diversity and inclusion are finally covered? One might think by holding this book.

Apparently, it can never be enough. As long as children and their families face inequality and exclusion and as long as important issues such as gaps in our knowledge are internationally identified, one can never claim that enough has been said. It seems that we need to break the barriers of our microcosm, widen our spectrum and eventually our perspective and enter into a more universal type of thinking and acting.

This edited volume is addressed to professionals and researchers in education, higher education students, policy makers, parents, school management and its staff or any other individual working on and interested in diversity and inclusion in education as well as in early childhood education in particular.

The vision while collecting material for this book was exactly the one aforesaid: to present the readers with seminal ideas, approaches and practices on inclusion that have been studied and implemented by expert researchers from diverse cultural backgrounds. The reader should expect to broaden perspective by acquainting oneself with the knowledge which emerges from different places of the world and which hopefully enables the exodus from one's microcosm.

It is a common truth, although not much realised, that our world has always been diverse. Therefore, diversity is not merely a phenomenon of our days. Yet, the transnational mobility of people has been constantly increasing over the last decades due to socio-economic, academic, professional, political or other reasons. The challenge of developing a better awareness and understanding of an individual's diversity, while—at the same time—working towards supporting and preserving one's own identity has nourished a novelty of ideas and facts to be explored and worked on. This fact is particularly evident in the field of education and especially in early childhood education where issues of children's diversity and their inclusion in the educational system have generated new points of concern and debate. Admittedly, one would easily assert that there is still a long way to go in many parts of the world, when it comes to valuing diversity and providing equal opportunities for all in education.

One good start would be for people to begin viewing diversity as a strength and a rich resource to support learning for all, rather than a problem to be overcome (Booth et al., 2000). But in order to do that, people need to first reconcile their own notions, biases, conflicts and failings (McCracken, 1993).

McNaughton (2006), in her *Respect for Diversity: An International Overview*, Working Paper 40, identifies four different types of diversity: 'cultural and racial diversity', 'developmental diversity', 'gender diversity' and 'socio-economic diversity'. At the same time, she describes five broad schools of thought that have provided the basic philosophy for the creation of educational policies and practices on valuing diversity among young children. These schools were identified as the 'laissez-faire school', the 'special provisions school', the 'cultural understandings school', the 'equal opportunities school' and the 'anti-discrimination school'. These reflections on diversity though, are only indicative of those many existing throughout the relevant international literature.

On developing a language for inclusion and inclusive education, Booth et al. (2000, p. 13) clearly point out that 'it is not another name for special needs education', whereas in a later version, Booth adds that 'it is an unending *process* of increasing learning and participation for all students. It is an ideal to which schools can aspire but which is never fully reached' (Booth & Ainscow, 2002, p. 3, emphasis in original).

Of course, inclusion in education is not a matter of location, as aptly pointed out, meaning that if children share the same space, they are not necessarily all included (Nutbrown, Clough & Atherton, 2013).

Many inclusive policies, approaches and projects can prove to be inadequate should there not be well-educated and trained teachers in the education of children that can positively utilise their knowledge and skills in order to achieve quality education—in other words, real inclusiveness. At the same time, all people in the environment of a child, as well as all ideas, beliefs, theories and practices that go on both inside and outside the school, have an important part to play in the inclusion process. Consequently, inclusionary education is inextricably connected with an inclusionary society. Undoubtedly, a society can only benefit from such a relation as, regardless of their differences, all its members' strengths, skills and talents are exploited and, as a result, progress is enabled (Thomas & Vaughan, 2004).

It is suggested that global outcomes in the education of young children 'can and are achieved by practices which are embedded in local cultures, values and ideals and, at the same time, informed by external influences' (Papatheodorou & Moyles, 2012, p. 5).

Having all the above in mind, this edited volume was created by bringing together a variety of texts that the editor hoped would trigger the readers' minds and excite their interest as to how diversity and inclusion in education is researched, viewed, approached, applied and dealt with in different parts of the world. Moreover, the editor's daily work in both higher education and early years services and schools had been constantly giving rich opportunities for thought, reflection and exploration of ideas and practices on inclusionary education, whether they are derived from the young children's in-service needs or the university student's intellectual searches and enquiries. These opportunities further stimulated the idea of creating this book.

At this point, it is appropriate to clearly outline the theoretical position and basic principles that have formed the basis of this book.

Thus, in the book that you now hold, we consider 'diversity' in education as the recognising and valuing difference in its broadest sense. At the same time, we advocate the creation of philosophy and practices that respect and embrace this diversity for the benefit of everyone involved in the educational process: children, practitioners, parents and other adults of the environment and wider community. As regards 'inclusion', we identify with the Early Childhood Forum (2003) position: 'Inclusion is a process of identifying, understanding and breaking down the barriers to participation and belonging'. Hence, the reader of this book will be able to find a variety of thematic chapters: some dealing with disability; others with special educational needs, language learning issues, personal, social, moral and emotional development within an inclusive framework; also, some with cultural and gender issues, and more.

We believe that inclusionary education goes hand in hand with quality education. Most importantly, we strongly support the idea of addressing issues of diversity and inclusion in education as early as possible. Early childhood, the period in the life of an individual that extends from birth to the age of eight years old, is the key period for working towards the valuation of diversity and the promotion of inclusion. Young children receive and absorb all messages around them and are affected by them even from infancy. It is important that the people who work with and teach young children are aware of this and adopt approaches and practices that enable children develop positive attitudes to differences. Being encouraged to see each other as special and appreciate the things about oneself that are similar to and different from others is the one big step towards quality education.

For these reasons, we consider early years education plays a fundamental role in valuing diversity and promoting inclusion for all, children and adults. People who work in early years education have the opportunity to help young children form positive self-concepts, develop critical thinking and enable them unlearn any unfair behaviour. On the other hand, all adults involved in early years education should be offered strategies and all necessary tools available in order for them to acknowledge their own beliefs and attitudes towards diversity and inclusion, and, consequently, adopt positive practices in their classroom that meet all children's needs. Considering that early years practitioners are preparing young children to live in tomorrow's society, it becomes evident how important their role is for better future citizenship.

This book presents case studies from various countries as well as theoretical frameworks, models, approaches and projects on diversity and inclusion in education. Each chapter of the book has its own, unique contribution to understanding aspects of inclusionary education at an international level of experience. Even though chapters may be read in any order the reader wishes to with the confidence that in every case a blend of information can be found while exploring them, the book has been thematically divided into sections for a better organisation of reading.

First, there is Section I which accommodates *research, studies* and *projects*.

The first chapter in Section I is titled 'Special Educational Needs and Early Childhood Practitioners in an Irish Context' and has been contributed by Mary Moloney and Eucharia McCarthy. This chapter looks at the concept of inclusion in ECE in Ireland by engaging with the experiences of children with SEN and early childhood practitioners in 14 early childhood settings during the implementation of a framework for action for the inclusion of children with SEN. It draws upon a national research study conducted by the authors to explore three interrelated concepts: early years practitioners' understanding and experience of inclusion, children with SEN experiences of Inclusion and the impact of a 'framework for action for the inclusion of children with SEN in early childhood settings' on inclusive practice.

The second chapter in the same section is titled 'Language Issues and Preschool Education in Kenya: A Reflection on Diversity, Challenges and Remedies', written by Mary Wangechi Kamunyu, and discusses the considerable achievements in ECD provisions in Kenya. It describes how ECD in Kenya concerns the holistic development of children between 0 and 5 years old and also explains how the current ETA in Kenya does not include ECD education and the problems arising due to the fact that many preschool teachers instruct young children in English which is not their first language. An important study is presented in this chapter which critically examines language issues and practices that affect the overall educational achievements of preschool in Kenya. The study has utilised a survey design in Narok North constituency of Narok County and the data of the study point out interesting issues for further consideration and action.

The final chapter of Section I (Chapter 3) is 'Training Innovative Preschool Students through an ICT Project: A Case Study from Turkey' by Hayal Köksal, and it describes in detail an international ICT project in Turkey. According to the author, the significance of the project which is entitled 'International ICT Seagulls Project©' lies in its age range. It is open to all age groups starting from kindergarten students and including undergraduates and graduates, and its aim is to train innovative, contemporary and qualified individuals. In the chapter, the main characteristics of the project are also explicitly outlined and the author explains how, through the project, awareness is created within the student–teacher circles (teams) concerning 'human dignity', 'cultural sensitivity' and 'tolerance' and the benefits that are there for all parties involved.

Section II follows with three more chapters, where *approaches* and *methods* are presented and explored.

The first chapter of the section (Chapter 4) is titled 'Inclusionary Education in Early Years through the Use of Persona Dolls: A Case from Greece' and has been written by Sophia Dimitriadi. In this chapter, the innovative Persona Dolls approach is presented, a powerful educational tool which embraces diversity and supports inclusion in the classroom. This child-friendly and non-threatening tool has successfully been used in the United States, the United Kingdom and other multicultural countries. A study is also presented, which is part of a longitudinal research of the author in Greek early years settings. The study described in the chapter involves the training of early years teachers on the use of Persona Dolls and the implementation of this approach in their early years classroom, as well as its outcomes.

Dorothy R. Howie in Chapter 5 and under the title 'Effective Pedagogy for Inclusive Education: The Role of Mediated Learning Experience' explores the importance of early mediation of learning by parents to their very young child, in a culturally appropriate way, as part of an effective pedagogy for diversity and inclusion. It outlines one internationally used approach to such mediation based on sound theoretical underpinnings, and discusses the wide-ranging research relating to the approach. The valuable information shared in this chapter significantly enriches the reader's knowledge on diversity and inclusion in early education.

Gülçin Alpöge in Chapter 6 titled 'Teaching Ethical Values to Preschool Children', the final chapter of Section II, describes a method of teaching values to preschool children. She explains why it is necessary to try to teach ethical values to young children at school and she also discusses the role of the home environment and how the limited time of parent–child engagement affects the process. The author has written a book in Turkish on teaching values to preschool children and identifies these values as universal: honesty, love, respect, responsibility, courage, fairness, friendship, goodness, peace and being able to make a choice. These values were chosen by a group of specialists on early childhood, considering the age of the children and the values most appropriate for them.

The next section is Section III which accommodates *educational frameworks, curricula* and *models*.

Agnes N. Toth in Chapter 7, 'Theory and Practice of Inclusive Education in Hungary', discusses the education system and its traditions in Hungary and gives a thorough description of inclusive education as well as teachers' attitudes towards inclusion in this country of Middle Eastern Europe. After the discussion of theoretical issues, a research follows, the objective of which is to verify whether mainstream teachers' attitudes towards inclusion have changed through the years: explore what they think of inclusion these days, find out what sorts of attitudes teachers have towards inclusion and whether these attitudes are positive or negative about integrative education in their school. The research sample is formed by 10 schools from three different counties of the Western Transdanubian Region in Hungary and the findings shared add valuable information to the reader.

The final chapter of Section III is Chapter 8, titled 'Multicultural Umbrella Model: Six Cs for Successful Integration' by Jean-Baptiste Quillien, Gabriela M. Theis and Veronica R. Quillien. It is the result of the authors' experience and discussions about diversity, cross-cultural boundaries and education. This chapter initially describes the MUM, an interdisciplinary model designed to help educators and policy makers implement efficient inclusion in the context of multicultural education. The purpose of this chapter is not to discuss the practices that are not working, but rather to illustrate with a case study—The Metamorphosis Project®—the application of a theoretical framework, the six Cs, in order to include diverse populations in education and, consequently, in society. The six Cs are: Communication, Cultures, Connections, Comparisons, Communities and, finally, Collaboration, a key element that the authors added in order to bring another dimension and refine the existing theoretical framework in terms of inclusion.

Lastly, there is Section IV which is thematically arranged on *literature review evidence* and *considerations* and accommodates two more chapters.

Amitav Mishra and Mousumi Bhaumik contributed the ninth chapter of the book, under the title 'Cross-Disability Approach to Inclusion of Children'. The chapter presents the Indian experience on early years education and inclusion and compares it with international developments. It identifies early childhood as a crucial phase of growth and development because experiences during this period can influence outcomes across the entire course of an individual's life. Important research studies are presented with the one related to the status of inclusion in early years education in India—and conducted by one of the authors—providing useful and important information for the international reader. Suggestions for promoting inclusion in early years education are discussed as well as adaptations in early years education curriculum. Finally, the importance of a cross disability approach to an inclusive early years education is highlighted and extensively analysed by the authors.

Last but not least is the chapter titled 'Young Children with Disabilities in India: Essential Competencies of Early Childhood Educators'. This is Chapter 10 of the book and is written by Ajay Das, Annamaria Jerome-Raja and Sushama Sharma. The chapter begins by providing some background information regarding the policy and programme initiatives of the GOI for the education of children with disabilities. The main focus of the chapter is the ECE teachers. An examination of their attitudes and its importance in the inclusion of children with disabilities is being conducted by way of the review of literature from both Indian as well as international literature. Finally, recommendations are being made regarding the skills and competencies that these ECE teachers need to possess in order to be successful in working with young children with special needs.

At the end of the book, the reader can find the conclusion offering a brief overview of the content of the book, highlighted ideas that formed the heart and soul of the chapters and some final thoughts for the future.

On behalf of the authors of this volume, we express our confidence that the audience of the book will be able to find a wealth of valuable information to add and reflect on its own knowledge. Finally, we wish and hope that this wonderful experience of ours involved in this project will be equally and productively shared with our readers.

References

Booth, T. & Ainscow, M. (2002). Index for inclusion: Developing learning and participation in schools. In M. Vaughan (Ed.), *CSIE and EENET*. Retrieved from http://www.csie.org.uk/resources/translations/IndexEnglish.pdf (accessed 8 August 2013).

Booth, T., Ainscow, M., Black-Hawkins, K., Vaughan, M. & Shaw, L. (2000). *Index for inclusion: Developing learning and participation in schools*. Bristol: Centre for Studies in Inclusive Education Ltd.

Early Childhood Forum. (2003). *Inclusion: Position statement.* Retrieved from http://www.ncb.org.uk/media/216977/ecf_inclusion_leaflet.pdf

McCracken, J. B. (1993). *Valuing diversity: The primary years*. Washington, D.C.: NAEYC.

McNaughton, G. M. (2006). *Respect for diversity: An international overview*. Working Paper No. 40. The Hague: Bernard Van Leer Foundation.

Nutbrown, C., Clough, P. & Atherton, F. (2013). *Inclusion in the early years* (2nd ed.). London: SAGE.

Papatheodorou, T. & Moyles, J. (Eds). (2012). *Cross-cultural perspectives on early childhood*. London: SAGE.

Thomas, G. & Vaughan, M. (2004). *Inclusive education: Readings and reflections*. G. Thomas & C. O'Hanlon (Series Eds). Maidenhead, Berkshire: Open University Press.

Section I
Research, Studies and Projects

1

Special Educational Needs and Early Childhood Practitioners in an Irish Context

Mary Moloney and Eucharia McCarthy

This chapter looks at the concept of inclusion in early childhood care and education (ECCE) in Ireland by engaging with the experiences of children with special educational needs (SEN) and early childhood practitioners[1] in 14 settings during the implementation of a draft framework for action (DFA) for the inclusion of children with SEN. It draws upon a national research study (Moloney & McCarthy, 2010) to explore three interrelated concepts:

1. Early years practitioners' understanding and experience of inclusion
2. Experiences of inclusion for children with SEN
3. The impact of a 'framework for action for the inclusion of children with SEN in early childhood settings' on inclusive practice

Drawing upon national and international policy, the chapter explores the historical trajectory towards inclusion in the Irish ECCE context. It discusses inclusion within the practice context and highlights the challenges

---

[1] In Ireland, staff working with children in ECCE settings are commonly referred to as practitioners.

and issues for parents, children and practitioners. The chapter then presents the findings from the implementation of a DFA for the inclusion of children with SEN in ECCE settings which was evaluated and piloted in 14 settings in Munster including County Clare, North Tipperary, County Kerry and Limerick City and County. It follows the stories of Sam (3½ years) and Matthew (2½ years) in particular and provides insight into the struggle for practitioners as they sought to develop inclusive practice and the transformation in their attitudes as the DFA was implemented.

According to the United Nations Educational Scientific and Cultural Organisation (UNESCO, 2005), inclusion is 'a dynamic approach of responding positively to pupil diversity and of seeing individual differences not as problems, but as opportunities for enriching learning' (p. 12). Thus, attitudes, values and expectations can be key factors in determining the child's level of participation within the setting. Consequently, the UNESCO (2005) definition, which portrays the child as rich in potential, calls upon practitioners to reflect upon their attitudes, values and expectations as well as their approach to working with and including children with SEN.

The ways in which parents, educators and the wider society work with and include children with SEN in individual contexts—home, preschool and school—are influenced by whether they see difference as problematic or opportunistic. This is particularly important during early childhood when children's experiences have a profound impact upon their development in later stages of life (Fox, Levitt, & Nelson, 2010; Shonkoff & Phillips, 2000). Indeed, the United Nations International Children's Emergency Fund (UNICEF, 2001) argues that 'choices made and actions taken on behalf of children during this critical period affect not only how a child develops but also how a country progresses' (p. 14). Hence, governments have a civic and moral responsibility to establish a comprehensive and appropriately resourced ECCE infrastructure that is responsive to and supportive of the diverse abilities and needs of all children.

International and National Policy Context

The journey towards inclusion has been greatly influenced by major legislative enactments such as the United Nations Convention on the

Rights of the Child (UNCRC, 1989) ratified by Ireland in 1992 and the Salamanca statement and framework for action on SEN (UNESCO, 1994). The UNCRC provided for a rights-based approach to inclusion by ensuring the right of all children to receive education without discrimination on any grounds, while the Salamanca world statement and framework for action holds that mainstream schools with an 'inclusive orientation are the most effective means of combating discrimination, creating welcoming communities, building an inclusive society and achieving education for all' (Article 2). Accordingly, inclusion and participation are 'essential to human dignity and the enjoyment and exercise of human rights' (ibid., p. 11). While historically, children with SEN were often hidden away (Alur, 2002; Griffin & Shevlin, 2011), today, their participation in education and society is a legal imperative guaranteed by the UNCRC. Their needs and rights are at the centre of educational policy and they are increasingly visible through their participation in ECCE settings, schools and the wider community.

Inclusion in Ireland

Ireland has long championed the cause of children with SEN within formal education. In fact, the first Inspector for Special Education was appointed in 1959. Since then, landmark policies include the Education Act, 1998, which contains the first legal definition of SEN in Ireland, the Education Welfare Act, 2000, whereby children must be enrolled in a primary school by the time they reach their sixth birthday and the Education for Persons with Special Education Needs (EPSEN) Act, 2004, which provides a statutory framework for the education of children with SEN. Critically, the EPSEN Act provides for assessment, the appointment of special needs assistants (SNAs), individual education plans and resource provision for children with SEN within formal schooling.

An entirely different picture emerges within the ECCE sector which does not have 'a clearly stated and communicated national inclusion policy' (Moloney & McCarthy, 2010, p. 144). Through its ratification of the UNCRC in 1992, Ireland committed to the provision of quality education for all children within a framework of lifelong learning.

The UNCRC was the impetus for the development of a broad range of policy initiatives that place inclusion at the core of ECCE provision, including *Ready to learn*—the White Paper on Early Childhood Care and Education (DES, 1999); the National Children's Strategy: *Our children their lives* (DHC, 2000); the Revised Childcare (preschool services) Regulations[2] (DHC, 2006); the National Quality Framework: *Síolta* (CECDE, 2006); the Early Childhood Curriculum Framework: *Aistear* (NCCA, 2009a) and the Free Preschool year in ECCE Scheme (Department of Children and Youth Affairs, 2010). Overall, ECCE policy is based upon an ecological approach to children's care and education giving due recognition to the key role played by parents, families and settings working together to support the child's emerging and existing abilities.

Shaping Inclusive Practice in an Irish ECCE Context

Ready to learn—the white paper on ECE (DES, 1999) sets out a comprehensive strategy for the development and provision of ECE up to six years. It places a 'particular focus on the target groups of the disadvantaged and those with special needs' (ibid., p. 45) and highlights the multiplicity of supports required to effectively support the inclusion of children with SEN: 'A high quality, intensive and clearly articulated programme, delivered by highly skilled and carefully trained personnel in contexts of small groups and individual instruction, and designed to specifically address individual identified needs' (ibid., p. 48).

ECCE is perceived as an early intervention where 'early childhood teachers who are trained in special needs education' (ibid.) can support families in adjusting to having a child with SEN and assist parents to acquire the skills they need to help their child develop to his/her potential (ibid.).

In terms of identifying and assessing children with SEN, *Ready to learn* highlights the benefits of multidisciplinary teams sharing recommendations and insights with ECCE practitioners. Such sharing is considered to

---

[2] Denotes statutory policy, that is, enacted by the Irish Government.

be of 'immediate value in preschool and in schools in developing education plans for pupils with disabilities' (DES, 1999, p. 85). It specifies the
need for curriculum, methodology, education plans and qualifications and
training. The core message is that inclusion does not happen by chance.
It is not 'about dumping children into an unplanned, under resourced
context' (Barton, 2002, p. 174); rather, it occurs in the context of a carefully
prepared environment, the support of appropriately trained practitioners
and the provision of resources.

Drawing heavily upon the UNCRC and building upon *Ready to learn*,
the National children's strategy: *Our children their lives* (DHC, 2000)
proposes three national goals for children: children will have a voice, their
lives will be better understood and they will receive quality supports and
services. Mirroring the broad thrust of the White Paper (DES, 1999), this
strategy recognises the capacity of ECCE to meet the holistic needs of
children as identified through a 'whole child' perspective, which takes as
its starting point the child's innate capacity for learning and development
that is present from birth (DHC, 2000, p. 51).

From an ecological perspective, childhood is seen as a complex set of
dynamic relationships ranging from the family to the State which acts as
the ultimate 'guarantor of their rights' (ibid., p. 68). As with the White
Paper (DES, 1999), the strategy highlights the need for practitioners and
others working with children to be provided with relevant training, as well
as encouraging inter-agency training to support improved coordination
between staff working in the voluntary and statutory sectors.

Two seminal publications resulted from the National Children's
Strategy: *Síolta*: The National Quality Framework (CECDE, 2006) and
Aistear: The Early Childhood Curriculum Framework (NCCA, 2009a).
Both pertain to children from birth to six years old. *Síolta* focuses upon all
facets of quality within ECCE including learning and development, while
Aistear helps practitioners provide appropriately challenging, positive and
enjoyable learning experiences (NCCA, 2009b). Each framework 'plays
a role in promoting and enhancing quality provision on a national level
and in this way they complement and support each other' (ibid., p. 5)
and both are underpinned by and share a number of common principles.
Particularly relevant to inclusion discourse are the principles of equality
and diversity. Crucially, equality is a critical prerequisite for supporting
the optimal development of children in Ireland:

> It requires that the individual needs and abilities of each child are recognised and supported from birth towards the realisation of her/his unique potential. This means that all children should be able to gain access to, participate in, and benefit from early years services on an equal basis. (CECDE, 2006, *User manual*, p. 7)

Inclusion is about much more than placement in or access to an educational setting. Effective inclusion means that children have a sense of belonging, participate fully in all activities of the setting and benefit in all areas of development just like their peers.

Aistear outlines children's learning and development through four themes: well-being, identity and belonging, communicating, and exploring and thinking. It is concerned with learning dispositions which are shaped by children's interactions with others and in the opportunities for learning presented to them within the ECCE setting. In an SEN context, it is the quality of the relationship between all those working with the child that leads to quality early intervention which 'constitute[s] a synergetic process: a mutually advantageous conjunction of distinct elements, of parents, carers, educators and therapists' (Cederman, 2006, p. 71). Accordingly, reciprocal relationships between all concerned with the young child's care and education are essential to promoting his/her best interests (CECDE, 2006; NCCA, 2009a).

Both *Síolta* and *Aistear* emphasise the need for practitioners to engage in cycles of 'observation, planning, action and evaluation' (CECDE, 2006, *User manual*, p. 57). They focus on the need to support children's early learning and development through formative assessment which is especially important for children with SEN. Dunphy (2008) suggests that assessment should focus not only on children's development of dispositions, attitudes and values but also upon their skills, knowledge and understanding. It should happen as part of everyday activities, tasks and routines (CECDE, 2006; NCCA, 2009a). In terms of inclusion, assessment fulfils a dual purpose: it demonstrates the richness of children's learning and development and identifies aspects that might benefit from attention and specific supports (Dunphy, 2008; Moloney & McCarthy, 2010). It helps to 'evaluate the interplay of factors related to child, environment and disability' (Jennings, 2005, p. 93) and forms the basis for better understanding the child's abilities, interests and needs, enabling practitioners to plan strategies to support development and learning.

Practice Context

On cursory inspection, Ireland has a rich tapestry of ECCE policy concerned with children's needs and rights. It upholds an ecological approach to working with children who have SEN and is concerned with a number of critical and interrelated factors: help and support to families of a child with SEN and cooperation between multi-disciplinary teams and practitioners (DES, 1999); differentiated curricula and supportive learning environments (CECDE, 2006; DES, 1999; NCCA, 2009a). Consistent with national and international research (e.g., Cederman, 2006; McGough, Carey & Ware, 2005; Sylva, Melhuish, Sammons, Siraj-Blatchford & Taggart, 2004), the ECCE policy further upholds the close relationship between highly trained practitioners and child outcomes.

Why then does the quality of ECCE provision in terms of children with SEN require urgent attention (Cederman, 2006; McGough et al., 2005; Moloney & McCarthy, 2010)? One reason may be that *Síolta* and *Aistear* have not been enacted and their implementation is predominantly dependent upon practitioner goodwill. As the only statutory policy governing the provision of ECCE, the Childcare (preschool services) Regulations, 2006, place an onus upon practitioners to be 'pro-active in ensuring that appropriate action is taken to address each child's needs in cooperation with his/her parents and following consultation, where appropriate, with other relevant services' (DHC, 2006, p. 36). While demanding the highest possible standards of care and education, these regulations simply require that 'a sufficient number of suitable and competent adults are working directly with the children in the preschool setting at all times' (ibid., p. 37). It is recommended that at least 50 per cent of practitioners would have a qualification appropriate to the care and development of children. In this respect, Irish research (Cederman, 2006; McGough et al., 2005; Moloney & McCarthy, 2010) consistently points to a considerable lack of appropriate training for practitioners who work with children who have SEN.

Interestingly, the voluntary Free Preschool Year in ECCE Scheme introduced in 2010 requires that preschool leaders working directly with children must be qualified in childcare/early education at a minimum of Further Education and Training Awards Council (FETAC)[3] Level 5 on the National Framework of Qualifications (NFQ). Designed to give children aged between three years and three months and four years and six months on 1 September each year access to a free preschool year of appropriate programme-based activities in the year before starting primary school, this scheme creates a direct link between quality ECCE and trained practitioners.

Worryingly, the overall poor lack of training across the sector necessitated the introduction of an interim measure to enable participating settings to ensure that practitioners acquired the minimum qualification by September 2012. Also of concern is the fact that these training requirements are only with respect to practitioners working with children from the age of 3 years and 3 months. Ultimately, the needs and rights of younger children attending ECCE settings are overlooked.

Clearly, practice is undermined by a range of factors that considerably impact children's experiences within ECCE settings: the voluntary nature of ECCE policy (Moloney, 2011), lack of a mandatory training requirement (Moloney, 2010, 2011) and inadequate resources (Moloney & McCarthy, 2010). Policy alone is not a guarantor of children's rights, for, in the absence of resources, 'policies espoused at a macro level risk floundering within the micro-environment of settings due to a mismatch between national ideologies and the practicalities of implementation on the ground' (Moloney, 2011, p. 17). It is against this backdrop that a DFA for the inclusion of children with SEN in early childhood settings in Ireland was developed.

---

[3] The NFQ, established in 2003, is a system of 10 levels. It is based on standards of knowledge, skill and competence and it incorporates awards made for all kinds of learning, wherever it is gained. School qualifications (awards) awarded by the State Examinations Commission, further education and training qualifications awarded by FETAC and higher education and training qualifications awarded by the Higher Education and Training Awards Council, Dublin Institute of Technology, other institutes of technology and the universities are all included in the Framework.

Study Scope and Methodology

The purpose of the study was to develop a framework for action for the inclusion of children from birth to 4 years of age with SEN in ECCE settings, design and implement an intervention based on the roll-out of the DFA in a range of ECCE settings and evaluate the impact of the DFA within settings from the perspective of practitioners and special needs support staff, parents and children.

It comprised two distinct research phases and was primarily underpinned by qualitative data collection strategies: child observations, focus groups and interviews with parents; practitioners working directly with the children with SEN; preschool SNAs (PSNAs), national disability agencies and various support services at local and national levels. Phase 1 involved an in-depth exploration of inclusion and examined practitioner understanding, children's experiences within settings, and the availability of supports and resources. Informed by phase 1 and guided by *Síolta* and *Aistear*, a DFA was developed, piloted and evaluated in 14 ECCE settings in Counties Clare, Kerry, North Tipperary and Limerick city and county. In this phase, 43 practitioners working directly with children who have SEN, 11 PSNAs (self-selected in phase 1) and 10 parents of children with SEN participated. The following section provides a brief synopsis of phase 1 findings which provide the context for the transformation in practice during the piloting of the DFA in phase 2.

Phase 1: Overview of Findings

The overarching finding which emerged was that while practitioners were willing to include children with SEN and had their best interests at heart, their understanding of inclusion and its implications for their practice was limited. It was clear that the mere placement of children with SEN in a setting does not automatically result in meaningful inclusion. Table 1.1 provides a synopsis of phase 1 findings.

Practitioner attempts to support inclusion were restricted by a range of factors including poor understanding of inclusion, limited, and often ineffective communication at multiple levels, inappropriate environments,

Table 1.1

Synopsis of Research Findings—Phase 1

Theme	Finding	Comment	Consequence
Practitioner understanding of inclusion	Uncertainty about what inclusion means	Practitioners asked: 'What is inclusion? Is it that the is physically within a room environment or is it that he is within a setting where he is in a room with somebody one-to-one?'	Children with SEN expected to adapt to the setting rather than the setting adapting to accommodate their diverse learning needs
Access to appropriate services by parents of a child with SEN	Limited access to speech and language therapy, occupational therapy, physiotherapy and support from psychologists and early intervention specialists	Availability of supports and resources determined by geographic location	Intervention services worked independently of ECCE settings; responsibility rested primarily with parents for passing information to practitioners in the hope that they would implement any programme developed by the intervention services for the child in the setting
Appointment of Preschool Special Needs Assistants (PSNAs) to children with SEN	PSNAs appointed on an ad hoc basis; lack of definition of the role of the PSNA	Absence of a coordinated, comprehensive, universal support mechanism	Two–three PSNAs appointed to the same child through different agencies; sharing of PSNAs between children; mismatch between PSNA hours and the child's hours of attendance
Physical environment	Practitioners had limited awareness of the impact of the physical environment on the child with SEN	The learning environment in some instances was crowded, noisy (radios playing in the background) and overstimulating	Children agitated by the numbers of children and noise levels

Communication between all those involved with the child	Limited communication at multiple levels	Practitioners were uncertain about how to share information with parents about their child with SEN; gaps in communication between practitioners, PSNAs and other professionals	Practitioners, PSNAs and support services all working in isolation; parents unsure about what their child was doing within the setting; limited team work within settings
Communication with children	Predominant focus upon verbal communication	Practitioners unaware of alternative forms of communication	Some children with speech and language delays were disempowered and unable to participate fully in the activities in the setting
Formal assessment of children's needs	Various models of assessment and support used within different health services executive regions	In some areas, assessment may have resulted in the development of an individual development plan (IDP) by an early intervention team (EIT) that was given to parents for their child. The IDP may or may not have been shared with practitioners	In the absence of an IDP/EIT support, practitioners were uncertain about how to plan for a child with SEN; delay in getting IDPs from the appropriate intervention services; PSNAs left without an IDP for an entire year; IDP reviews long overdue in some instances. In these cases, PSNAs did not know how to support the child's ongoing development
Formative assessment of children's needs	Child observations undertaken on a limited basis within settings	Even though practitioners were aware of the need to observe, many were uncertain about how or what to observe or how to use the data from observations effectively	Practitioners tended to abdicate responsibility for the child with SEN to the PSNA
Planning for children's learning	Planning was inconsistent with considerable variation between settings	Practitioners acknowledged that planning for children's specific needs can be challenging	Practitioners and PSNAs generally struggled with planning effectively to support children's learning

Source: Author's primary research data.

limited assessment and planning, absence of curriculum and weak professional development. Consequently, the DFA was underpinned by five core elements considered central to inclusive practice (e.g., CECDE, 2006; DES, 1999; McGough et al., 2005; NCCA, 2009a):

1. Professional development
2. Communication
3. Environment
4. Assessment for learning
5. Accessing the curriculum/programme

Phase 2: Implementing the DFA

Practitioners and PSNAs were introduced to and mentored in the effective use of the DFA at a series of training workshops in October 2009. Practitioners were asked to identify one action from each area within the DFA: communication; environment; assessment for learning and accessing the curriculum/programme. These actions were to be prioritised during the piloting of the DFA between 27 October 2009 and 29 January 2010. They were also asked to complete a reflective exercise at the end of each week. Thus, participants were facilitated to interpret and represent not just their own voice but that of children with SEN and their parents. Resources to support the implementation of the DFA (e.g., reflective journals and home/setting notebooks) were disseminated. Each of the 14 settings nominated one practitioner to complete the reflective journal. Thus, a total of 14 completed reflective journals, one from each setting, were submitted.

Phase 2: Findings

Inclusion is premised upon an ecological approach to working with children where parents, practitioners, PSNAs and intervention services work together to support the child's learning and development. As outlined, phase 1 findings highlighted ineffective communication at multiple levels. During the piloting of the DFA, while communication between practitioners and parents, practitioners and PSNAs, practitioners and colleagues was considerably enhanced, communication with children was transformed.

Communicating with Parents

All 14 settings sought to enhance communication with parents. Six settings used a home/setting notebook to share information with parents: details of emerging friendships, the child's likes and dislikes, whether the child was upset/happy, as well as details of progress in developing or enhancing specific skills. The following home/setting notebook excerpts provide a sample of the nature and scope of information shared. In the first, Harry (3½ years) communicates with his parents; in the second, the practitioner writes on behalf of Matthew (2½ years).

Excerpt 1: Community Setting (1)
Hi Mom and Dad, I had a nice day today. I did painting; I did it by flicking the straw and Susan painted my hand and put it on paper. Maria sang Humpty Dumpty and fell on the floor off the chair. I laughed at Maria; I enjoyed it.

Excerpt 2: Community Setting (2)
Today, Matthew watched worms wriggling in the wormery. He joined his hands together and wriggled them to indicate worms and tried to say 'worm'. He used his index finger to wriggle finger paint down a long sheet of paper. He showed his hand to Lucy and chatted about the worms with her using his joined hands.

Although six settings used the home/setting notebook, only three parents shared information with settings in this way. The following parental response demonstrates how Harry's parents took their lead from the practitioners so his voice prevailed as information was shared through the home/setting notebook.

Parental response
Hi everyone, after school I went to Nana and Granddad's house, then I went for a sleep with my teddy bear. When I woke up I had great fun with

my Nana and Granddad and Uncle Simon. I was writing and drawing with Uncle Simon and drew a picture of Nana and Granddad. Then I gave Dad his birthday card and he loved it.

Confirming the effectiveness of the home/setting note book, parent response 4 reads:

They are using a note book for school and home coordination and they are keeping a scrapbook so we can see his progress. We know how well he is doing now.

Four settings also set up a system of progress meetings with parents. The reflective journal (see Table 1.2) reveals how these meetings provided a safe environment for the child's mother to express her feelings and to discuss her hopes and expectations for him. It shows that all those working with the child in the setting established a shared understanding of how to work with him to support his ongoing development both at home and in the setting. This child had the support of three different PSNAs, each appointed by different agencies and each of whom attended the setting on different days. The journal highlights the practitioner's struggle to engage with one PSNA and how this impacted their relationship.

Communicating with PSNAs

While poor communication between practitioners and PSNAs continued to be a challenge throughout phase 2, findings indicate that a certain level of progress was made. One setting, for instance, set aside 'specific time' each week to 'consult and to share information' about the child with the PSNA which resulted in 'better understanding [where the PSNA] knows what we expect and we know what to expect as well. Everybody knows where they stand.' Crucially, 'we work better as a team now' (private practitioner (PP) 5: Reflective journal). While experiences of working with the PSNA were predominantly positive, two settings continued to experience difficulties. For instance, in community setting (3), the PSNA 'takes total control' of the child with SEN, which hindered his progress within the setting. The practitioner's frustration was evident in week 5:

Table 1.2

Reflective Journal Completed by Community Setting (1)

	Describe the Action Taken from the DFA in the Area of Communication	*What Worked Well*	*What Challenges Did You Encounter*	*Implications for Inclusive Practice*
Week 1	As room leader, I am communicating more with the SNA. Child's mother is communicating through Big Mac and journal	I feel we are all working together now. From reading the DFA we are all singing from the same hymn sheet	Trying to get everyone together outside of the room to meet; trying to find time to do so	Communicating more with the child— letting him communicate back by giving lots of choices and not assuming what he wants
Week 2	Planned a meeting with the PSNA for Thursday	I felt that the child would benefit more if all communicated more with him and I got this across at the meeting	One of the PSNAs did not attend to go through the outcomes of the meeting again	Planned a meeting with child's mother to find out what she wants for the child while he is in our service
Week 3	Met with child's mother today to find out what she wants for him (goals)	Communication between child's mother, PSNAs and staff in the room—now we all know what child's mother wants	PSNA	From this communication, we will adapt all activities so that child is always included
Week 5	Another meeting arranged with child's mother	Long meeting with child's mother—lots of information shared	child's mother talked at length; began to cry. We all cried together— child's mother, PSNA, manager and I	Child's mother is happy with what we are doing. It is so hard sometimes adapting to a routine

(Table 1.2 Contd.)

(Table 1.2 Contd.)

	Describe the Action Taken from the DFA in the Area of Communication	What Worked Well	What Challenges Did You Encounter	Implications for Inclusive Practice
Week 6	Communicated to child's mother about carol service for parents. Child will participate	I was nervous for child's mother as she wasn't sure whether he would get upset or not	Talking to child's mother about it. She wanted to know every detail; all songs to be sent home	We sang the songs into a tape recorder so she and the child would be familiar
Week 9	Child is communicating so much better using his eyes. Child's mother has asked for the work she did over Christmas to continue	Talking to child, asking him; eyes up for 'yes', down for 'no'. We feel he is understood more	Child's mother communicated to us that the support agency doesn't think that he would be able for mainstream school	Shouldn't he be able to go to school where the parents want him to go (inclusive practice)?
Week 11	Child's mother communicates by phone if she needs to and in book	Child's mother seems very relaxed around us now	I find it hard communicating with one of his [child's] PSNAs. I have tried many times	I find it hard on the one day that this PSNA is in to include her and the child. She just doesn't seem to fit in

Week 12
Communication between the [disability agency] and child's mother, to us is very good. From communicating with child's mother, we are all aware of where the child is and what child's mother expects from us and her child. The team is working well together; the staff and PSNAs all want the same thing for the child and his family. The challenges are far and few between. Thank you for all your ideas about putting a communication book together for the PSNAs around our setting and the method in the room. I have learned so much—how important communication is with family, outside agencies and PSNAs.

Source: Author's primary research data.

I am really finding it difficult to find ways to try and distance the PSNA from smothering him and preventing him from discovering for himself. She tends to interfere and spoils what may have been interesting scenarios with other adults and children. This situation is leading to frustration amongst the staff who recognise a problem but also feel helpless. (Community practitioner [CP] 3: Reflective journal)

In general, however, practitioners believed that the DFA

> ... helped to make all of the staff aware of what we were trying to do and we became very focussed. This has spilled over to our daily work not just with special needs and we are trying to make time to meet to discuss our days with each other. (Interview with PP 6)

Communicating with Colleagues

Each of the 14 settings organised a staff meeting at the outset of phase 2 to 'explain what [the DFA] was about and to make sure that we were all involved [it gave settings a] real focus, we discussed how we might work together to improve what we were doing with all children not just the child with special needs' (CP 6: Reflective journal). As with PSNA involvement, practitioners encountered difficulties in trying to motivate their colleagues: 'getting everyone involved was difficult. Some took [the DFA] and were involved totally; others didn't get involved at all' (PP 4: Reflective journal). However, where staff were '100% committed to the DFA and to improving how we communicate and work with the children', the benefits were 'enormous' (Interview with CP 1): 'We're all on the same page now. We know what we want the child to achieve and we work together to help her to achieve her goals. It's a real team effort and it's easier for us all' (Interview with PP 2).

Children Have a Voice and Are Listened to

Notwithstanding that 21.73 per cent (N = 36) of children presented with a speech and language delay, practitioners did not know how to support or facilitate this aspect of development. Consequently, there was a pre-dominant focus upon verbal communication including rapid fire questions and multiple instructions. As a result of the pilot study, practitioners claimed to be more aware of 'how to communicate' with a child who has SEN. Tellingly, PP 3 articulated how she 'just took it for granted that he understood what I wanted, it never crossed my mind that maybe he didn't understand.' Likewise, PP 5 explained how, prior to the pilot study, 'we were only half caring for children; we hadn't time to get to know them, to communicate with them.'

Six settings made picture schedules to encourage and support communication with children who had a speech and language delay. They were used to 'offer choice', to 'explain what's going to happen next', to 'offer another way of expressing himself', to 'let other children and staff see that there are other ways to communicate' (Reflective journal extracts). Critically, the picture schedule 'helps everyone; staff, the PSNA and the other children' (CP 5: Reflective journal).

Ten settings altered their group size, so that the child with SEN was part of a small group of four to six children rather than a large group of twenty children. This strategy had a significant impact upon inclusion. Children were able to 'form friendships with specific children in a safe environment' where they were not overwhelmed by the large numbers of children and their 'voice was heard' (Interview with PP 4). In three settings, practitioners acknowledged that children with SEN may have been 'intimidated by the numbers and the noise' (Interview with PP 4). Through their involvement in smaller groups, children with SEN developed the 'skills and confidence to participate better in larger group time like circle time and outdoor play' (CP 6: Reflective journal). Commenting on the impact of the small group size, and pointing to the impact upon their son's experience, parent response 6 reports 'a massive change in Colin ... in every way; his speech has come on, he is making little friends and he seems happy, smiling more. We are delighted at the change in him ... it's like he is able to cope now.'

Five settings appointed a key worker who had responsibility for the child with SEN. Following the appointment of a key worker, Sam who 'never spoke or interacted with anyone' was described as 'a different child. When he comes into the preschool he hugs us now and he always smiles at us and the children. He even said "hello" on Wednesday. That was a major breakthrough' (PP 4: Reflective journal). Because they viewed Sam more positively and saw his potential rather than his special need, practitioners described how they 'have such hope for him now and we can encourage him to say more words, to keep going and reach his potential' (PP 4: Reflective journal).

In addition to the strategies outlined, practitioners sought to enhance communication with children by:

1. Using a distinct and slower method of talking to the child during this programme.
2. Getting down to the child's level now to get his attention.
3. Making eye contact with him when we are communicating with him.
4. Pausing and wait for a response when I am chatting to her. I didn't know how to do that before and would always ask too many questions or just keep talking. It never crossed my mind that she didn't respond ... I never noticed.

Similarly, PP 3 recognised that prior to engaging with the DFA, the child was not included, *'before we kind of assumed that he wanted to do the things we decided ...'*. The impact of increased communication upon children and parent's experiences was evident through parent responses.

There is more labelling in the room now ... more meetings/communication. Staff are more aware of our child's needs, they have definite goals. We get more feedback about what he is doing ... they're using more visual aids and using symbols in songs and rhymes. (Parent response 5)

Observations

Practitioners in all 14 settings undertook child observations in phase 2. We take up Sam's story who was perceived as having 'very little ability' and where 'everyone, the intervention team, the speech and language people and us ... we all seem to give a negative picture to his Mum' (Interview with PP 4). In spite of the fact that Sam had attended the setting for 12 months prior to the pilot study, practitioners did not 'really know a lot about him [and] wouldn't know where to start if we were to plan a programme for him' (PP 4: Support visit, November 2009). Throughout phase 2, the key worker observed Sam solely to build a picture of his strengths, to focus upon what he could do. Observation A provides insight into Sam's ability.

Key worker Observation A, 13 November 2009

Table Top Activity

Sam is playing at a table with bricks with his PSNA. He is stacking the bricks on top of each other.[4] There is one other child at the table. Sam is manipulating the bricks to fit together. He is very good at this activity. Concentration level is very high. He ensures that pieces fit together correctly. Sam and the PSNA take turns to stack the bricks. One brick at a time each. The PSNA leaves the table. Sam continues to stack the bricks. He gathers all the bricks together on the table. He tries to pull his bricks apart. He is very persistent. He gets upset when he can't pull them apart. Sam gets up and walks over to another child in the room to ask him to help him. The child is unable to help him. Sam walks over to me (practitioner). I help him pull them apart. Sam shouts 'yah' and returns to his table.

As the key worker became more competent in undertaking and sharing observations with her co-practitioners, everybody began to see Sam in a 'more positive way' and expressed 'surprise' that he 'can do so much'. He had previously been described as a 'happy little fellow [who] just flitted from one thing to another … he didn't seem to concentrate on anything' (PP 4: Site visit, January 2010). The attachment of blame to Sam clearly indicates that practitioners lacked awareness of their role in supporting his inclusion within the setting.

A concern for practitioners was their belief that Sam had '*no speech*' and again, abdicating their responsibility, 'he doesn't make any attempt to talk' (PP 4: Site visit, January 2010); hence, their 'amazement [that he] is so clever' (Key worker, February 2010) '… we couldn't believe all the things he is able to do. There is an awful lot going on in his head' (PP 4: Support visit, February 2010). Critically, Sam was no longer perceived as having 'very little ability'; rather, 'he has huge potential' (PP 4: Support visit, February 2010). Indicating a shift in thinking and approach

---

[4] Mentoring during site visits enabled the key worker to make sense of and understand what had been observed.

to working with parents, practitioners were 'eager to share what we have observed with [Sam's] mother ... it will be great for her to hear something positive for a change' (PP 4).

Curriculum

Undoubtedly, this aspect of the DFA was the most daunting for practitioners. Reflective journals bear testimony to the challenges associated with curriculum planning and implementation. Nine journals reported that 'the child is included in all areas of the curriculum'. In these settings, a series of disconnected activities (e.g., water play, finger painting, blowing bubbles) were offered to children in the absence of an overall plan to extend or integrate activities to support development. By contrast, the other five settings made a concerted effort to engage with the guidelines in the DFA around curriculum.

Developing Inclusive Practice

Here we take up Matthew's story. Having considered the guidelines for curriculum development in the DFA, practitioners established a number of core objectives. These were to:

1. Take their lead from Matthew's interests
2. Build upon and incorporate these interests into the overall curriculum of the setting
3. Enhance Matthew's speech and language development
4. Support Matthew's social development
5. Encourage and support Matthew to be independent

Alongside observations, practitioners photographed Matthew engaging in a range of activities. Not only were the photographs used to document Matthew's involvement in the curriculum, they were used to further build on his interests. Therefore, when practitioners 'found a butterfly, it was photographed, when a frog came to visit, it was photographed' (Interview with CP 4). These photographs were compiled into a series of picture books for Matthew that 'he likes to take off the display and look and talk about the children and the pictures. He returns to the picture books often' (Interview with CP 4). The books empowered Matthew to associate pictures with activities, he 'learned the names of animals and birds ... he looked at pictures of the other kids and pointed to them in the classroom; so he learned who they were and sometimes they sat beside him looking at the books too' (Interview with CP 4). Because the books were readily available and accessible, Matthew was empowered to develop friendships, his emerging language and, crucially, independence. During week 4, practitioners 'extended his awareness of the natural world' by introducing a nature box to the setting. Although the activities undertaken were directed towards supporting Matthew's development, 'everyone benefitted; all the children, the staff ... it was a brilliant experience for all of us and so worthwhile' (CP 4: Final site visit, March 2010).

Discussion and Conclusion

This pilot study had a profound impact on inclusive practice within participating settings enabling practitioners and PSNAs to transform their practice. Practitioners experienced a sense of 'I can do' through engagement with the pilot study which impacted positively on their attitudes towards children with SEN and their capacity to respond to children's diverse abilities. There was a real shift in thinking where practitioners were empowered to respond positively to the children's learning needs and to see individual differences not as problems but as opportunities for enriching learning (UNESCO, 2005), not just for the child with SEN but for all children.

Today, children with and without SEN play, develop and learn together at home, preschool, school and within wider society. This reflects a shift away from previous practices where children with SEN were isolated from their peers. It also reflects societal values about promoting and supporting children's learning and development and creates a sense of belonging for every child and family. However, as mentioned, inclusion is about much more than placement in or access to an educational setting. This study provides empirical evidence of the need for settings to be ready for inclusion. Through piloting the DFA, practitioners achieved the ultimate goal of enhancing the quality of children's experiences within settings, thus giving children a voice, while better understanding their lives and providing quality supports and services (DHC, 2000). During the final workshops in March 2010, practitioners claimed that their success stemmed from the initial training workshops together with the ongoing mentoring and support provided throughout the pilot study. Practitioners further claimed that the DFA which they described as their 'bible' was instrumental in helping them to reflect upon their practice and implement positive change throughout the intervention. Undoubtedly, the model of targeted professional development combined with ongoing support enabled practitioners to change some of the key behaviours on the ground in terms of organising the learning environment, enhancing communication with children, parents, colleagues and other profession-als, observing and interpreting children's participation in the day-to-day activities of the setting and consequently planning appropriately for their learning and development. The importance of professional development cannot be overstated. Thus, professional development informs and shapes all aspects of inclusive practice—communication, the learning environ-ment, assessment for learning and curriculum. Ultimately, professional development is the engine that drives inclusive provision and practice in the early years (Moloney & McCarthy, 2010, p. 132). By embracing inclusive practice and implementing evidence-based strategies, ECCE practitioners were empowered to 'see' the 'child' and not the 'need'. Thus, they saw the potential for maximising outcomes for young children with SEN. When we take the time to reflect upon our practice, to see the child, to truly listen to and understand his/her differing abilities and our role in supporting development and learning, we realise the trust and respon-sibility that is bestowed upon us as practitioners. Following this study, a framework for action was developed together with a comprehensive accredited Certificate in Inclusive Care and Education for the early years. The roll-out of this training commenced in September 2012 in Limerick. It is hoped to influence positive change in attitudes, shape the process of inclusion and ultimately enhance children's experiences within settings, leading to improved outcomes for children.

References

Alur, M. (2002). Status of disabled people in India: Policy and inclusion. *Exceptionality Education Canada, 12*(2 & 3), 137–167.

Barton, L. (2002). Inclusive education and the management of change in Britain. *Exceptionality Education Canada, 12*(2 & 3), 169–185.

Cederman, K. (2006). *North Tipperary Early Intervention Service—Synergy: An exploration of high quality early intervention for children with special needs in diverse early childhood care and education settings.* Dublin: CECDE.

Centre for Early Childhood Development and Education (CECDE). (2006). *Síolta, the national quality framework for early childhood education.* Dublin: CECDE.

Department of Children and Youth Affairs. (2010). *Free pre-school year in early childhood care and education.* Retrieved from www.dcya.gov.ie (accessed 23 September 2013)

Department of Education and Science (DES). (1998). *Education Act.* Dublin: The Stationery Office.

———. (1999). *Ready to learn: The white paper on early childhood education.* Dublin: The Stationery Office.

Department of Health and Children (DHC). (2000). *National children's strategy: Our children their lives.* Dublin: The Stationery Office.

———. (2006). *Childcare (pre-school services) (Amendment No. 2) Regulation, 2006.* Dublin: The Stationery Office.

Dunphy, E. (2008). *Supporting early learning and development through formative assessment: A research paper.* Commissioned by the National Council and Curriculum and Assessment. Retrieved from www.ncca.ie (accessed 23 September 2013).

Fox, S. E., Levitt, P. & Nelson, C. A. (2010). How the timing and quality of early experiences influence the development of brain architecture. *Child Development, 81*(1), 28–40.

Griffin, S. & Shevlin, M. (2011). *Responding to special educational needs: An Irish perspective.* Dublin: Gill & Macmillan.

Jennings, J. (2005). Inclusion matters. In L. Abbott & A. Langston (Eds), *Birth to three matters* (pp. 89–104). Maidenhead, UK: McGraw-Hill/Open University Press.

McGough, A., Carey, S. & Ware, J. (2005). *Early years provision for children from birth to six years with special needs in two geographical areas in Ireland.* Dublin: CECDE.

Moloney, M. (2010). Professional identity in early childhood care and education: Perspectives of pre-school and infant teachers. *Irish Educational Studies, 29*(2), 167–187.

Moloney, M. (2011). From vision to practice: Are children at the centre or clinging on at the periphery of practice within early childhood care and education provision? *New Zealand Research in ECCE Journal, 14*, 3–22.

Moloney, M. & McCarthy, E. (2010). *Development of a framework for action for the inclusion of children with special educational needs in early childhood care and education settings*. Research study commissioned by the Department of Education and Skills, Ireland. Limerick, Ireland: Curriculum Development Unit, Mary Immaculate College. Retrieved from www.cdu.mic.ul.ie (accessed 23 September 2013).

National Council for Curriculum and Assessment (NCCA). (2009a). *Aistear: The early childhood curriculum framework*. Dublin: NCCA. Retrieved from www.ncca.ie (accessed 23 September 2013)

———. (2009b). Aistear: the Early Childhood Curriculum Framework and Síolta, The National Quality Framework for Early Childhood Education. *Audit: Similarities and differences*. Retrieved from www.ncca.ie (accessed 24 July 2014)

Shonkoff, J. & Phillips, D. (2000). *From neurons to neighbourhoods: The science of early childhood development*. Washington, D.C.: National Academic Press.

Sylva, K., Melhuish, E., Sammons, P., Siraj-Blatchford, I. & Taggart, B. (2004). *The effective provision of pre-school education: The final report*. London: Department for Education and Skills/Sure Start Publications and the Institute of Education.

United Nations Convention on the Rights of the Child (UNCRC). (1989). *Convention on the rights of the child, 20 November* 1989. United Nations Treaty Series, Vol. 1577. Retrieved from http://www.refworld.org/docid/3ae6b38f0.html (accessed 24 July 2014).

———. (2001). *Understanding and responding to children's needs in inclusive classrooms: A guide for teachers*. Paris: UNESCO.

———. (2005). *Guidelines for inclusion: Ensuring access for all*. Paris: UNESCO.

United Nations Educational, Scientific and Cultural Organisation. (1994). *The Salamanca statement and framework for action on special needs education*. Retrieved from http://www.unesco.org/education/pdf/SALAMA_E.PDF (accessed 14 September 2014).

———. (2005). *Guidelines for inclusion: Ensuring access to education for all*. Retrieved from http://unesdoc.unesco.org/images/00140224e.pdf (accessed 17 September 2014).

United Nations International Children's Emergency Fund (UNICEF). (2001). *The state of the world's children 2001*. Retrieved from www.unicef.org (accessed 23 September 2013)

2

Language Issues and Preschool Education in Kenya: A Reflection on Diversity, Challenges and Remedies

Mary Wangechi Kamunyu

Kenya is the only African nation with an established early childhood education programme, and the initiative has had a significant impact on its citizens. Compared to other countries at similar levels of economic development, Kenya has made considerable achievements in early childhood development (ECD) provision (MOEST, 2005). ECD in Kenya concerns the holistic development of children between 0+ and 5+ years old under the auspice of the Ministry of Education Science and Technology (ibid.). The current Education and Training Act does not include ECD; the only policy framework that directs the MOEST's provision of ECD is the Partnership Policy (ibid.). Early childhood curriculum internationally and in Kenya emphasises the use of the mother tongue or the language of the catchment area in the instructional strategies for teaching preschool children. This is important because young children come to school when they are fluent in their mother tongue or in a language spoken in their home environment. Language is very instrumental in the early learning since the formative stage of learning forms the bedrock for future literacy development.

However, studies have found that the majority of preschool teachers instruct young children in English, though it is not their first language.

When children don't speak the school's language, they may struggle to make progress, or drop out early. They may find it harder to cope in school because they are often less exposed to other languages outside the home. Many ECD centres place so much emphasis on literacy and numeracy skills that they are essentially 'early primary education' centres, rather than ECD centres (Mwangi, 2011). The importance of language use cannot be overemphasised, yet many preschool children enter school with language disorders which are either not diagnosed at all or are misdiagnosed due to lack of sufficient well-trained language pathologists in the ECD centres. The overall literacy achievement in a child is embedded in language proficiency, and any difficulties in language translate into a loss in total educational outcome for the child. The objective of this study is to critically examine language issues and practices that affect the overall educational achievements of preschool in Kenya.

Methodology

This study has utilised a survey design in Narok North constituency of Narok County. It has sampled 20 preschools from a target of 158 ECD centres. The main descriptive methods used were tabulation of frequencies and percentages. Twenty teachers responded to structured interviews, coupled with observation schedules of classroom language use. Data were analysed using the Statistical Package for Social Science (SPSS).

Findings

The Role of Preschool in Kenya

The study sought to establish the role preschool was playing in the Kenyan society, like other world societies. The rationale for doing this was to examine how language facilitated the performing of such roles. Eighty-five per cent of the respondents revealed that in some instances preschool group care functions as an alternative to home care, and focuses on protecting health, promoting nutrition and providing enjoyable experiences to the children served. In addition, they reported that in other cases, preschool group care is designed to help children develop interpersonal skills and to become members of a peer group. In still other situations, group care is seen as 'preschool', where activities are organised into a 'curriculum' designed to promote cognitive development, language and early literacy skills. One dominant thread of thought that tied these views was that language is very instrumental in the development of interpersonal skills, playing activities and cognitive development typified in numeracy skills, singing, oral drills, etc.

Language Planning in Preschool

One thing that was dominant in the target population was that Narok North Constituency was cosmopolitan. Children came from diverse multilingual ethnic backgrounds, so the preschool teacher must, therefore, decide the language of instruction to choose under such circumstances. Sixty per cent of the respondents pointed out that their planning was often complicated by children themselves being either bilingual or multilingual, or expected to develop those skills. Especially where children came from intermarriages, it was found that some children were first confronted with the need to learn a new language during their initial exposure to formal education. Another lingering issue that was observed was that out of the 20 teachers observed, only 12 spoke the three major languages spoken in the region: Maa, Gikuyu and Ekegussii. This issue takes us back to the use of the lingua franca—Kiswahili, which is the Kenyan official and national language. Regrettably, 90 per cent of the respondents reported that most of the children are not fully competent in Kiswahili, while others were in the process of its acquisition. Therefore, language planning for preschool in Kenya is one besetted with challenges and hurdles which need to even out for real educational outcomes to be achieved. It must harmonise the multilingual realities of the children and their teachers by devising language and instructional choices suitable for all.

It was observed that during learning, some children were not participating well due to language problems. Out of the 20 teachers interviewed, 65 per cent said that they had not received formal training in teaching ECD centres. So, they intimated that they did not know what normal language development looked like. This means that they cannot diagnose language disorders or prescribe intervention measures. They also reported that they could not know which children were showing slow or deviant development and may need special help. It is in this light that they owned up to the fact that they could not design environments to ensure optimal language development for the children. This disturbing scenario proves that majority of the teachers are ill-equipped to train children and there is a dire need by the government of Kenya to train its ECD teachers before hiring them.

Strategies of Using Language in Preschool Learning

A research done by Mwangi (2011) on preschool teachers' use of oral instructional strategies in teaching in English—a study in Kasarani division, Nairobi province, Kenya—found that the instructional strategies most used by preschool teachers were giving directions, asking questions, code switching and repeating words and phrases. Expanding on children's utterances, giving explanations, substituting words with real items, giving examples and contrasting meanings were the least used instructional strategies when teaching in English.

In this study, when the respondents were asked which language strategies they employed when teaching children, 85 per cent revealed that one helpful style of interaction is a highly responsive one, in which the teacher lets the child decide what to talk about, expands on that topic, works hard to figure out what the child means, suggests new activities and pays more attention to what the child wants to say than about whether it is being said correctly. Such a strategy was found to be very viable in language development for children; however, it required intensive use to catalyse language acquisition for those children with language handicap. This picture is of an optimal language teacher who assumes the role of cooperative conversational partner rather than taking an explicitly didactic or directive role.

One common denominator that emerged from all the respondents interviewed was that language activities must be planned with the mental maturity of the child in mind. Language teaching is most useful to young children if it is presented in the context of their own activities and attempts at expression. Seventy-eight per cent of the respondents observed that as children get older, they could use language to learn language; they no longer needed to encounter every new language skill within a meaning-ful context. Furthermore, they become increasingly capable of learning intentionally, of attending to and benefiting from explicit instruction, and of using models as sources of learning.

Sixty-two per cent of the respondents further added that talking about a wide variety of complex topics, modelling an enriched vocabulary, engaging in talk about talk itself, discussing word meanings, challenging children to explain themselves and to justify their own thinking, setting higher standards for comprehensibility and explicitly correcting errors are important in the language development of 4-, 5-, and 6-year-old children.

It was also noted that some teachers preferred to scaffold as a strategy of language development. In this case, children in the age range of 4–6 were expected to control certain language-related literacy skills that prob-ably emerged from being read to, from experience in looking at books with adults, and from experience with letters, with pencils and paper and with the observation of adult literacy activities. However, 55 per cent of the respondents felt that only children who acquired the language benefited from this strategy. Scaffolding was seen to create frustration to those children whose language proficiency was low. It was needful for the teachers to know the language needs of the children before utilising such approaches.

With respect to group care settings, one study has shown that the qual-ity of the language environment of the day care centre has a large impact on the language development of the children enrolled (McCarthy, 1994). The amount of expressive verbal interaction with caregivers has a specific effect on the children's language development. Children's language level is related to opportunities to initiate conversations with caregivers and is negatively related to the number of conversations initiated with peers. For example, observational studies that compare children's talk at home and at school consistently find that homes are the richer environment.

One of the persuasions of this study was to find out how we can increase and maximise opportunities in schools where children use language in as good a manner as in home environment.

One such comparative study was carried out in England (Tizard, 1981; Tizard & Hughes, 1984). The researchers discovered that the average child had almost three times as many conversations per unit of time with a parent at home as with a caregiver in nursery school and that the home conversations continued for twice as many adult/child turns. As Tizard notes, a brief conversation between children and adults may suffice for children to make demands, which can be either met or denied. Through such conversations, encouragement may be given, suggestions are made, information or orders are given, or questions are answered.

In this study, 70 per cent of the teachers interviewed revealed that one way of creating language-rich environments where numerous opportunities were created to have one-on-one talk with interested and responsive children was necessary for language development of children. Through this strategy, children learnt important rules for playing, conversing, negotiating and arguing with peers. Teachers cautioned that children with strong esteem and confidence rated more highly in holding one-to-one talk with the teacher unlike those with low self-confidence. Again, for any deep exchange of meaning that takes time to be achieved, sometimes, the teacher needs to encourage the children to hold the conversation through verbal positive reinforcement.

During the preschool years, language and cognition are very closely related. It was observed that teachers engaged in a variety of activities to stimulate the language development of children. Sixty-five per cent of the teachers interviewed reported that stimulating children's language involved enriching their vocabulary. This involved the use of wall charts with objects and animals drawn with their manes below them. Also, language games and chants with new words were used frequently as a way of reinforcing acquisition of vocabularies.

Another key activity of facilitating language use was making children understand how things work, for instance, simple domestic chores like cooking, washing, etc. Such activities presented children with new action words which they hitherto did not know. Other aspects of learning language involved their knowledge about numbers, about weather, about how things grow, about how people live in other parts of the world and dozens more such topics.

Furthermore, preschool programmes that prepare children for schools in which reading and writing are central activities need to plan ways to stimulate the development of pre-literacy skills. All teachers interviewed mentioned that children in the age bracket of 4–6 were more positioned to read and write, but this depended on how well they had been exposed earlier. The teachers mostly noted pronunciation challenges of certain phonemes, especially if such sounds were redundant in the child's mother tongue.

McCarthy (1994) notes that although 3-year-olds do not need to start learning how to read formally, they can learn through preschool activities a great deal about letters and the sounds they stand for, about how to write important words like their own names, about the many purposes writing is used for, about books and the stories in them. Children who start formal reading instruction with this kind of background have a head start over children with little exposure to either the forms or the uses of literacy.

Ways of Reinforcing Preschool Literacy Experiences

The study went out to establish how the teachers were reinforcing literary experiences among the children. Eighty per cent of the teachers said that one way was to encourage the children to decipher the written language code. This involved the children following along as the teacher read aloud. It also involved asking children questions about words in books or signs in the social environment. The children were then asked to write for themselves—even in invented spelling—because it served to focus their attention on written language symbols and on how they combine to represent oral language.

Another way of promoting language development among preschool children was by encouraging comprehension of text meaning. Sixty-nine per cent of the teachers said that they often encouraged discussions with the children about the text being read; this enabled the child to derive the meaning of words from the physical interpersonal context. Wells (1985) adds that the fact that books often contain more varied vocabulary and sentence patterns than everyday conversation is an added benefit.

The third way of encouraging language use by preschool children was by appreciating the function of reading and writing. Fifty-four per cent of the teachers admitted that being read to contributes to children's motivation to learn to read, and seeing people writing helps children understand that writing is a useful activity in their community. While these benefits of deciphering, comprehension and appreciation are important for all children, 70 per cent of the teachers intimated that these approaches may be especially important in schools since most children did not have books to look at and materials to write with at home. They also added that such approaches proved handy in cases where children did not see adults engaged in literacy activities outside of school settings. One of the gains associated with these literary experiences was that it reduced the risks of primary school failure when the children left the preschools. For effective development of literary experience, availability of learning resources is paramount. We need to interrogate the type, quality and quantity of such materials.

Resource Materials for Language Development

Creating rich language-learning environments requires materials— especially books for teachers and/or children to read and caregivers who are literate, or interested in becoming literate, in the language being used in the preschool. In Kenya, the government has provided free primary education for its children but this is in exclusion of ECD learning. Initially, the MOEST used to provide ECD teachers with a teacher's course book and wall charts. Mostly, the beneficiaries were urban ECD centres, while rural ones did not benefit. Sixty-five per cent of the teachers interviewed revealed that the MOEST no longer provides ECD centres with any learning materials. The ECD heads usually rally parents to raise funds for buying such materials. Even when such materials are affordable, most parents think that free education caters for all learning including ECD and so they are reluctant to offer a hand. In the end, ECD teachers are left to work with insufficient resources, at times improvising and devising the best possible local solutions.

Language Difficulties Observed among the Preschools

All the teachers interviewed revealed that they observed many language difficulties facing the children which acted as a great impediment to language development. These included trouble in modulating voice, for example, the child's voice can be too loud or too soft. It was reported that some children always seemed not to hear what others tell them. Other children showed difficulty in understanding, repeating and following instructions. Some other children had a very limited vocabulary. It was found that some children spoke slowly or without fluency, stuttering or not finishing sentences. Other language difficulties included having trouble naming familiar people or objects or struggling to retrieve familiar words from memory, struggling with rhyming or retelling familiar stories and having a hard time keeping a conversation on the topic.

Challenges Facing Inclusive Practices in the Preschool Programmes

Programme Efficacy

Substantial research literature on inclusion efficacy show that children benefit from services provided in inclusive settings, showing gains in specific competencies as well as in broad social and interactive skills (Guralnick & Groom, 1988). Early integration efforts demonstrate that simply integrating children does not ensure positive outcomes. Instead, benefits depend on planned efforts to facilitate them (Lamorey & Bricker, 1993). One challenge facing inclusive placements in the preschool programme in Kenya was poorly constructed intervention plans and strategies. Sixty-nine per cent of the teachers interviewed said that quality assurance and standards were missing in the preschool programmes since it has not been factored by the government. Effectiveness of various types of inclusionary programmes for children, for example, speech and language intervention programmes for children with communication disabilities may go undiagnosed or not be overcome properly. This has presented challenges to the preschools in achieving desired outcomes.

In the same vein, lack of opening inventories on the language disorders noted in children and the intervening measure undertaken for each case proved to be a hurdle in tracking such problems. Seventy per cent of the teachers interviewed reported that their training in ECD curriculum did not delve much on diagnostic studies on communication disorders among children. Hence, they were well equipped in differentiating different disorders or prescribing intervening measures for them. So, much of their attempts in handling such issues depended on trial and error which was a very infective way of handling language difficulties; indeed, such crude measures were said to worsen the children's learning problems. It was also reported that not a single language pathologist visited the preschools. The one and only language pathologist working in Narok District Hospital was not always available because many locals are poor and cannot afford to pay for therapy.

Cost-Effectiveness and Administrative Issues

Administrative support for or resistance to inclusive models may rest with funding concerns and perceptions of inclusion efficacy (Salisbury & Chambers, 1994). In this study, it was found that the Kenyan government does not fund preschools. The funding is left to the parents and the community. Seventy-eight per cent of the respondents commented that this lapse has created hurdles in the general learning in the preschools, such as shortage of learning materials and teaching resources as well as salaries of the teachers. The financial limitations affect the cost of providing speech, language and hearing services in integrated settings.

Personnel Qualifications

Inclusive practices necessitate alternative roles, responsibilities and qualifications for personnel. While serving children and youths with communication disorders in inclusive programmes, speech–language pathologists, general and special educators, various related service personnel and family members will inevitably engage in collaborative role sharing. In this model, concerns may arise regarding personnel qualifications and preparation (Campbell, Stremel-Campbell & Rogers-Warren, 1985). In regard to this, 78 per cent of the respondents observed that because of the poor grounding and training in ECD curriculum, the ECD teachers were incapable of developing, monitoring and implementing programming for children with speech, language or hearing impairments as the primary problem.

Effects on All Learners

One concern in the implementation of inclusive practices is the influence of children with disabilities on the instructional environment of the classroom. There is the belief that the presence of a learner with special needs may compromise the ability of non-disabled peers to benefit from instruction (Sharpe, York & Knight, 1994). Due to lack of necessary resources in the ECD centres, 72 per cent of the respondents said that they faced difficulties in efforts to accommodate the needs of the child with disabilities in general education as well as controlling the influence of the child with disabilities on the education of other students. Prizant (1995) has suggested that modifications to the environment, activities and child interactions should all be considered when planning for a variety of inclusive experiences. Additional research is needed to evaluate the influence of inclusive practices on all learners.

Conclusion

A major item on the developmental agenda for the child up to age 6 is language. Accomplishments during this period typically include development of control over one's native language sufficient to enable participation in social interaction with peers and with adults, to provide the resources for telling and understanding stories, to offer and understand explanations of interesting phenomena and to use language to solve problems (Prizant, 1995).

Language development during this period typically culminates in the development of abilities that will contribute to the achievement of literacy during the early school years. Despite the centrality of language achievements in the developmental agenda of the first five years, language issues are rarely at the forefront of thinking about how to plan environments for young children.

When designing programmes to provide care and promote development during the preschool period (whether these programmes are formal and classroom-based, or more informal, community or home-based), optimising the language environment usually becomes an issue only in cases where complex linguistic situations highlight it (MOEST, 2003). For example, in multilingual societies where group care involves native speakers of several different languages, or in societies where preschool teachers are likely to use a national language different from that spoken by children, some form of language planning for preschools might occur. We would argue that the quality of the language environment deserves attention for every young child, especially those in group care settings, whether monolingual or multilingual.

Repeated failure on the part of the teachers to respond to the child's communicative attempts (either because of disinterest, because of commitment to more adult-centred activities or because the adult and child do not share a language) constitutes another environmental obstacle. Failure on the part of the teachers to value the child's native language as a useful and valid communicative system similarly constitutes a risk to the child's language development. Failure on the part of the teacher to recognise the need to attend to all children, including those who may seem shy, less interested in the group activities, less responsive, or less competent, can further diminish the quality of the environment for children (Wells, 1985).

A strong programmatic emphasis on teaching academic skills (letters, numbers, colours, rote memorisation of materials) may absorb energies that could better be devoted to real communicative activities and language-enriching conversations. The absence of appropriate books and materials that provide the context for conversations that build oral vocabulary and readiness for literacy may likewise reduce the value of the language environment to the child.

Recommendations

There is a need to ensure that all children are supported and taught in optimum settings so that their language and developmental needs are met. Teachers and administrators should receive annual opportunities for training in issues of communication problems in order to create the most optimum classroom climate respectful of all students. Teachers and administrators should receive periodic training in language needs and intervention measures.

ECD principles have been accepted, but action plans and strategies to implement the principles in the particular context of Kenya need further elaboration. A solid policy framework based on prioritisation and phasing strategies is urgently needed in addressing communication needs of the children.

To develop a policy framework, some conceptual and terminological clarifications are needed. Most importantly, a clearer and more rational provision structure needs to be put in place for the training of teachers, caregivers and parents as well as for inspection and monitoring before any efforts are launched to develop training, inspection, monitoring and evaluation systems.

Providing ECD teachers with minimum government support would be essential to mobilise supplementary resources from parents and prevent the collapse of ECD centres. Finally, efforts must be focused on the drafting of relevant legislation in order to ensure policy implementation.

References

Campbell, C. R., Stremel-Campbell, K. & Rogers-Warren, A. (1985). Programming teacher support for functional language. In S. Warren & A. Rogers-Warren (Eds), *Teaching functional language* (pp. 309–339). Austin, Texas: Pro-Ed.
Guralnick, M. J. & Groom, J. M. (1988). Peer interactions in mainstreamed and specialized classrooms. *Exceptional children*. Bloomington, Indiana: Phi Delta Kappa.
Lamorey, S. & Bricker, D. (1993). Integrated programs: Effects on young children and their parents. In C. Peck, S. Odom & D. Bricker (Eds), *Integrating young*

children with disabilities into community programs (pp. 249–270). Baltimore, Maryland: Paul Brookes.

McCarthy, M. (1994). Inclusion and the law: Recent judicial developments (Research bulletin No. 13). Bloomington, Indiana: Phi Delta Kappa.

Ministry of Education Science and Technology (MOEST). (2005). *Background report of Kenya for the UNESCO/OECD Early Childhood Policy Review Project.* Government of Kenya.

Mwangi, M. W. (2011). *Pre-school teachers' use of oral instructional strategies in teaching English: A study in Kasarani division, Nairobi province, Kenya.* Retrieved from http://ir-library.ku.ac.ke/etd/handle/123456789/1821 (accessed 22 November 2012).

Prizant, B. (1995). *Issues and strategies in providing inclusive learning experiences for children with language and social communicative challenges* (Unpublished thesis). Emerson College, Boston, Massachusetts.

Salisbury, C. & Chambers, A. (1994). Instructional costs of inclusive schooling. *Journal of the Association for Persons with Severe Handicaps, 19*(3), 215–222.

Sharpe, M. N., York, J. L. & Knight, J. (1994). Effects of inclusion on the academic performance of classmates without disabilities: A preliminary study. *Remedial and Special Education.* Cambridge: Harvard University Press.

Tizard, B. (1981). Language at home and at school. In C. B. Cazden (Ed.), *Language in early childhood education.* Washington, D.C.: National Association for the Education of Young Children.

Tizard, B. & Hughes, M. (1984). *Young children learning.* Cambridge: Harvard University Press.

Wells, G. (1985). Preschool literacy-related activities and success in school. In D. R. Olson, N. Torrance & A. Hildyard (Eds), *Language, literacy and learning* (pp. 229–255). New York: Cambridge University Press.

3

Training Innovative Preschool Students through an ICT Project: A Case Study from Turkey

Hayal Köksal

We live in an era of information, technology and communication. Not only has the mode of communication or business changed, but education has also changed through the use of technology in the global world. Information and communication technology (ICT) plays an important role in the improvement of generations. Its significant role lies in the spread of the knowledge produced and/or gained, creative thinking, sharing and collaboration with others.

The author, as the Director of the Eurasian and Turkish Center for Schools of Quality, has aimed at paving the way for establishing such an understanding within various degrees of school students, who are considered the future leaders of the world.

The goal of the project was determined to be to teach collaboration through technology use and thus, to serve humanity by training qualified future citizens (Ennals & Köksal, 2011). It is open to all countries to include all the colours of the humanity into it. With the project, students are expected to internalise the scientific approach in conducting a project, and also to understand the differences between cultures and the importance of being environmentally literate and empathetic. In other words, at every stage of the project, students are motivated to realise the importance of being creative and original, dealing with time effectively, keeping well-designed portfolios and obeying the ethical rules which are considered to be the characteristics of every effective study.

In this chapter, the '©ICT Seagulls Project' and a sample case conducted by the 5-year-old students in Istanbul in 2006 will be described step-by-step to the readers, and will be referred to merely as the 'Project', from this point on.

Main Characteristics of the Project

The project is called '©International ICT Seagulls Project' and it has three main characteristics: diversity, inclusion and collaboration. Even though there is a tendency to separate the terms diversity and inclusion, such that diversity is used to address issues surrounding culture, whereas, inclusion is interpreted as including children with special needs and disabilities, this project holds those two concepts together by including all groups from all cultural backgrounds (Bruce, 2006).

It is designed for all volunteer teams, which are called students' quality circles (SQCs), from preschools to universities, from all countries of the world. In other words, it includes all age groups from kindergarten to college, hugging the gifted and the disabled ones. This reflects the true diversity and richness of variety (Pimentel, 2006).

SQCs is a team of students who work to solve their problems using a participatory approach (Ennals & Köksal, 2011; Köksal, 2004, 2012). This helps to develop the leadership quality attributes of the members working in the team (Chapagain, 2006, p. 63; Köksal, 2006b). Teachers and parents might take part as the supporting bodies. Students actively participating in SQCs activities develop a number of leadership traits, skills and habits, such as self-confidence, self-discipline, interpersonal and public relations skills, empathy, social responsibility, time management skills, scientific and analytical skills, communication skills, creativity and the working habits of a team member with a broad vision (Chapagain, 2006).

In addition to this, the use of ICT affects young children positively, for children are surrounded by ICT in their immediate environments and they are exposed to very developed technologies from a young age.

New technologies support, influence and shape their lives, such as inter-active whiteboards, electronic toys and games, mobile phones, cameras, walkie-talkies, remote controlled toys and even computers. All children at every age can benefit from learning with and about ICT (Mehrotra, 2012). In order to live in a healthy and fruitful future world, it is needed to train qualified generations. According to Bonstingl (1992), in the new paradigm of learning, students should be in such educational processes provided by families and schools that they should gain the needed courage to improve their abilities, interests and love for learning continuously. The main concern of the project is to develop new ways and approaches to expand the learning potential for all age groups. One of the best ways of achieving that is to design and develop some projects for young people supported by the people around them. Use of technology must be an important ingredient, for the world has been in an era of technology since the final quarter of the 20th century, as mentioned above.

Children learn in different ways, have different styles and build on very different backgrounds of experience. Classrooms increasingly contain groups of children with a wide range of individual differences. These dif-ferences include a wider range of capabilities than they have usually been permitted to show in the regular classroom. Another important issue is the age factor. The younger they are when they meet new ideas and technolo-gies, the more creative and successful they become. Therefore, the target of educators as well as parents must be to open the necessary channels and to provide the necessary environment for those future leaders. Today's kindergarteners will be retiring in the year 2068 according to Ali (2011). It is not clear to us what the world will look like in five years, much less 60 years, so it is very important for us to prepare students for life in that world. Many schools have been seeking alternatives for providing chal-lenging fields for the students and, thus, they aim at satisfying parents, students and also themselves as the leading institutions.

Project management is one of the best ways of opening such windows for the young. Through project design, students develop awareness in respect of their responsibilities as far as their own future is concerned; they develop skills to do career-based projects and also learn and imple-ment the main principles of 'project management' (Köksal & Meyer, 2003). Through that kind of study, students deal with many emerging issues such as global warming, famine, poverty, health issues and other environmental and social issues.

The essence of the project focuses on total quality person (TQP) training and aims at 'catching kids young'. It is known that early intervention programmes and projects help to make children ready for school by supporting their cognitive development and team spirit. It is thought that this readiness for school will have a positive effect on a child's attendance by facilitating the child's adaptation to school. As it was mentioned above, 'age' is an important criterion for all kinds of educational processes. A 'project-based approach' provides valuable learning experiences to young children. It is internalised easily and accurately. The reason lies within the methodology. Children at early ages perceive 'project management' as a kind of game, and that kind of implementation gives fruitful results at the end of any teaching learning process (Köksal, 2006a).

Childhood, as is known by everyone, is the age when development and learning take place the quickest, and experiences gained in this period construct a base for the following years. Therefore, instead of waiting for a child's later years to take part in innovative projects, motivating him to be a part of a project at a very early age, such as in kindergarten, might be more fruitful for him/her. Waiting for further school years to support the development of areas which are supposed to be completed in the first six years of his/her life becomes very late after that time, and this can cause retardations the compensation of which is impossible. Results of research in that area have shown that project involvement makes children ready for school and for further studies by supporting their cognitive development (Kartal, 2007). Modern researchers have shown that the years between 3 and 10 are of the greatest importance in the child's physical, emotional and intellectual development. At this stage, the child should be introduced to the joy of learning through collaboration. Recreational activities gain importance at that age. It is wise to guide a child in the proper habits of life and a healthy mode of living, as well as in the cultivation of social habits, which play a pivotal role later on for community life. It is felt that most of the mental and emotional problems that arise in later childhood owe their origin to the maladjustment of children during the preschool period (Sinha, 2005). Therefore, empowering students through projects will be one of the keys to attaining peace and productivity.

Detailed Information about the Project

In the following part, some more details about the contents and steps of the '©International ICT Seagulls Project' will be shared.

History

In 1999, the Ministry of National Education started the Total Quality Management in Education (TQE) campaign in 70,000 Turkish schools. The Turkish Center for Schools of Quality, which aims at spreading that philosophy and its practices in educational environments, was founded by John Jay Bonstingl and the author on 22 January 2000 in Istanbul. The author, as the Director of the Center, decided to design an ICT project to teach the total quality (TQ) philosophy, its tools and methodology to school children and teachers in Turkey in 2002. The project would last an academic year, and the outcomes would be shared through the Internet to reach every school in each town and city within the country.

Since one significant symbol of Istanbul and Bosporus is 'seagulls', the project was named as 'ICT Seagulls Project'. The teamwork would be the main ingredient focusing on collaboration, sharing and caring rather than developing hostile feelings of rivalry. Since the project aimed at teaching the practical side of TQE, it also followed its philosophy, that is, continuous improvement. Each year, participants share their reflections to improve the project and necessary modifications are done based upon them.

A good example of those modifications is about the guidance of the school teams: During the first years of the project, a 'face-to-face' model was used and seminars for teaching the 'methodology of project management' and 'web page design' were conducted at the conference halls of the schools. However, for the last five years, everything has been shared in the cyber world. A training folder is sent through emails, or the training CD is sent through the postal service to each team. If the need appears, schools are visited to give guidance.

Another change was about the inclusion of various groups. For instance, non-governmental teams were included in 2005, kindergarten teams in 2006, international teams in 2007 and teams with disabled participants in 2008.

The other change was about the portion of assessment grades. The role of peer assessment increased over the years. It was 30 per cent during the initial years but now it is 60 per cent.

Within nine years, nearly 300 projects were finalised successfully. In 2003 six, in 2004 five, in 2005 twenty-four, in 2006 thirty-one, in 2007 ninety-three, in 2008 thirty-two, in 2009 nineteen, in 2010 twenty, in 2011 thirteen and in 2012 twenty projects were conducted. In each team, there are eight students and two teachers; in other words, almost 3,000 people were trained and affected by the project. They learned how to apply analytical skills while managing a project. If it is assumed that their parents and people have also been influenced, it is clearly understood how influential a project is.

Topics

Through the Project, awareness will be created within the student–teacher circles (teams) concerning 'human dignity', 'cultural sensitivity' and 'tolerance'. Gaining a historical perspective about the studied problem areas (themes), internalising the team spirit, using quality tools affectively, improving technological and environmental literacy, managing time and conflict, focusing on ethics—especially respecting the copyrights of others and improving communication and problem-solving skills are considered to be other benefits. Through the project, students as well as the leading teachers understand the necessity of feeding the 'mind, body and spirit' in a positive way. Young generations are motivated to be more creative, productive and investigative, regardless of what they study. Participants develop a positive attitude towards the importance of sharing the results of their projects in a very extraordinary style. By using their imaginations, they fly towards and beyond all limitations, just like 'Jonathan Livingstone Seagull', not only at national but also at international platforms.

Methodology

Project circles study based upon the PDCA mindset (Plan–Do–Check–Act) by using quality tools and following the 'SQC' logic. They use ICT at an optimal level. It was proved after a nine-year experience that the project adds a large amount of knowledge and skills to students through its contribution to character development of the young. They gain and improve the philosophy of life-long learning. It is worth noting that those outcomes are approved not only at the national level but also at the international platforms (Köksal, 2009a). For instance, the project has been supported by the World Country for Total Quality and Excellence in Education (WCTQEE) which was founded by 25 countries in India. It is heartening to have SQCs from all over the world.

Main Steps

After the completion of the registration procedures between the coordinator and the administration of the volunteer school, the necessary training seminar is given to the Project Circle (Team) through PowerPoint (PPT) sharing and also teleconferencing sessions in the cyber world via Skype. All the team members and the leading teachers start their project journey after getting the detailed information about the steps of the project. Projects must be prepared based upon the PDCA mindset as mentioned above. Teams take the following steps after getting the needed training:

1. They identify the project topic concerning the problem area with the participation of all members of the circle including volunteer parents and students.
2. They conduct a detailed research (literature review) about the problem area.
3. They draw the 'road map' of the project by using quality tools, such as brainstorming, Ishikawa diagram, Matrix, Pareto, etc.
4. They find out and determine some strategies, tactics to solve the problem after the determination of the main and root causes of the problem.

5. They prepare data collection tools.
6. Then, the implementation step starts. They collect and analyse the data related to the problem. In order to do that, they prepare surveys, interviews or observation tools.
7. They implement those strategies to bring about the solution to their problem.
8. Meanwhile, they try to involve the whole community in those planned activities. Thus, they create awareness about the problem.
9. Finally, they measure the success rate of the change they created as a result of their implementation phase.
10. They share all the outcomes with the community through various technological ways, such as web page design, blog or PPT.

As it was pointed earlier, that methodology is called the PDCA mindset; in other words, they plan in advance, apply the problem solving tools, check the result and, after the necessary modifications, recommend the solutions to the public through ICT.

Assessment Process

ICT Seagulls projects are assessed in three steps:

1. The Preliminary Step

It is a simple overall checking of the project steps by the general coordinator. Only after her approval, the team members start the peer assessment of the all approved projects. The following criteria are taken into consideration during that step:

a. Obeying time restrictions (managing time)
b. Following the general rules of the project during the project steps
c. Designing and sharing the outcomes of the project according to the rules
d. Delivering all the documents and CDs in a complete and timely manner

2. Peer Assessment Step

All the teams/circles from various schools of different countries assess other projects (excluding theirs). Their grades form 60 per cent of the whole grading process. Circle members are also expected to correspond with the other circles' members living in different countries. The circles from the same schools cannot assess their schoolmates. An assessment form, which is shared through the web page of the project, includes the following criteria. Team members come together under the leadership of their teachers and assess all the teams based upon the following items:

a. The identification of the project topic must be done in a democratic manner and the main problem should be clearly defined.
b. The literature review of the problem area must be conducted from the Internet and from the library resources. All the members should understand the main theme accurately.
c. The data analysis and determination of the main and root causes must be done accurately through various quality tools such as brainstorming, fishbone and matrix diagrams.
d. Strategies and solutions determined by the members must be clear and affective.
e. Changes after the implementation should be stated openly in the strategic plan. They must be measured, and the improvement/ change rates must be given in percentages.
f. The outcomes of the project should be well clarified. The project diary exists on the web page.
g. The web page designs must hold all the needed characteristics and sections (easy access, logos, links, contact, circle members, …).
h. The web page must have PPT presentations to show the way to the web visitors, both in the mother tongue and in English.
i. The advisor/expert in the problem area should be mentioned on the web page with due gratitude.
j. All the quoting should be done accurately.

3. Jury Assessment Step

The honorary jury members from different countries assess all the projects based on the same criteria mentioned above. It constitutes 40 per cent of the whole assessment. Jury members are asked to use the following General Criteria while assessing the projects:

    a. Correct use of the PDCA mindset and SQC methodology including quality tools
    b. Appropriateness to the student level
    c. Creativity and authenticity
    d. Scientific approach
    e. Team spirit

Age Group

As it was stated before, the project is open to all age groups. However, for the assessment step, the grouping is done as follows:

    1. Preschool education/kindergarten circles/teams
    2. Elementary school circles (1–8 graders)
    3. High school circles (9–12 graders)
    4. University circles (undergraduate, graduate, post-graduate)
    5. Circles supported by non-governmental organisations (NGOs) (all age groups)
    6. Circles supported by the business world (all age groups)
    7. Disabled circles (all age groups)
    8. Gifted students' circles (all age groups)

School types do not make any difference in evaluation phase, that is, there is no difference between the circles that belong to state or private schools. They are assessed within the same group. However, different criteria are used for the young and adult ones. This is also valid for the disabled circles.

Awards

Every project circle completing the whole process successfully is a 'winner'. However, after the assessment period, they are also awarded by various titles, such as 'The Most Creative Circle' or 'The Best High School Project Leader', etc.

There is no financial award of this project. The ones who complete the project successfully learn how to conduct a scientific project, how to manage time and conflict, how to apply quality tools and the PDCA mindset and how to use technology in a collaborative way. The reward is internalizing the methodology and gaining national and international reputation through press releases, social media and web page announcements from the project.

A Sample Preschool Education ICT Seagull Project

In this section, a preschool ICT Seagulls project, which was studied within the International ICT Seagulls project in 2006 by the students of a private school, will be shared with the readers.

General Information

Seven children of the age of five years of a local school in Istanbul participated in the project under the guidance of their teachers in November 2005. The group consisted of four boys and three girls. Two class teachers and an IT Teacher guided the team. The team called itself the 'Green Dot Circle'.

They used to meet every Wednesday and Friday during their project hours within the classroom during the academic year of 2005–2006. The project was delivered to the coordinator as a hard copy in addition to the PPT presentation. The results appeared in June 2006 and the Award Ceremony of 2006 ICT Seagulls projects was held in September 2006 at

Albert Long Hall of Boğaziçi University. There, a synopsis of the presentation of their project was presented before the audience in English. The author would like to acknowledge all students involved in the Green Dot Circle and their parents, their teachers and also the school administration, who supported and contributed so much during the project and presentation steps.

Contents

The Green Dot Circle first brainstormed to find out their problems and identified one theme on environmental issues. The project title was: 'Our Contributions to Recycling and Disposing of Waste'. The team members designed a logo and they determined their slogan as: 'The journey of the recycled items', which were the prerequisites of the project.

The goal of the project was: Starting recycling awareness within the school and teaching ways of safe disposal of non-recoverable waste.

They listed their objectives as:

1. Learning the meaning and the steps of the recycling system in Turkey.
2. Creating awareness among the school and its surrounding community.

Since the project is based upon the PDCA mindset, the leading teachers started the project with 'planning'. They determined other steps as:

1. Activities related to the project topic
2. Processes and activities
3. Evaluation of the project

Leading teachers also decided to link the project topic to one of the units of the preschool programme. Thus, they would give more time to the team members for their study and all the other students of the class were able to get information about what was going on in the project. The Green Dot Circle first brainstormed to find out their problems and identified 'recycling' as a theme to bring about some solutions to their environmental problems. Teachers included the project topic into the curriculum with the unit of 'The Life and the Harmony in the World: Recycling'. The main idea of the unit was to learn about recycling, making use of waste materials and using natural resources more effectively. After a detailed literature review, they brainstormed about the probable activities to be done in their school.

They prepared a unit action plan to learn the names of the materials to be recycled, and about recycling systems and citizen responsibilities related to recycling.

They prepared a list for their future work:

1. 'Mind mapping' about recycling
2. Collecting and grouping the waste materials, items
3. Forming a container to put all the collected materials in
4. Signs and cards of recycling and learning their meanings
5. Playing with those cards
6. Organizing an 'Environment Project' within the borders of the school
7. A research assignment for all members
8. Informing the school people about the ICT Seagulls Project in general and what they plan to do.

Activities

1. The first step was 'mind-mapping'. The following thoughts appeared as the result of the brainstorming activity which focused on the question: 'What items can we recycle?'. The answers were: cardboard and paper, a milk box (a toy house can be made out of it), papers and glue, napkin, a broken glass, plastics and leather, cotton; after tearing a sweater, it is made again; also, blankets, leather shoes and trees.
2. Then, the following activities were realised during the year:

    a. Preparing a special corner for the project. It included a project calendar, a PC to work on for the project, a play corner, a math corner

    b. Preparing bulletin boards in Turkish and English

    c. Field trips

    d. Some drawings to show the recycling journey of paper

    e. Working with waste materials

    f. Collaborating with all subject areas concerning the project topic

    g. Preparing a survey

    h. Experiments (material burying, day and night game, volcano game)

    i. Activities in the kitchen of the school

3. Final evaluation included a mind mapping exercise to investigate what they had already learned. It included their PPT presentation, portfolio and reflections.

   Mind mapping was interesting to see their reflections:

   Member 1: I have learned that solid waste should not be thrown into the waste baskets. If we do so, recycling process will not be possible.

   Member 2: It was interesting to learn that glass is made from silica and it is filled with air. If we had not done recycling, the world would have been much polluted.

   Member 3: I have learned that we should put the white glass into white glass bins, and the coloured ones into coloured glass bins before sending for recycling. And we must not waste any material around us in vain.

   Member 4: I have learned the meanings of recycling marks. If we do not recycle, the right of human beings and animals is limited and all the terrible smell covers everywhere.

   Member 5: Tetra Pak boxes are used as counters in kitchens if they are recycled. How interesting it is!

   Member 6: We saw how glass beads are made in Glass Workshop.

   Member 7: For recycling we should separate all the solid waste from others. Otherwise, everything is useless.

Final evaluation showed the outcomes of the project. Here are their own words:

- Recycling is a big problem in our country.
- Recycling is necessary not to waste money.
- If we do not do recycling, we waste the ones in nature.
- The world is being polluted.
- We waste our natural resources.
- Erosion is another outcome of that problem.
- While walking around, the grass seems so dirty.
- Environmental pollution causes accidents. For instance, you can step on a banana skin and fall down.
- We must throw our waste in different cans with different contents.
- This country was covered by waste in ancient times.

4. Solutions were also shared by the kids:

- We must have separate waste baskets.
- The waste containers should be placed near apartments.
- If the municipality works harder, we have a cleaner environment.
- We must use the batteries which have recycling signs on them.
- We cannot meet recycling boxes very often, everywhere.
- Our people do not care.
- Very old people do not know this; we should go and teach them.
- To not kill nature we should do recycling.
- All municipalities should have recycling centres.
- Hospitals are very important places to keep the waste in different boxes.
- Municipalities should place different kinds of waste baskets everywhere. Thus, we can throw our waste accordingly.

After the completion of the project, they prepared their PPT with their teachers and also added their e-mail accounts to answer the questions of the participants. They presented their projects and shared their experiences before the audience. They were awarded as the 'Champion project leaders of the preschool education level'. They were just like little stars shining with light and energy. A seven-month project journey had added many experiences to the future leaders of the world.

Final Words

According to the findings, gained from the experience through a six-month collaboration with kids, and also from the observation during the final presentations, it was understood that 'early childhood education projects' had an effect not only on the cognitive but also the affective and psycho-motor development of children who participated in the project (Barell, 2003; Bonstingl, 1992; Chapagain, 2006; Kobrin, 2004; Köksal, 2007; Mehrotra, 2012). These findings revealed the importance of involving kids in projects at very early ages.

Inclusion of preschool students into such projects might be more effective if early childhood education programmes start for those children who live in disadvantageous environments. This point must be taken into account, because environmental conditions affect children's development, especially in the early years. Such kind of support causes children to start to school more prepared, to adapt more easily and to be more successful in school, as was stated in many studies (Köksal, 2009b).

For this reason, preschool education must not be ignored, and a scientific approach should be introduced within the syllabus of alternative early childhood courses and projects. Furthermore, the use of ICT might add more enthusiasm and interest among the kids. Providing such diversity to educational institutions will create an early state of tolerance for cultural differences. This is the essence of a peaceful and collaborative world.

References

Ali, W. S. (2011, 22–24 October). Values and skills through child-friendly quality education. *Proceedings of the Seventh National Convention on Students' Quality Circles* (7th NCSQC'11), Shuvatara School, Nepal (pp. 28–29). Lalitpur: QUEST-Nepal.

Barell, J. (2003). *Developing more curious minds*. Alexandria, Virginia: ASCD.

Bonstingl, J. J. (1992). *Schools of quality*. Alexandria, Virginia: ASCD.

Bruce, T. (Ed.). (2006). Diversity & inclusion. *Early childhood: A guide for students* (pp. 127–130). New York: SAGE.

Chapagain, R. D. (2006). *Guide to students' quality circles*. Kathmandu: QUEST.

Ennals, R. & Köksal, H. (2011, June). Creating collaborative advantage through students' quality circles. *Proceedings of IAMB 2011 Conference*, Istanbul.

Kartal, H. (2007). The effect of mother–child education program. *Elementary Education Online*, 6(2), 234–248.

Kobrin, D. (2004). *In there with the kids*. Alexandria, Virginia: ASCD.

Köksal, H. (2004). *Eğitimde Güç Birliği için İmece Halkaları (SQCs for the unity of power in education)*. Istanbul: Academy Publishing.

———. (2006a). *Bir demet etkinlik (A bunch of in-class activities)*. Istanbul: Paymaş Printing.

———. (2006b). *Projects of the year 2006*. Retrieved from http://bilisimcimartilar. com/english/projects/2006-projects/

———. (2007). *İçimdeki Çocukla Sürekli Öğrenen Ben (Me: Life-long learner with the child within)*. Istanbul: Prisma Printing.

———. (2009a). Hugging all the nations through TQE. In A. Baykal & H. Köksal (Eds), *The international convention book on students' İmece circles* (pp. 115–118). Istanbul: Visual Art Center.

———. (2009b, 2–5 December). Using technology to support future critical thinkers and problem solvers (TQPs). *Proceedings of 12th ICSQCC at City Montessori School, Lucknow, India*. Lucknow, India: City Montessori School.

———. (2012). SQCs in Turkey as 'imece circles'. In R. Ennals & D. Hutchins (Eds), *AI & Society*. doi: 10.1007/s00146-012-0380-8

Köksal, H. & Meyer, A. (2003, 15–18 June). A project-based activity for the world's cultural heritage. Paper presented at the UNESCO Conference on Intercultural Education, University of Jyvaskyla, Finland.

Mehrotra, D. (2012). *Implementing six sigma in education towards TQM in academics*. New Delhi: S. Chand.

Pimentel, R. (2006). Using ICT to support children's development and learning. In T. Bruce (Ed.), *Early childhood: A guide for students* (pp. 21, 24). New York: SAGE.

Sinha, D. K. (2005, 2–5 December). Empowering students through the renewal of primary school curriculum and evaluation procedure. *Proceedings of the eighth ICSQCC at City Montessori School, Lucknow, India*.

Section II
Approaches and Methods

4

Inclusionary Education in Early Years through the Use of Persona Dolls: A Case from Greece

Sophia Dimitriadi

All children should have the right to equal opportunities in education, meaning that all children should have opportunities to fulfil their potential and be included within an educational system. Inclusion involves acknowledgement of the diversity of people in its broadest sense, not only those with impairments and those having special educational needs, but all those—children and adults—who are vulnerable to exclusionary pressures. Addressing issues of diversity and working towards inclusion in early years education is about improvement of delivered education—for both children and practitioners[1]—through the process of restructuring policies and practices. The primary aim should be to increase the participation of children in the learning process, thus providing an effective schooling for all.

In this chapter, an innovative and effective educational tool that addresses issues of diversity and promotes inclusion in education and, generally, in society will be introduced to those not familiar with it. In addition, a research study that took place in Greece will be briefly presented.

---

[1] The term 'practitioner' is used to refer to every professional working in the education and care of young children under the age of five, irrespectively of the type of early years settings he/she works for.

This learning medium that provides young children a safe platform for embracing diversity is known by the name of 'Persona Dolls'.

History of Persona Dolls

Persona Dolls originally appeared in the multicultural United States, during the 1950s. Kay Taus, a nursery teacher in California, and her colleague, Ruth, pioneered the concept of Persona Dolls in order to deal with prejudice and discrimination in their classrooms (Etienne, Verkest, Kerem & Meciar, 2008; Nutbrown, 2002). At that time, there were very few resources to reflect the lives of children from ethnic minority families or other diversity backgrounds (Centre for Education for Racial Education in Scotland, 2004), so these two resourceful teachers decided to take action and do something about this inequality of resources. Therefore, they made dolls out of card trying to represent the physical features and skin tones of the children in their classroom environment. The teachers dressed the dolls and gradually built stories around their lives and lifestyles, providing them with a certain persona—personality. These dolls had a certain family background, a certain cultural background, a certain way of life, likes and dislikes, favourite food, books, TV programmes, best friends, etc. Then, the teachers were telling the children the stories that the dolls had 'told' them (Taus, 1987). The carton dolls developed into real dolls later in the 1980s as Kay Taus became a member of the Anti-Bias Curriculum Task Force (A.B.C. Task Force) team which developed a whole philosophy and classroom practice against discrimination and prejudice, widely known as the Anti-Bias Curriculum (Derman-Sparks, 1989). Those dolls were called Diversity Dolls or Anti-Bias Persona Dolls (Centre for Equality and Innovation in Early Childhood, 2012).

The Persona Dolls approach gradually transformed into a method and, drawing on the work of their US colleagues, was brought to Australia and Europe almost simultaneously, in the late 1990s, by innovative and enlightened educators (Gaine & van Keulen, 1997; MacNaughton, 1999; MacNaughton & Williams, 1998).

However, starting from the UK and South Africa, Persona Dolls became internationally known as a non-threatening and effective means for tackling exclusion due to discrimination, thanks to the efforts and work of Babette Brown, an inspired and dedicated nursery school teacher from South Africa who became a political exile in Britain in 1963 (Brown, 1998, 2001, 2008; Persona Doll Training, 2012). Babette Brown, as the founder of the Early Years Trainers Anti-Racist Network (EYTARN), worked hard to communicate and highlight the power these Dolls have in training young children—and the adults in their environment—to unlearn prejudices, challenging exclusion and discriminatory behaviours, as well as in inspiring the implementation of inclusive practices and policies in early years settings and schools (Persona Doll Training, n.d.). Since then, Brown has been authoring books on Persona Dolls, organising training sessions on the making of and using the Dolls and, finally, providing constant inspiration for other authors and researchers in the conducting of relevant research on the effectiveness of the use of Persona Dolls (Cook, as cited in Brown, 2008; Etienne et al., 2008; Irish, 2009; Konstantoni, 2009; McClement, as cited in Brown, 2008; Nutbrown, 2006; Smith, 2005, 2006a, 2006b). In 2000, Babette Brown founded Persona Doll Training, a registered charity based in the UK that supports and educates practitioners in the use of Persona Dolls (Mickelburgh, 2012; Persona Doll Training, n.d.).

In Greece, Persona Dolls are not so widely known. For more than 15 years, this chapter's author has been working and collaborating with a wide number of preschool settings around Athens—the capital city of Greece—and has been researching on issues of equality and inclusion in early years education. During this period, no evidence of teachers working with Persona Dolls in their classroom was found. In addition, one can easily support this fact by establishing the complete absence of relevant Greek bibliography and only identifying some individual, recent efforts, limited, though, to a conference presentation level (Βίτσου & Αγτζίδου [Vitsou & Agtsidou], 2008) or to graduate and post-graduate dissertation research efforts (Δεληγιάννη, Κολλάρα & Μιχαλή [Deligianni, Kollara & Michali], 2012; Λιόλιου [Lioliou], 2011).

What Is a Persona Doll?

Persona Dolls are exactly what the words mean: dolls with their own personas (Pagett, 2005). They are not like ordinary dolls; they are not dramatic play dolls used in symbolic play or the home corner and, most certainly, they are not puppets (Bisson, 2001; Brown, 2008; Taus, 1987). They are 'people' who 'talk' to the teacher by 'whispering' in his/her ear (Persona Doll Training, 2011).

What is unique though about the use of Persona Dolls is that it is not the children's doll rather it is the teacher's (Brown, 2001; Persona Doll Training, 2011, n.d.).

Persona Dolls are child-like girls and boys, approximately 70 cm tall in height (see Photo 4.1). Like the children in a setting, the Dolls are fat, thin, short and tall. They have different skin tones (reflected by different colours in fabric) and different colour, length and texture of hair (e.g., short, black, curly hair; long, straight, ginger hair in two bunches, etc.). Their facial characteristics (shape and colour of eyes, nose and mouth) are ethnically appropriate addressed too. The clothes of the Dolls represent all types of clothing of children in a setting (Brown, 2001): they wear jeans, tee-shirts, dresses, trousers, sweat-shirts, etc. as well as *salwar kameez* (a type of suit, worn especially by Asian women, with

Photo 4.1

Persona Dolls

Source: Personal archive; photo taken by Sophia Dimitriadi.

loose trousers and a long shirt), sari, *rumaal* (piece of clothing similar to a handkerchief), hijab, turban, etc.

In order for the Dolls to further promote issues of diversity and inclusion and enable children (and adults) to heighten their awareness and understanding as well as appreciate similarities and differences, it is important that some of the Dolls reflect a variety of impairments. For example, as in everyday life, Dolls can wear glasses, or—in case they are blind—they can have a white stick or even a guide dog. They can also have a hearing aid, a wheelchair or even crutches (Brown, 2001). There are only a few suppliers who can provide schools with these Dolls, but there are also training sessions provided for practitioners who want to learn how to make their own Dolls.

The Persona Doll Approach

As previously stated, Persona Dolls have their own personas just like every child in a setting has. This means that the Dolls have a certain family background with one father and one mother, or only one parent, or a stepfamily, or just living with the grandparents, etc. They can have siblings or not. They have a certain name, place they live, place of origin and they speak one or more languages. They have things they like and things they don't like. They have favourite food as well as food they don't eat at all and there are things that they're good at and others that they are not so good at (Bisson, 2001; Brown, 1998, 2001, 2008; Enßlin & Henkys, 2003; Whitney, 1999).

The Persona Doll approach is a non-threatening, innovative and effective way to engage young children (and the adults working with them) in an interactive learning about diversity and inclusion through storytelling and discussion (Smith, 2006a). The Dolls and their stories challenge the values, stereotypes and prejudices that underpin exclusion and discrimination. As stated in the 'Persona Dolls in Action' Support Book (Persona Doll Training, n.d.): 'Practitioners use the Dolls to help children understand that words and actions can be hurtful, to encourage empathy and motivate them to want to stand up and show their support to people experiencing discrimination and unfairness' (p. 3). In support of this evidence, Smith

(2006a) explains that the Dolls also provide psychosocial support and address human rights issues such as inclusion and diversity, disability, gender, racism and xenophobia, social class, health, culture and faith. Similarly, Brown (2002) reports that through the use of the Dolls children learn to appreciate the differences and similarities between themselves and other children in their group, without feeling superior or inferior.

Why in Early Years?

The early years setting being the first social group that children meet outside their family environment, it is the perfect place to unlearn any unfair and unjust message that children have absorbed, as well as any stereotypical behaviour that has already been built in their minds (Dimitriadi, 1997, 2011). During preschool years, children develop their self-identity and their ideas about others and about the world they live in. All the experiences that preschool children gather from home, school and their surroundings will determine the development of their positive or negative self-concept as well as their images about people different from themselves (Lindon, 1998).

Research shows that young children of the ages between two and five might already have developed certain ideas and images about others and about self which reveal stereotypic and even discriminatory attitudes. Not only do they recognise differences, they also absorb values about which differences are positive and connected with power and which are negative and connected with 'inferiority' and isolation (Derman-Sparks, 1989; Milner, 1983). Everyday school practice seems to support this research evidence (Δημητριάδη [Dimitriadi], 2001; Δημητριάδη & Σταμούλου [Dimitriadi & Stamoulou], 2009).

At the same time, young children also notice how parents and teachers act towards differences and what ideas seem to hold about them. Adults' attitudes towards issues of diversity and discrimination will considerably determine a child's forming of either positive or negative ideas about people other than them (Neugebauer, 1992).

With this data in mind, Persona Dolls seem to provide an excellent educational tool that can be used as a starting point for equity education with young children and the adults in their environment.

Persona Dolls in Practice

Persona Dolls represent our society's diversity. They can be used in early years settings that have children as young as 18 months of age (Etienne et al., 2008). They can also be used with young children who attend the first two grades of primary school, especially in order to reinforce their personal, social and emotional development and lately—with great success—for issues of victimisation and bullying. However, most emphasis in the use of the Dolls is being put into the age range between three and six years of age (Brown, 2001, 2008; Pagett, 2005; Persona Doll Training, 2011; Respectme, n.d.).

The Dolls 'visit' children at their school, usually at circle time, and while sitting on the practitioner's lap, the Dolls share with the children their happy and not-so-happy experiences. It is advised that the first Doll the children are introduced to be a boy Doll, so that the interest of the boys in the classroom is aroused equally, as most of them think of dolls being only girls and also being only for girls. Practitioners need to be trained in the use of the Dolls beforehand by experienced professionals and then create a strong bond with the Dolls. This bond can be achieved by practitioners' working in small groups together in order to create the Dolls' personas, that is, their individual personality and background. The individual stories and details of personal backgrounds of the Dolls are agreed between the practitioners and remain as constant as those of the real children in the classroom. Through this procedure, the practitioners get the opportunity to be aware of their own beliefs and practices towards diversity and inclusion, put them under new perspective as well as extend their own intellectual horizons on understanding the world around them. It is highly recommended, though, that this special information along with the individual stories of the Dolls are kept in a special diary, accessed by all adults in the setting (and maybe children's parents, too) in order to avoid any possible confusion to the children, help them connect to the Dolls and make the stories and their impact even more powerful. New facts can be added to each Doll's personal information background and consequently to their individual diary, just as it happens to real children while their experiences are being built up. Still, it is important to keep a consistency in each Doll's life story and maintain its identity, always within an inclusive and anti-discriminatory framework (Brown, 2001, 2008; Persona Doll Training, n.d.; Taus, 1987; Whitney, 1999).

Practitioners should not make funny voices pretending that the Dolls are talking. On the contrary, practitioners should use their real, everyday speaking voice, thus, becoming the means through which the Dolls share their stories with the children. Occasionally, the Dolls 'whisper' in the practitioner's ear in order to answer to a child's question.

With the power of storytelling, children:

- Quickly accept the Dolls as real people and think of them as friends (although they know they are dolls)
- Listen to the Dolls' stories and think critically
- Realise that there are other children too that have experienced situations like the ones of their own and have been hurt or felt excluded, as they might have in the past
- Engage with the Dolls actively by asking them questions or reporting their own uncomfortable situations
- Express their thoughts, attitudes and feelings
- Provide the Dolls with solutions to their problems

According to Bannon (2011, p. 3), Persona Dolls promote:

- Speaking and listening skills
- Community cohesion and citizenship
- Empathy and appreciation of diversity
- Anti-discriminatory practice and equal opportunities

Practitioners act as facilitators during Persona Doll storytelling sessions. They choose to tell stories that happened to the Dolls with themes that are either familiar to children, or themes that children are unfamiliar with, especially as a response to observations that adults in the classroom have made. Ideally, when introducing a Doll for the first time, the practitioner shares basic information about the Doll with the children (drawn from the special diary which was made with the collaboration of the other practitioners of the school), such as the name, the age, the family background and where this 'visitor' lives. It is a good idea to ask children in the classroom to make this new 'person' feel comfortable and welcome, as it is the first time he/she visits the school. The Doll can then share a short, 'happy' story with the children, as it is wise to avoid introducing sad and problematic situations during his/her first visit in the class (Bisson, 2001; Brown, 2001, 2008; Mickelburgh, 2012; Persona Doll Training, 2011). The goal is for the children to get to know the Doll and become friends. However, due to the fact that some children of this young age cannot listen to a lengthy story and concentrate for a long time, the first stories should be kept simple and short, not exceeding five minutes (Brown, 2001).

The second visit of the same Doll will include some more information around the Doll's life which will enable children to get to know their 'friend' better. Once the children have bonded with the Doll's character, it is the perfect time to develop and share another short story, preferably with content similar to the children's current experiences, such as changing schools, having a new sibling, wearing glasses, etc. The practitioner should encourage children to express their feelings and thoughts, by asking open-ended questions. Yet, the practitioner should try not to impose own ideas, rather he/she should provoke a discussion and encourage the children to participate actively by doing most of the talking (Brown, 2001; Whitney, 1999).

The third visit is an important one. The children have now bonded with the Doll, whom they consider to be their friend. They know a lot about the life of their friend and most of them have already identified themselves or situations that have happened to them with those of the Doll. It is high time that a 'deeper' story is introduced to the children that has to do with the Doll's experiencing an uncomfortable, unfair and exclusionary situation, such as teasing due to an impairment, exclusion from a game due to a disability, name-calling, bullying, racism, cultural exclusion, etc. (Bisson, 2001). The practitioner unfolds the story that the Doll has come to share and, as a facilitator, she/he triggers active participation by asking open-ended questions which develop the children's empathy towards the Doll's unfair situation, enables them to put their emotions into words, encourages them to carefully listen to each other without interrupting one another, gives them a lot of opportunities to talk about what has happened to the Doll, reinforces their critical thinking and, finally, encourages them to suggest practical and realistic solutions (Persona Doll Training, 2011).

The ending of the story should be a resolution (Etienne et al., 2008). Children's contributions of ideas and possible solutions are incorporated in a simple and short ending story that the Doll might revisit to share with the children and thank them for helping her/him out. Children must feel reassured that the Doll is much happier now that she/he has received their support and has also taken their advice. Finally, as children of that young age might need to touch and feel the Doll, practitioners could let children pass the Doll around the circle at the end of the session, thus allowing them to cuddle, hug, or simply greet the Doll, reminding them though that their friend doesn't like it when someone pulls her/his hair or undresses her/him (Brown, 2001). After this short closing ritual, the Doll leaves the classroom.

A Case from Greece

As indicated earlier in this chapter, Persona Dolls are not so widely known, needless to say, used in early years and primary education in Greece. This evidence can be further supported by the fact that neither exists nor is adopted by any particular framework for a diversity-based and/or inclusionary framework in early childhood education and generally, in all the different kinds of early years settings in the country (Δημητριάδη [Dimitriadi], 2001; Δημητριάδη & Σταμούλου [Dimitriadi & Stamoulou], 2009; Dimitriadi, 1997, 2011; Dimitriadi, Papadaki & Makrogkika, 2010).

Therefore, after more than a decade of the author's researching the field of diversity and inclusion practices in early years education, as well as working in the early years classroom, the idea of exploring and implementing an educational tool so simple and child-friendly, yet so powerful, became an irresistible challenge.

As a result and since her first acquaintance with the approach in early 2000, the author introduced Persona Dolls to practitioners of Greek nurseries and other preschool education settings. In addition, she monitored their implementation of the approach in their classrooms and, at the same time, explored and researched the tool's impact and potential. The vision and aim had always been to enable practitioners and their settings to acknowledge diversity responsibly and, consequently, provide an inclusive environment for all parties involved.

As the author has established a professional collaborative network of a large number of early years education centres that has been developed through her academic responsibility of monitoring and supervising more than 160 school-based student teachers per year, the case to be presented is part of her research project on diversity and the Persona Dolls approach that took place in the above settings.

Obviously, the Persona Dolls approach has been introduced to early years practitioners of varying levels of hierarchy in school (teachers, assistant teachers, nursery nurses, student teachers, etc.) and of varying years of working experience. Yet, in this chapter, it has been chosen to present a sample of the research work and its outcomes that has been done with the sample group of six early years teachers. At that time, these teachers had been working with groups of three to six-year-old children, for more than five years.

Methodology Issues

According to Clough and Nutbrown (2002), the methodology that a researcher chooses to use is the result of the principles and values as well as of the philosophy and ideology he/she has and, as a result, structures his/her research work. The more variety of values and principles a researcher has, the more methodologies his/her research might incorporate (Roberts-Holmes, 2006). From this point of view, we chose to adopt a 'child-centred methodology' (Dhalberg, Moss & Pence, 1999; James & Prout, 1990; MacNaughton, Rolfe & Siraj-Blatchford, 2004), as well as an 'anti-bias/inclusionary methodology' (Jacobson, 2003; Lindon, 1998; Mallory & New, 1994; McCracken, 1993; Millam, 2002; Neugebauer, 1992; Pugh, 1996; Siraj-Blatchford, 1995; Siraj-Blatchford & Clarke, 2000; Siraj-Blatchford, J. & Siraj-Blatchford, I., 2002).

As regards sampling, participants were not chosen from a random selection, but rather 'hand-picked' from personal contact with practitioners who wished to get involved in the project, as it required a time-consuming training before actually participating in the research. This kind of sampling, where participants are selected according to convenience of access and availability, is entirely legitimate and acceptable, especially in a small-scale study of a single researcher, although the findings are limited to the sample itself (Δημητρόπουλος [Dimitropoulos], 2001; Siraj-Blatchford, I. & Siraj-Blatchford, J., 2004). In research methodology, this kind of sample selection is reported as 'purposive sampling' (Denscombe, 2003; Roberts-Holmes, 2006, p. 143), 'convenience sampling' (MacNaughton et al., 2004, p. 156), 'opportunity sample' (Bell, 1993, p. 83) or σκόπιμη δειγματοληψία ['deliberate sampling'] (Δημητρόπουλος [Dimitropoulos], 2001, p. 60).

On the other hand, the research practice of 'triangulation' was also employed so that the research project would acquire validity and the outcomes would become convincing (Hughes, 2004). Through triangulation, different sources of evidence are compared and combined (Cohen, Manion & Morrison, 2000), at least three (Hucker, 2001), by using a variety of research methods, thus, getting different perspectives (Robert-Holmes, 2006). In our case, 'secondary research methods' were used (literature search, documents, reports, the Internet, etc.), as well as 'primary research methods' (interviews, questionnaires, observations) (Hucker, 2001).

Being a qualitative research project, the most broadly used form of its design was employed, that is, the 'case study' (Edwards, 2004). Finally, 'ethical issues' while conducting the research, such as children's participation and protection, awareness and respect of the diversity of people involved, avoidance of using language bias, informed consent when documenting via videotaping, etc., were all tried to be given due consideration throughout the process of the research project (Coady, 2004; Hucker, 2001; Roberts-Holmes, 2006).

Training on Persona Dolls

Our research interests and projects on diversity and inclusion in education, and especially on the role that Persona Dolls can play in these matters, have been greatly influenced originally by the work of Derman-Sparks (1989), and later—after becoming a member of the EYE (formerly known as the EYTARN) in the late 1990s—by the work of Babette Brown and the Persona Doll Training Organisation. Therefore, it becomes apparent that both our work and approaching style while implementing the tool of Persona Dolls in early years education are derived from the Persona Doll Training resources that we have collected for more than a decade now and which include books, training packs, videos, CD-ROMs, support material and a small number of Persona Dolls.

The project started by working with the selected early years teachers in small groups and not altogether as it was desired, due to difficulties in organising a convenient-for-all set of meetings. However, despite the difficulties in finding out-of-school spare time to devote to the project, all early years teachers were equally and strongly committed to working towards an inclusive practice.

First, the early years teachers who participated in the project were all engaged in exploring their own ideas, feelings, beliefs and attitudes through various team exercises. This process involved, among other things, the presentation of the award-winning television programme 'The Eye of the Storm' (Peters, 1970) which documented a shocking experiment that Jane Elliott, a third-grade teacher in the United States (Peters, 1987), implemented on her students regarding unfair exclusion in the class. It also involved video watching and exercises from the 'In Safe Hands' resource and training pack (Save the Children & The Refugee Council, 2001), the 'Celebrating Diversity: Inclusion in Practice' video and support book, as well as from the 'Persona Dolls in Action' training pack (Persona Doll Training, n.d.). The exercises involved 'getting to know each other' games, brainstorming, worksheets that challenge bias and exclusion, etc. Some indicative exercises drawn from the 'Persona Dolls in Action' Support Book (pp. 13–20) were:

'Who Am I?' (p. 13)
Each participant introduces him/herself by adding an adjective starting with the first letter of his/her name, e.g. the first person says, 'shy Stephanie' (her name); the next person says 'shy Stephanie and funny Fiona' (her name); the next says 'shy Stephanie, funny Fiona and persistent Peter' and so on.

'That's Where I Belong' (p. 17)
All participants suggest which groups are discriminated against in their country. The suggested groups are written down in a list. Then, every participant spends a few minutes to think and decide which of the listed group most closely identifies with. If there are other participants that identify

with the same group, then they work together and contribute their ideas on questions such as:

- What do they like and what they do not like about being a member of this group?
- What jokes and negative comments they don't like to hear about the group they belong to?
- How do the media present their group?
- How would they like others to treat them as a group?

'Removing Physical Barriers' (p. 19)
Participants think about their workplaces and consider whether children and adults with disabilities have access to all areas of the building, are able to use all facilities and able to participate in all activities.

Especially for this last exercise, it was with amazement that the teachers participated in the project realised that their settings had accessibility obstacles, not only to people with disabilities, but also to parents with prams too.

After these sessions, the teachers worked in groups and

- Challenged ideas of diversity and discrimination
- Shared own experiences of bias and exclusion
- Examined own values and attitudes
- Became more aware of their own stereotypes
- Agreed on a new, improved philosophy for their classroom and on adopting an inclusive policy and practice in their setting
- Explored ways that they could address these issues

Creating the Doll's Persona

After presenting the purchased Dolls to the teachers, each one was encouraged to choose the Doll he/she wanted to bond with and create its personality. They exchanged ideas and opinions on what background they would build for each Doll and tried in a variety of ways (by getting information from the children's parents and from friends, by reading relevant material, by browsing through the internet, etc.) to avoid stereotyping and consequently, to create a persona that would be accurate and bias-free. The teachers built their Doll's persona (and along the way, while using it in the class, they added more details concerning the Doll's life) and kept diaries on that information that all adults in their setting could have access to, thus ensuring consistency and continuity in the stories shared with the children.

Some questions considered in order to turn the Doll into a 'person' were:

- What's the Doll's name?
- How old is the Doll?
- What's the Doll's family background (Does she/he have siblings, a mother and a father, grandparents and other members in the family, and what are their names)?
- Where does the Doll live (flat, house, boat-house, tent, etc.)?
- Which members of the Doll's family live with her/him?
- What are the jobs of the Doll's parents?
- What does the Doll like to eat and what doesn't she/he?
- What are the Doll's favourite games?
- What are the Doll's favourite TV programmes, songs, actors,...?
- Which school programme activities does the Doll like best and which doesn't she/he?
- Are there any things that the Doll is really good at and others that she/he isn't and which are these? Why can't the Doll do certain things (due to physical characteristics, disability, temporary impairment, etc.)?

The Doll Enters the Classroom

During group sessions in which the teachers were creating each Doll's personality and history background, several opportunities were given to them in order to bond with this new 'person'. They even had the chance to take their Doll home and buy or create some extra clothes for her/him (so that the Doll does not show up in a classroom with the same clothes every time she/he visits). This way, the teachers got to know their Doll and felt more confident introducing it to the children in their classroom.

When the teachers introduced their Dolls for the first time to the children at circle time, they told them that a child of their age had come to visit from another school. All six teachers preferred to sit the Doll on their laps, instead of providing a 'special chair' (Brown, 2001, p. 22) for her/him, thus enabling them to have a better control of the Doll. The visit did not take long as the primary aim was to establish an initial relationship with the children, by giving some small details about her/him as regards habits, likes and dislikes, etc. So, no stories were told at that time; the children were rather encouraged to identify common grounds with the new 'friend', as the Dolls asked questions through the teacher. The Doll 'whispered' in the teacher's ear and the teacher said: 'Dimitri[2] wants to know if you like outdoor play too …'. Then, children took turns in responding.

All teachers were careful as to when the Doll left the classroom; it did so as a 'real' child would do. This means that they never put the Doll in a bag in front of the children, nor did they ever allow children see the Doll kept in a cupboard.

It Happened to Dimitri …

This is a sample story created by one of the teachers who participated in the project and shared with her classroom of four-year-olds:

Last time Dimitri came to visit us, he was very happy. Do you remember that he went on a short vacation with his parents and little sister to a small island by boat? They had a wonderful time there, they built beautiful castles in the sand, they swam and they even tried some water sports! Do you remember who Dimitri said made the biggest castle?
[Children's responses]

But today, Dimitri is feeling very sad. How can you tell when one is sad?
[Children's responses]

Yes, that's right. He doesn't feel like playing with the others, his face looks differently and he doesn't want to talk much. Would you like me to tell you what happened to make Dimitri sad?
[Children's responses]

---

[2] All Persona Doll names and characters appearing in the text are fictional and do not refer to a real child in the classroom.

Well, yesterday he went to school as usual. He couldn't wait for his favourite time of the day to come, that is, playing outdoors! He feels so excited when he runs and climbs up trees and rolls down the small hills in their school's garden! He was eager to show his friends how to build castles in the sand box area too! But as he approached a group of children to play with, they said they didn't want him to join their play because he wore glasses. They told him that children with such thick glasses can't run fast enough and are not as good as the others in activities, thus, making their team lose when they compete.

When Dimitri said that this wasn't true, they started teasing him and calling him 'Four eyes, four eyes!'.

How do you think that made Dimitri feel?

[Children's responses]

Dimitri has asked me to ask you if you have ever been excluded from a game at school and teased and laughed at. What happened? How did that make you feel?

[Children's responses]

Dimitri doesn't know what to do. He really likes playing outdoors with his friends and does not believe that wearing glasses prevents his team from winning any game. What do you think he should do?

[Children's responses]

Dimitri says you have given him a lot of good ideas. He says he will try your ideas at school and see if they work. He thanks you for helping him out and promises to visit again and let you know how it went.

The teacher made sure that Dimitri revisited after a week to tell her class how he gave a solution to his unfair exclusion by incorporating the children's ideas and suggestions.

Similar scenarios were devised and told to children by the other teachers who participated in the project. Their stories were about children who had been discriminated against and excluded from play by their peers: a boy called Hassan, excluded due to his skin colour; a girl called Katerina, excluded due to her obesity, a boy called Yiannis, excluded due to his gender; a boy called Petros, excluded due to wearing a hearing aid and, finally, a girl called Mariella, excluded because she didn't speak Greek well.

Persona Dolls in Greek Early Years Settings— The Outcomes

As developed over a lengthy period of time and due to the use of methodological and data triangulation (Denzin, 1978), the outcomes will only be summarised and not presented in full in this chapter.

Children's Benefits

- Became aware of their own diversity and of others
- Started valuing diversity in their classroom and in society positively and gained awareness of the richness there is in the different lifestyles
- Became more able to resist stereotyping and exclusion due to diversity
- Became more confident of their own identity, as well as their group's, and enhanced their self-esteem
- Explored ideas of what is fair and what is not and learned to stand up for themselves and for others
- Learned to enjoy storytelling, developed listening skills and active participation
- Developed critical thinking
- Broadened their vocabulary
- Practiced problem-solving skills
- Learned to respect each other when talking
- Learned to express feelings and respect the feelings of others
- Became actively involved for a mutual cause
- Became compassionate and caring for the problems of other people

Teachers' Benefits

- Became more aware of their own biases and non-inclusive attitudes
- Increased knowledge and understanding of diversity and inclusion issues

- Unlearned certain discriminatory attitudes and improved their equal opportunities practices
- Learned to stop being judgemental
- Developed an inclusionary policy in their classroom and tried to convince colleagues and their directors to implement this policy in the whole setting
- Learned not to impose their own minds on children
- Learned to help children express their feelings by using a broad and accurate vocabulary
- Learned to work co-operatively with their colleagues
- Learned to respect each other more and empathise with the problems of others
- Learned to help children deal with their fears
- Became more confident in raising 'difficult' and 'uncomfortable' issues
- Exercised their storytelling skills
- Developed a more responsible, bias-free attitude when answering to children
- Learned the basic principles of having a constructive dialogue with the children and with other adults

Nevertheless, teachers faced some problems when implementing the Persona Doll approach as well. Teachers reported that it took them very long to become confident in storytelling. They also encountered difficulties managing the children in the classroom during the initial sessions. In addition, quite a lot of times were recorded when the teachers did not respond to the children's questions and remarks in a bias-free manner. One other issue was their reluctance to have the Doll on their lap and speak for her/him, as they thought they seemed 'silly' and felt more like an actor rather than a teacher; the mutual feeling among all participants was that they felt exposed. However, most of them overcame this feeling very quickly in the sessions that followed.

Finally, teachers reported to have received ambivalent feedback from the parents. There were others that expressed very enthusiastic messages for the project, volunteered to get involved and help in any way they could. Those parents were impressed by the positive impact the Dolls had had on their children and wanted to learn more about the study and become engaged in this process. On the other hand, there were parents who expressed strong complaints about teachers raising 'delicate' issues through the Dolls, such as racism, disability, religion and family lifestyles. They thought that their children were too young to be introduced to such issues and there were times that exclusionary attitudes were expressed by a minority of parents. Unfortunately, those were the parents who avoided coming to the parent–teacher sessions prepared exactly to address these issues. Luckily though, the percentage of opposing parents was relatively low.

Conclusion

The Persona Doll approach is a powerful, non-threatening, educational tool at the educator's service. Persona Dolls are designed for children in early years education as well as for children in the first grades of primary school. Through storytelling, young children are engaged in active learning and discussion about diversity and inclusion. The children develop better awareness of self and of others, become problem-solvers and learn to make a difference by standing up for themselves and for others.

Persona Dolls as a medium for learning and adopting inclusionary practices in education was implemented in Greek early years settings as well. The findings are in consistency with the findings reported in the relevant bibliography on the use of Persona Dolls (Brown, 2001, 2008; Etienne et al., 2008; Persona Doll Training, 2012, n.d.; Smith, 2006a, 2006b; Taus, 1987; Whitney, 1999).

Although the tool is designed mostly for trained professionals, it was tested with early years student teachers as well with great success (Δεληγιάννη [Deligianni] et al., 2012; Dimitriadi, Kollara & Michali, 2013).

Currently, we are exploring the power that Persona Dolls have in combating bullying at schools. It is our strong belief that equality in education is every child's right and should appear first in the priority list of every educational policy of all countries. Children are never too young to learn and it is important that they learn to counteract the negative and damaging messages surrounding us as soon as possible. Early years education programmes should set the fundamental stone to encourage inclusion for all, as today's children will form tomorrow's citizens.

References

Bannon, K. (2011, July 16). *Persona Dolls*. Retrieved from http://www.everylittlegirl.com/blog/personadolls/ (accessed 2 April 2012).

Bell, J. (1993). *Doing your research project: A guide for first time researchers in education, health and social science*. Maidenhead: Open University Press.

Bisson, J. R. (2001). *Story telling with Persona Dolls*. Retrieved from http://www.teachingforchange.org/wp-content/uploads/2012/08/ec_personadolls_english.pdf (accessed 19 November 2012).

Βίτσου, Μ. & Αγτζίδου, Α. [Vitsou, M. & Agtsidou, A.] (2008). Persona Dolls: Ο Αντισταθμιστικός Ρόλος τους κατά των Διακρίσεων [Persona Dolls: Their counterbalancing role against discrimination]. Στο Δ. Μ. Κακανά & Γ. Σιμούλη (Επιμ.), Η Προσχολική Εκπαίδευση στον 21ο Αιώνα: Θεωρητικές Προσεγγίσεις και Διδακτικές Πρακτικές (σσ. 275–282). Αθήνα: Επίκεντρο. [In D. M. Kakana & G. Simouli (Eds.), Early childhood education in the 21st century: Theoretical approaches and teaching practices (pp. 275–282). Athens: Epikentro].

Brown, B. (1998). *Unlearning discrimination in the early years*. London: Trentham Books.

———. (2001). *Combating discrimination: Persona Dolls in action*. London: Trentham Books.

———. (2002). The power of Persona Dolls [Supplemental material, loose-leaf pages]. *Practical Pre-School, 31*, 13–14.

———. (2008). *Equality in action: A way forward with Persona Dolls*. London: Trentham Books.

Centre for Education for Racial Education in Scotland. (2004). *Origin and purpose of Persona Dolls*. Retrieved from http//:www.education.ed.ac.uk/ceres/Projects/Persona.htm (accessed 21 January 2011).

Centre for Equality and Innovation in Early Childhood. (2012). *About diversity dolls*. Retrieved from http://www.geocities.com/glendamacnaughton/DDolls/intro.html (accessed 28 May 2012).

Clough, P. & Nutbrown, C. (2002). *A student's guide to methodology*. London: SAGE.

Coady, M. (2004). Ethics in early childhood research. In G. MacNaughton, S. A. Rolfe & I. Siraj-Blatchford (Eds), *Doing early childhood research: International perspectives on theory and practice* (pp. 64–72). Buckingham: Open University Press.

Cohen, L., Manion, L. & Morrison, K. (2000). *Research methods in education* (5th ed.). London: Routledge.

Δεληγιάννη, Α., Κολλάρα, Σ. & Μιχαλή, Μ. [Deligianni, A., Kollara, S. & Michali, M.] (2012). Παίζοντας με τις Κούκλες: Πρακτικές στο Βρεφονηπιακό Σταθμό (Playing with the dolls: Practices in early years education settings). Σ. Δημητριάδη (επιμ.) [In S. Dimitriadi (Ed.)]. Αδημοσίευτη πτυχιακή εργασία (Unpublished dissertation). Αθήνα: Τμήμα Προσχολικής Αγωγής, Τ.Ε.Ι. Αθήνας [Athens: Department of Early Childhood Education, T.E.I. of Athens].

Denscombe, M. (2003). *The good research guide*. Maidenhead: Open University Press.

Denzin, N. (1978). *The research act* (2nd ed.). New York: McGraw-Hill.

Derman-Sparks, L. (1989). *Anti-bias curriculum: Tools for empowering young children*. Washington, D.C.: National Association for the Education of Young Children (NAEYC).

Δημητριάδη, Σ. (2001). Διερεύνηση των Ζητημάτων Διαφορετικότητας και Διακρίσεων στην Εκπαίδευση των Μικρών Παιδιών (Exploring diversity and bias in early years education). Στο Α. Κοντογιάννη & Ε. Ντολιοπούλου (Επιμ.), Μετα-πτυχιακά: Εξελίξεις και Προοπτικές στην Προσχολική και Πρωτοσχολική Αγωγή, 3, 191–200. Αθήνα: Ελληνικά Γράμματα. [Dimitriadi, S. (2001). Exploring diversity and bias in early years education. In A. Kontogianni & E. Doliopoulou (Eds), Post-gratuate: Developments and prospects in early childhood education (pp. 3, 191–200). Athens: Ellinika Grammata.]

Δημητριάδη, Σ. & Σταμούλου, Α. (2009). Απόψεις και Στάσεις παιδαγωγών σχετικά με τη Διαφορετικότητα και τις Διακρίσεις στον παιδικό σταθμό (Teacher's views and attitudes towards diversity and discrimination in the nursery). Στο Α. Τριλιανός & Ι. Καράμηνας (Επιμ.), Ελληνική Παιδαγωγική & Εκπαιδευτική Έρευνα (Greek Pedagogical & Educational Research) τ. Α΄(σσ. 606–617). Αθήνα: Ατραπός. [Dimitriadi, S. & Stamoulou, A. (2009). Teacher's views and attitudes towards diversity and discrimination in the nursery. In A. Trilianos & I. Karaminas (Eds), Greek pedagogical & educational research (vol. A, pp. 606–617). Athens: Atrapos.]

Dhalberg, G., Moss, P. & Pence, A. (1999). *Beyond quality in early childhood education and care: Postmodern perspectives*. London: Routledge.

Dimitriadi, S. (1997). *Addressing issues of diversity and discrimination in the education of young children and promoting an anti-bias curriculum in early childhood education: An examination of practices in pre-school settings in Greece* (MEd dissertation thesis). Hull University, Hull, UK.

———. (2011). Being alike, being different: An exploration in Greek nurseries and pre-school centres. *Journal of Educational Chronicle, 2*(2), 1–14.

Dimitriadi, S., Kollara, S. & Michali, M. (2013, May). *Introducing Persona Dolls to the pre-school classroom*. Paper presented at the eighteenth International Conference of the APPAC (Association of Psychology & Psychiatry for Adults and Children), Athens, Greece.

Dimitriadi, S., Papadaki, T. & Makrogkika, E. M. (2010, May). *Equal opportunities: Principles and practices in Greek Early Years Classroom.* Paper presented at the fourth World Congress of the APPAC, Athens, Greece.

Δημητρόπουλος, Ε. [Dimitropoulos, E.] (2001). Εισαγωγή στη Μεθοδολογία της Επιστημονικής Έρευνας: Ένα Συστημικό Δυναμικό Μοντέλο [Introduction to scientific research methodology: A systemic, dynamic model]. Αθήνα: Έλλην [Athens: Hellin].

Edwards, A. (2004). Qualitative designs and analysis. In G. MacNaughton, S. A. Rolfe & I. Siraj-Blatchford (Eds), *Doing early childhood research: International perspectives on theory and practice* (pp. 117–135). Buckingham: Open University Press.

Enßlin, U. & Henkys, B. (2003). Vielfalt ins Gespräch bringen mit Persona Dolls (Diversity with Persona Dolls). In C. Preissing & P. Wagner (Eds), *Kleine kinder-keine vorurteile? Interkulturelle und vorurteilsbewusste arbeit in kiTas (Small children—no prejudices? Intercultural and anti-bias work in nurseries).* Freiburg: Herder.

Etienne, R., Verkest, H., Kerem, E. A. & Meciar, M. (2008). *Developing practice-based research with Persona Dolls for social and emotional development in early childhood.* London: Children's Identity and Citizenship in Europe (CiCe).

Gaine, B. & van Keulen, A. (1997). *Anti-bias training approaches in the early years: A guide for trainers and teachers.* Utrecht: MUTANT.

Hughes, P. (2004). Paradigms, methods and knowledge. In G. MacNaughton, S. A. Rolfe & I. Siraj-Blatchford (Eds), *Doing early childhood research: International perspectives on theory and practice* (pp. 31–55). Buckingham: Open University Press.

Hucker, K. (2001). *Research methods in health, care and early years.* London: Heinemann.

Irish, N. A. (2009). *Evaluating the effectiveness of an ububele Persona Doll: Emotional literacy programme for preschoolers from Alexandra township* (MEd [Educational Psychology] dissertation thesis). University of the Witwatersrand, Johannesburg, South Africa.

Jacobson, T. (2003). *Confronting our discomfort: Clearing the way for anti-bias in early childhood.* Portsmouth: Heinemann.

James, A. & Prout, A. (Eds). (1990). *Constructing and reconstructing childhood.* Basingstoke: Falmer Press.

Konstantoni, K. (2009, 2–5 September). *Why do you think nobody wants to play with Emma?: Persona Dolls, participatory methods and methodological issues in researching young children's views on exclusion.* Paper presented at the ninth Conference of European Sociological Association, Lisbon.

Lindon, J. (1998). *Equal opportunities in practice.* London: Hodder & Stoughton.

Λιόλιου, Ε. [Lioliou, E.]. (2011). *Διερεύνηση Αντιλήψεων και Στάσεων Παιδιών Προσχολικής Ηλικίας σε Ζητήματα Ετερότητας με την Αξιοποίηση της Μεθόδου Persona Doll* [Exploring opinions and attitudes of pre-school children on issues of 'the other', using the Persona Doll method] Διπλωματική Εργασία [Phd thesis]. Πανεπιστήμιο Θεσσαλίας, Βόλος. [University of Thessaly, Volos].

MacNaughton, G. (1999, 17 June). *Changing attitudes with Persona Dolls.* Keynote address presented at the *Persona Doll Project Conference*, London.

MacNaughton, G., Rolfe, S. & Siraj-Blatchford, I. (Eds). (2004). *Doing early childhood research: International perspectives on theory and practice.* Buckingham: Open University Press.

MacNaughton, G. & Williams, G. (1998). *Techniques for teaching young children: Choices in theory and practice.* Melbourne: Longman.

Mallory, B. L. & New, R. S. (Eds). (1994). *Diversity and developmentally appropriate practices: Challenges for early childhood education.* New York: Teacher's College, Columbia University.

McCracken, J. B. (1993). *Valuing diversity: The primary years.* Washington, D.C.: NAEYC.

Mickelburgh, J. (2012). Persona Dolls. *In Early Years Foundation Stage Forum.* Retrieved from http://eyfs.info/articles/article.php?Persona-Dolls-133 (accessed 19 November 2012).

Millam, M. (2002). *Anti-discriminatory practice: A guide for workers in childcare and education.* London: Continuum International Publishing.

Milner, D. (1983). *Children and race: Ten years on.* Hong Kong: Ward Lock Educational.

Neugebauer, B. (1992). *Alike and different: Exploring our humanity with young children.* Washington, D.C.: NAEYC.

Nutbrown, C. (2002). *Research studies in early childhood education.* London: Trentham Books.

———. (2006). *Key concepts in early childhood education & care.* London: SAGE.

Pagett, S. (2005, 22–29 December). Persona Dolls: Hello Dolly! *Nursery World*, 105(4000), 19.

Persona Doll Training. (n.d.). *Celebrating diversity: Inclusion in practice* [Support Book & Video]. London: Persona Doll Training.

———. (n.d.). *Persona Dolls in action* [Support Book]. London: Persona Doll Training.

———. (2011). *Understanding bullying: Understanding children who are bullied and challenging those who bully.* London: Persona Doll Training.

———. (2012). *Equality in practice, learning by doing.* Retrieved from http:// www.persona-doll-training.org/ukhome.html (accessed 23 October 2012).

Peters, W. (Producer & Director). (1970). *The eye of the storm* [Television documentary]. USA: ABC News.

———. (1987). *A class divided: Then and now* (Expanded ed.). Chelsea, Michigan: Yale University Press.

Pugh, G. (Ed.). (1996). *Contemporary issues in the early years: Working collaboratively for children* (2nd ed.). Weston-super-Mare: Paul Chapman Publishing/National Children's Bureau.

Respectme. (n.d.). *Persona Dolls*. Retrieved from http://www.respectme.org.uk/Persona-Dolls.html (accessed 05 March 2012).

Roberts-Holmes, G. (2006). *Doing your early years research project: A step by step guide*. London: Paul Chapman.

Save the Children & The Refugee Council. (2001). *In safe hands: A resource and training pack to support work with young refugee children*. London: Save the Children.

Siraj-Blatchford, I. (1995). *The early years: Laying the foundations for racial equality*. London: Trentham Books.

Siraj-Blatchford, I. & Clarke, P. (2000). *Supporting identity, diversity and language in the early years*. Buckingham: Open University Press.

Siraj-Blatchford, I. & Siraj-Blatchford, J. (2004). Surveys and questionnaires: An evaluative case study. In G. MacNaughton, S. A. Rolfe & I. Siraj-Blatchford (Eds), *Doing early childhood research: International perspectives on theory and practice* (pp. 149–161). Buckingham: Open University Press.

Siraj-Blatchford, J. & Siraj-Blatchford, I. (2002). *Educating the whole child: Cross-curricular skills, themes and dimensions*. Buckingham: Open University Press.

Smith, C. (2005). *Report on Persona Doll Valley Pilot Training Project*. Cape Town, South Africa: Persona Doll Training/Western Cape Education Department.

Smith, C. (2006a, 20–24 September). *Persona Dolls: Human rights, inclusion and diversity in practice*. Paper presented at the thirtieth IBBY Congress: Children's Books and Social Development, Macau, China. Retrieved from http://www.ibby.org/index.php?id=678 (accessed 22 March 2012).

———. (2006b). *Persona Dolls: Making a difference* [Manual and DVD]. Kalk Bay, South Africa: Persona Doll Training.

Taus, K. (1987). *Teachers as storytellers for justice* (Unpublished master's thesis). Pacific Oaks College, Pasadena, CA.

Whitney, T. (1999). *Kids like us: Using Persona Dolls in the classroom*. St. Paul, Minnesota: Redleaf Press.

5

Effective Pedagogy for Inclusive Education: The Role of Mediated Learning Experience

Dorothy R. Howie

This chapter explores the importance of early mediation of learning by parents to their very young child, in a culturally appropriate way, as part of an effective pedagogy for diversity and inclusion. It outlines one internationally used approach to such mediation based on sound theoretical underpinnings, and discusses the wide-ranging research relating to the approach.

Human Mediation and Mediated Learning Experience

There is a strong theoretical and empirical base for the role of human mediation in learning. Vygotsky (1978), in his sociocultural theory of learning, stresses social interaction, and within that social interaction, the human mediation of cultural tools, as central to learning.

Feuerstein (Feuerstein, Feuerstein, Falik & Rand, 2006) has not only put forward a Theory of mediated learning experience which is similar to that of Vygotsky's human mediation, but also operationalised the criteria for this human mediation. Feuerstein sees the human mediator as playing an essential role in the child's learning and thinking by coming between the child and the child's world to organise and mediate that world to the child.

Feuerstein first lists a set of universal criteria which he considers to be found in every culture, as follows:

1. Mediation of intentionality and reciprocity-sharing of the learning goal
2. Mediation of meaning—giving a sense of the need for and value of learning
3. Mediation of transcendence—going beyond the immediate learning goal

He then lists non-universal criteria, which could be found to differing extents in different cultures. These are:

1. Mediation of feeling of competence
2. Mediation of regulation and control of behaviour
3. Mediation of sharing of behaviour
4. Mediation of individual and psychological differentiation
5. Mediation of goal-seeking, goal-setting and goal-achieving behaviour
6. Mediation of challenge: the search for novelty and complexity
7. Mediation of awareness of the human being as a changing entity
8. Mediation of the search for an optimistic alternative
9. Mediation of the feeling of belonging

These mediation criteria, and particularly those delineated as universal criteria, match closely with criteria for effective pedagogy, for example, as outlined in the New Zealand National Curriculum document (New Zealand Ministry of Education, 2007). The Scottish Borders use these mediated learning experience criteria to prepare all teachers, and key members of the school communities, including parents, for high quality teaching–learning processes (Howie, 2011).

Both Vygotsky and Feuerstein have important messages about the cultural nature of such mediation, which encourage us to ensure that early human mediation to the young child is culturally sensitive and appropriate.

Vygotsky's sociocultural theory of learning sees learning and thinking as being embedded within the unique social context of the learner, because it is socially mediated. This is shown in a key quote of Vygotsky: 'Every function in the child's development appears twice: first *between* people (interpsychological) and then *inside* the child (intrapsychological) ... All the higher functions originate as actual relations between human individuals' (1978, p. 57, emphasis original).

Vygotsky's experience with the learning of children from minority cultural groups in Russia led him to take a very positive view of the role of culture in an individual's learning, and to see the study of such children's learning as needing to involve a study of the interaction of their culture with their learning (Vygotsky, 1929, cited in Sutton, 1988).

Rogoff (1990, 2003) has extended this theory to the work of early childhood learning, and discussed the significance of its cultural implications for that work.

Feuerstein (Feuerstein et al., 2006) believes that if there is inadequate mediated learning experience from human mediators in one's own culture, an individual will be culturally disadvantaged. He also sees mediated learning experience as the key to cognitive modifiability, and the ability to overcome possible barriers to cognitive development caused by 'distal' factors, such as poverty. Colleagues of Feuerstein have shown the cognitive modifiability of young children through mediated learning experience across a range of low, medium and high socioeconomic contexts (Tzuriel, 2000; Tzuriel & Ernst, 1990).

The Pnina Klein Approach to Mediation in Early Parent–Child Interactions

Professor Pnina Klein, currently in the School of Education at Bar-Ilan University, Israel, has for some years carried out international research on her Mediational Intervention for Sensitising Caregivers (MISC) programme for addressing the intellectual and social-emotional needs of very young children in relation to mediation. She developed the MISC to improve the quality of early adult–child interactions in order to promote the young child's learning potential.

The MISC programme is based on the first three universal mediation criteria delineated by Feuerstein for quality human mediation, and includes also two additional criteria outlined by Feuerstein and considered by Klein to be of considerable importance in quality adult–child interaction. However, the empirical definition of each of these chosen criteria is unique to Klein, and each is informed by research preceding and following MISC intervention in relation to the criteria (P. Klein, personal communication, 2 August 2012). The definitions of these chosen criteria (Klein, 2003, pp. 71–72) are as follows:

1. *Intentionality and reciprocity*: Any act or sequence of acts that is directed towards affecting a child's perception or behaviour. Reciprocity occurs when the child responds, vocally, verbally or non-verbally.
2. *Mediation of meaning*: Behaviour that expresses verbal or non-verbal affect, excitement, or appreciation in relation to objects, concepts or values.
3. *Transcendence*: Behaviour that is directed, beyond what is necessary to satisfy the immediate need that triggered the interaction, towards expanding a child's cognitive awareness.
4. *Mediated feeling of competence*: Behaviour, verbal or non-verbal, that identifies a specific component or components of the child's behaviour that are considered contributive to the experience of success.
5. *Mediated regulation of behaviour*: Behaviour that models, demonstrates and/or verbally suggests to the child to regulate his or her behaviour in relation to specific task requirements or to any other cognitive process required before overt action.

The meditational processes, which address both intellectual and emotional needs, are named and exampled in the MISC programme as follows:

1. Focusing (intentionality and reciprocity), which is exampled as making the environmental stimuli compatible to the child's needs
2. Exciting (meaning), which is exampled as expressing excitement vocally, verbally or non-verbally over experiences, objects, people, etc.

3. Expanding (transcendence), which is exampled as explaining, elaborating, associating and raising awareness of cognitive aspects of thinking
4. Encouraging (feelings of competence), exampled as giving praise which is meaningful to the child, and clear identification of the reasons for success
5. Organising and planning (regulation of behaviour), exampled as regulating with regard to speed, precision, force and preferred sequence of activities

As described by Klein in her article on 'Interaction-oriented early intervention in Ethiopia' (Klein & Rye, 2004), the MISC is a method for sensitising caregivers (mothers, teachers, etc.) to the positive aspects of their existing interactions with their child. She sees it as drawing on three theoretical frameworks:

1. An eco-cultural approach, which highlights the caregiver's own goals and aims for child-rearing, looking at the caregiver's view of the ideal child, ideal parent, etc., so the use of the MISC measure of mediation is preceded by effort made to understand the cultural and contextual environment in which the children are learning, and to take these factors into account in planning an intervention.
2. A developmental approach, with attention to the dynamic interactions between the caregiver and child, and how these affect each other and their environment.
3. A meditational approach, based on Feuerstein's Theory of Cognitive Modifiability and Vygotsky's Sociocultural Theory of Mediation.

The typical features of MISC as described in this 2004 article involve sensitising and raising consciousness about the caregiver–child relationship. Attempts are made to raise parental awareness of their own philosophy of child rearing, how they perceive their child, and themselves as parents, how they perceive their child's cognitive and emotional needs, and how they perceive their interactive behaviours with the child.

Interviews and questionnaires are used, along with observations of the child in their natural learning contexts (home and early childhood setting) and parent–child and teacher–child interactions are videotaped and analysed in partnership with the caregiver (parent and teacher). Videotaping and analysis are the main methods used, with a rich variety of aspects attended to, including the emotional climate of the interaction, the sensitivity to the child's communicative cues, the extent to which the parents allow their child to initiate interactions, encourage them or follow their lead, with building on positive parental strengths. Observing mediational interaction (OMI) (Klein, 1996) is used to observe the extent to which the meditational criteria outlined for the MISC programme are used, and an individualised programme is developed to strengthen the use of these criteria, by paraprofessionals who are part of the caregiver's own cultural context.

There has been considerable empirical work carried out using this OMI instrument, and exploring and enhancing parental/caregiver early mediation using Feuerstein's criteria, and particularly the MISC approach, in a number of differing cultural contexts.

In Israel, Klein and Feuerstein (1985) carried out an early study with parents of first-born infants, Tzuriel and Eran (1990) carried out a study with parents of young kibbutz children, Tzuriel and Ernst (1990) carried out a study with low-, medium- and high socioeconomic status (SES) parents of young children, Tzuriel and Weiss (1998) carried out a study with mothers of Grade 2 children with a heterogeneous background and Klein and Alony (1993) carried out a study of low-SES, high-risk mothers, all in Israel.

Klein, Weider and Greenspan (1987) carried out a study with low-SES, high-risk mothers in the United States.

Klein was involved with research colleagues in a number of other studies in a variety of cultural contexts, using both the MISC programme and the OMI instrument, many reported in her publication 'Early Intervention: Cross-cultural Experiences with a Meditational Approach' (1996). Examples of these studies are a study by Pramling (1996) of parental mediation in Sweden, a study by Fuglesang and Chandler (1996) of parental mediation in Sri Lanka, a study by Hundeide (1996) of parental mediation in Indonesia and studies by Teferra and Tckle (1996) and Melese (2001a, 2001b) of parental mediation in Ethiopia.

Taking the MISC programme intervention in Ethiopia as one example, it is clear that in the poor communities worked with in Addis Ababa, with selected children aged 1–3 years, strong efforts were made to ensure that the programme was owned by the community, with project team members also trying to communicate respect for parents' opinions and behaviours and an openness to learn from them. The intervention was carried out by paraprofessionals from the communities of the families, who were trained to understand the philosophy of child-rearing, views of the ideal child, parent, caregiver or teacher, held by the family, and to encourage parents and others to value their own ideas for meaningful, challenging and affectionate interactions. There were both home-based individual intervention meetings and group-based sharing by parents, the latter found to be of value in the pilot study. Both types of intervention involved explaining the basic criteria of mediation through the use of videotaped home parent–child mediation sessions, focusing on positive aspects of the mediation and encouraging increase in frequency of such mediation. Parents were also encouraged to think of ways of using such mediation in other situations.

There was a clear improvement noted in the quality of the mother–child interactions following the MISC intervention, which persisted over time and was noted in the six-year follow-up study (Melese, 2001b). Both the mothers and their children became more active participants in their interactions, as did other family members who attended the home sessions. One interesting finding is that parents in the MISC intervention group engaged significantly more in the expansion of ideas, explanations and storytelling than did the parents of the compared non-intervention group. Also, there was positive change in the frequency of parental encouragement in the MISC intervention group, which is noted to run counter to the Ethiopian cultural objectives in child-rearing of developing modesty and humility. However, it is considered by the researchers that the intervention did serve parental needs to help enhance their children's learning ability without contradicting their cultural objective of raising polite and obedient children.

Klein notes in relation to the universality of the three central mediation criteria chosen for her MISC intervention programme that 'the profile reflecting the quality of the interaction in different cultures and contexts may be different'. She considers this to lead to unique thinking behaviours. For example, 'children not receiving sufficient expansion have difficulties in connecting ideas' (personal communication, 2 August 2012). It is of particular interest to the writer to look at 'peak' or unique parent–child interactions which relate to unique cultural values, and how these translate into unique and positive child thinking behaviours, such as creative thinking behaviours and emotionally laden holistic thinking behaviours.

Concerns and Questions in Relation to Early Mediation Programmes Such as Klein's MISC Programme

Key researchers in this area highlight the need for a culture-sensitive 'eco-cultural' approach to enhancing early parental mediation. Tzuriel (2000) states: 'The reciprocal effects [of mediation] should be integrated within an ecological framework' (p. 239). As noted earlier, Klein (Klein & Rye, 2004) sees an 'eco-cultural' theoretical framework as important in her intervention approach. It is suggested that in any planned early interventions to enhance parental mediation, Bronfenbrenner's updated ecological theory (Bronfenbrenner & Morris, 1998) be used as a framework for exploring and enhancing parental mediation in an ecologically integrated way.

An important question is to what extent criteria currently included within Feuerstein's theory of mediated learning experience, and making up Klein's MISC programme and OMI checklist, are appropriate and adequate in differing cultural contexts, especially when the aim of the intervention is to build up cognitive strengths which are valued and important within each cultural context. Vygotsky, in his attention to the cultural embeddedness of learning, reminds us of the key cultural meanings and values that parents and learners bring to the learning situation. Vygotsky wants there to be a positive understanding of such meanings, revealing the positive characteristics of thinking within any unique culture (Sutton, 1988).

Feuerstein considers that the three key universal criteria in his theory of mediated learning experience are universal, that is, found in every culture.

Kozulin, a research colleague of Feuerstein and leading Vygotskian scholar, suggests in his overview (2003) of a number of studies carried out by Tzuriel between different cultures (Ethiopian immigrants and native Israeli) and different SES families (low SES versus high SES) that there are considerable differences in parental mediation by such parents, including in the first three criteria which Feuerstein considers universal. For example, there is some evidence in these studies that parents who are more Western-orientated and have more schooling provide more mediation of the transcendence criteria, while parents who are less Western and have less formal education provide more mediation of the control of behaviour. He suggests that 'the criteria of mediation, at least as they are identified by Western observers, are education and culture dependent' (A. Kozulin, personal communication, 2 August 2012).

Kozulin (2002) considers that 'there is little doubt that certain forms of mediation are universal' but draws attention to the question: 'What constitutes this universal core of mediation and which forms of mediation are culture specific?' (p. 24). He also states that 'it is important to enquire whether the "same" aspects of mediation have identical meanings and importance in different cultures and with different social groups' (ibid.).

My own work with Maori parents and caregivers in the New Zealand context (Howie, 2003a) suggests that they have unique constructions of the meaning of mediation, which offer rich additional criteria for mediation of learning valued in their culture. Affirming cultural meanings is imperative to any intervention in partnership with the Maori in our bicultural and multicultural society (Howie, 2003b).

There is some suggestion within the literature associated with intervention with Klein's MISC approach, such as that reported by Klein (2003), that there may be two general forms of mediation: a Western, analytic style and a traditional, holistic style. Klein argues that the analytic style 'is currently the objective of most parents', so 'it creates a special need for experiences of analytic mediation prior to school entry' (p. 81). However, her associate, Hundeide (1996), in the excellent chapter 'Facilitating Cultural Mediation: Indonesia', actually emphasises a number of different forms of cultural mediation: the analytic, inquiring mode; the storytelling, narrative mode; dialogic storytelling; dramatisation and role playing; music, songs, dance and gestures, graphic and iconic forms of mediation; and the cultural repertoire of metaphors and prototypes. Hundeide stresses that storytelling and dramatisation are 'the natural way in which mediation takes place in many cultures' (p. 115) and states: '[T]hrough seminars and discussions with educators and parents in different traditional societies, I have found that there are different forms of cultural mediation, some of which may be just as informative and important for us as ours may be useful for them' (Hundeide, 1996, p. 117).

There are two concerns here. The focusing in mediation on one more Western mediation framework may overlook key cultural meditational values and practices which are of importance to the unique cultural group being worked with. For example, Hundeide (1996) describes the importance to parents in a slum area of Jakarta of the promotion of moral qualities in their children, and also questions the relevance of the conception of intelligence implicit in our Western programmes of cognitive enrichment for such families. The second is that unless we understand and embrace the holistic and multifaceted approach to mediation suggested by Hundeide's outline of the different forms of cultural mediation, we will not be enriched by including and celebrating the richness of the diverse cultural world experienced by families with which we work, and the world in which we live.

References

Bronfenbrenner, U. & Morris, P. (1998). The ecology of developmental processes. In W. Damon & R. Lerner (Eds), *Handbook of child psychology: Theoretical models of human development, Vol. 1*. New York: Wiley.

Feuerstein, R., Feuerstein, Ra. S., Falik, L. H. & Rand, Y. (2006). *The Feuerstein instrumental enrichment program*. Jerusalem: International Centre for the Enhancement of Learning Potential.

Fuglesang, A. & Chandler, D. (1996). Child focus through mediated learning experience in Sri Lanka. In P. S. Klein (Ed.), *Early intervention: Cross-cultural experiences with a mediational approach*. New York: Garland.

Howie, D. R. (2003a). *Thinking about the teaching of thinking*. Wellington: New Zealand Council for Educational Research.

———. (2003b). *Crossing boundaries: The cultural imperative*. Paper presented at the ninth International Conference of the International Association for Cognitive Education & Psychology, Seattle.

———. (2005). *Early learning and mediation*. Paper presented at the tenth International Conference of the Association for Cognitive Education & Psychology, Durham.

———. (2011). *Teaching students thinking skills and strategies: A framework for cognitive education in inclusive settings*. London: Jessica Kingsley.

Hundeide, K. (1996). Facilitating cultural mediation: Indonesia. In R. S. Klein (Ed.), *Early intervention: Cross-cultural experiences with a meditational approach*. New York: Garland.

Klein, P. S. (Ed.). (1996). *Early intervention: Cross-cultural experiences with a meditational approach*. New York: Garland.

———. (2003). Early intervention: Mediational intervention for sensitising caregivers. In A. S. Seng, L. K. Pou & O. Tan (Eds), *Mediated learning experience with children*. Singapore: McGraw-Hill.

Klein, P. S. & Alony, S. (1993). Immediate and sustained effects of maternal mediating behaviours on young children. *Journal of Early Intervention*, *17*(2), 177–193.

Klein, P. S. & Feuerstein, R. (1985). Environmental variables and cognitive development. In S. Harel & N. J. Anastasiou (Eds), *The at-risk infant: Psycho/socio/medical aspects*. Baltimore, Maryland: Paul Brookes.

Klein, P. S. & Rye, H. (2004). Interaction-oriented early intervention in Ethiopia: The MISC approach. *Infants and Young Children*, *17*(4), 340–354.

Klein, P. S., Weider, S. & Greenspan, S. L. (1987). A theoretical overview and empirical study of mediated learning experience: Prediction of preschool from mother–child interaction patterns. *Infant Mental Health Journal*, *8*(2), 110–129.

Kozulin, A. (2002). Sociocultural theory and mediated learning experience. *School Psychology International*, *23*(2), 7–35.

———. (2003). Psychological tools and mediated learning. In A. Kozulin, B. Gindis, V. Ageyev & S. Miller (Eds), *Vygotsky's educational theory in cultural context*. New York: Cambridge University Press.

Melese, E. (2001a). *Early psychological intervention in Ethiopia* (Unpublished doctoral dissertation). University of Bergen, Norway.

———. (2001b). The more intelligent and sensitive child (MISC). In P. S. Klein (Ed.), *Seeds of hope: Twelve years of early intervention in Africa*. Oslo: University of Oslo/Unipub Forlag.

New Zealand Ministry of Education. (2007). *National curriculum*. Wellington: New Zealand Government.

Pramling, I. (1996). Upgrading the quality of early childhood education: Sweden. In P. S. Klein (Ed.), *Early intervention: Cross-cultural experiences with a mediational approach*. New York: Garland.

Rogoff, B. (1990). *Apprenticeship in thinking: Cognitive development in social context*. Oxford: Oxford University Press.

———. (2003). *The cultural nature of human development*. Oxford: Oxford University Press.

Sutton, A. (1988). L. S. Vygotskii: The cultural–historical theory, national minorities and the zone of next development. In R. M. Gupta & P. Coxhead (Eds), *Cultural diversity and learning efficiency*. London: Macmillan.

Teferra, T. & Tckle, L. W. (1996). Mediational intervention for sensitising caregivers: Ethiopia. In P. S. Klein (Ed.), *Early intervention: Cross-cultural experiences with a mediational approach*. New York: Garland.

Tzuriel, D. (2000). Developmental perspectives of mediated learning experience theory. In A. Kozulin & Y. Rand (Eds), *Experience in mediated learning: An impact of Feuerstein's theory in education and psychology*. Oxford: Pergamon.

Tzuriel, D. & Eran, Z. (1990). Inferential cognitive modifiability of Kibbitz young children as a function of mother–child mediated learning experience (MLE) interactions. *International Journal of Cognitive Education and Mediated Learning, 1*(2), 103–117.

Tzuriel, D. & Ernst, D. (1990). Cognitive modifiability of young children and mother–child mediated learning experience (MLE) in low, medium and high-SES. *International Journal of Cognitive Education and Mediated Learning, 1*(2), 119–135.

Tzuriel, D. & Weiss, S. (1998). Cognitive modifiability as a function of mother–child mediated learning strategies. Mothers' acceptance–rejection, and children's personality. *Early Development and Parenting, 7*(2), 79–99.

Vygotsky, L. S. (1978). *Mind in society: The development of higher psychological processes*. Cambridge, Massachusetts: Harvard University Press.

6

Teaching Ethical Values to Preschool Children

Gülçin Alpöge

This chapter explains why I prepared this book, to help teachers who want to develop ethical values in preschool children. At the beginning of such a project many questions spring to mind. Why young children? Why in school? What kind of values? Let me start by explaining why I thought it was necessary to teach ethical values in school, to preschool children. Then I will go on to explain each value and finally I shall describe methods which, I believe, will achieve this aim of installing ethical values in preschool children.

Ethical Values and Their Significance

Each society has customs that they value but which may change over time and which is not customary in other societies. For example, not smoking in the presence of your parents or other elderly people or rising as teacher enters the classroom are ways in which people show respect. These customs can change over time or from society to society. But the value 'respect' is accepted in most societies. I have chosen 10 values which are universal and which are considered by most societies necessary to be able to live together peacefully. Research done in different parts of the world shows that even children say that telling a lie or being irresponsible are things people should not do because they can be harmful to others or to ourselves (Nucci, 2000). The 10 values I have chosen are:

1. Choosing
2. Honesty
3. Love
4. Respect
5. Courage
6. Goodness
7. Responsibility
8. Justice
9. Friendship
10. Peacefulness

Reason for Teaching Values to Very Young Children

It is important to learn these values early because children who have internalised them have more self-confidence, can decide for themselves and can solve most of their problems by themselves. More important still, those children who have accepted these values and keep them in mind while making a choice become happy children (Önder, 2003). Those who do not abide by these values become outcasts in the society, are unsuccessful and therefore unhappy (Eyre & Eyre, 1993). To have societies that function well, you need citizens who respect these values. If values are virtually non-existent, then that society is unstable.

Research shows that children start to internalise values at an early age (Grusec & Kuczynski, 1997). Usually value education starts at home. Parents are role models for their children. Also they can explain how we behave in certain situations and why. Thus, the young child can understand the importance of values and why they are important. In our day most mothers work, so you have two working parents who, understandably, have little time to devote to their families' problems, and to give children explanations concerning their behaviour. There are also single parent families where the parent is both physically and emotionally overloaded and can have little time even for conversation. Children who are left alone watch a lot of TV and are negatively affected by some of the programmes in which they watch a lot of incidences which they cannot comprehend. When they watch TV alone, they cannot differentiate between what is right and what is wrong, what is good and what is bad, what is just and what is unfair in these episodes. Rare messages from the parents are weak in comparison to the messages they get from the screen. They come to accept the messages from TV even if they misunderstand most.

There are also families who are constantly on the move. Having no real roots can affect children adversely. They cannot easily develop values as each society is, to a certain extent, different. Thus, when mixing with different cultures, they naturally become confused and do not know which values to actually accept.

How to Teach Values to Very Young Children

Ethical values cannot be easily learned by trial and error. Either parents or teachers need to help children understand them. Preschool children cannot form abstract concepts. Values are abstract concepts. Therefore, there is a need to give children some concrete materials to work with, so that they can begin to appreciate the meaning of values. In order to achieve this goal, I have attempted to give examples and supply materials by which to work. First of all, I have tried to explain what I mean by each value, so that the teacher or parents know what I am talking about. To be able to teach these values, the teacher must have a clear picture of what each value represents. Afterwards, I have written an open-ended story describing each value to enable the adults discuss the story's inherent value with the children. In the book, I have gathered activities, games, songs or poems, tales or stories and drama activities concerning each value to help children understand and deal with these values. In this chapter, I am going to try to explain what I mean by these values and how to talk to children about them.

How to Begin and Which Methods to Follow

As children spend relatively little time with parents and considerable time in school, I feel strongly that teachers should shoulder the task of helping children with value concepts. Teachers aim to change children's behaviour by the teaching–learning process. While teaching, they express themselves in phrases that contain these values, because teachers have these values at the back of their minds. They are familiar with them. So they easily become role models for children most of the time. But it is important to guide the children not by 'telling' all the time but by asking questions which will make them aware of what they are saying and why they are behaving the way they are. This is not so easy with young children because it is important to get the child to realise that he is forming a judgement and to get him to understand why. Asking questions to give the child awareness is called 'a clarifying response technique' (Raths, Harmin & Simon, 1978). The teacher questions the child without judging when he/she makes a statement or behaves in a way which contains a value judgement. The teacher simply repeats what the child has said to start with. For example, if the child says, 'Girls are dumb', the teacher can respond saying, 'So you think girls are dumb.' The teacher can then ask more questions: 'Have you felt this way for a long time?' and again, 'Can you tell me why you think girls are dumb?' Of course, the tone of voice and the attitude of the teacher are very important to assure the child that he is not being judged. Here are some examples for questions:

1. Is that something you prize?
2. Are you glad about that?
3. How did you feel when that happened?
4. Have you felt this way for a long time?
5. Was that something that you yourself choose?
6. What do you mean?
7. Are you saying that … (repeat what he said)?
8. Did you say that … (repeat in some distorted way)?

Raths has 30 questions for this technique. These questions are used to get the child to understand why, what he said without thinking is 'unfit' and that it can be understood in other ways or that it can be hurtful. The teacher can use the 'clarifying response' to get the children to be aware of values, but for young children to get to understand each value he/she needs more concrete materials. Also, the teacher needs to be clear on each value he/she is teaching. So, there needs to be an explanation of each value. Let us consider these values.

Choosing

Choosing means:

1. Being able to choose independently without any influence. We must remember that children can be influenced by their peers also. If one child wants a blue balloon, everyone wants a blue balloon.
2. There must be a real choice. If the alternatives are too similar, this is not a real choice. When offering a choice it should be 'Are you going to play ball or do you want to ride a bike?'
3. Being able to accept the consequences. It means being able to think about the results and accepting them or choosing accordingly. Going to the zoo may mean missing a favourite cartoon programme.

If the child chooses something that does not meet with your approval, it is preferable to warn him about the consequences of his choice rather than telling him that it is a bad choice and making him feel guilty about making a bad choice. He should not be made to feel ashamed.

Examples

When talking about choice, the subject should be something the child can understand.

1. For example, talk about a child who makes a beautiful picture. The teacher tells her that she will frame it and hang it in school, but on the other hand if she takes it home her mother will put it up on the fridge. She must decide what to do.

2. Another example is about a boy. His father gives him an allowance each week. He can get stickers for that amount, but if he saves for three weeks he can get a ball. So what should he do?

If children learn to choose intelligently and freely, then when they confront a value they can internalise it and accept the results. So, choosing is a first step to values education.

Love

Love can be considered in two parts: loving yourself and loving others. If a person is not happy, or is not at peace with himself/herself, then that person is going to have difficulty loving others.

Loving Yourself

Loving yourself means accepting yourself as you are. It means being at peace with yourself. It means being happy to be alive. Teachers must remember that children are influenced by their friends. If other children make fun of a child, he/she can be so hurt that he/she feels unworthy. Teachers must be alert to these kinds of behaviour. Teachers can help children to appreciate themselves by talking to them about the things they could not do when they were younger and can do now. They can talk about how each child is unique and does not have an exact equal. A good way of demonstrating this is to have a mirror covered by cloth in a separate part of the room and to ask each child to go to meet a special person. The children are asked not to reveal the person they met until everyone has a turn. Then the teacher can explain that each child is special and unique.

Loving Others

Loving others means being good to others because you like them.

A game may put the children in the mood. Each child chooses a partner and when the music starts, they all start to dance. When the music stops, they hug each other. Then the music starts again and the children dance. When the music stops, this time, four or more children should join in and hug each other. Finally, when the music stops for the last time, all children are huddled together hugging each other.

When we talk to the children about love we can talk about how:

1. Love is a good feeling
2. Love is paying attention, and listening
3. Love is protecting
4. Love is showing tolerance towards others
5. Love is sharing with the one you love

When we are explaining love to the children with the topics listed above, we must not forget that these children expect the same kind of attention, protection and tolerance from us.

Respect

Respect is also considered in two parts: respect for yourself and respect for others.

Respect means to value someone or something. Therefore, respect includes people, animals and plants as well.

Self-Respect

Self-respect means that you value yourself and are happy and proud of who you are and what you have done. It is being able to take care of yourself and being proud of this. In order to explain this to young children, it helps to ask them the things they are able to do. Self-grooming is important. Talk about how they felt when they were ill. So to keep well they need to take care of themselves. It means you take care of your body and your mind. It means doing things you will not regret or be ashamed of. If you have self-respect, it becomes easier to respect others.

Respecting Others

To respect others is hard to explain to preschool children who are egocentric and think of others only after themselves. Respect means being polite and using the magic words of 'please', 'thank you', 'excuse me', 'don't mention it', etc. It means treating others the way you would like to be treated. If you push someone, you will probably get pushed back. If you treat them politely, you may get the same treatment. Respectful treatment of others includes all others, everyone. The way you treat people lets them know what you think of them. Respect is about relationship. If people act respectfully, there would not be so much violence. The best way to explain respect to young children is to be a role model. If parents and teachers show respect to children, then the children can learn to respect others. To show respect to children means to pay attention when they talk, to have eye contact when you talk, to show that you like it when they are respectful, and to say you are sad (not angry) when they are not (Borba, 2001).

Courage

Courage means facing fear. We must not confuse being shy with being fearful. Sometimes shy people can be very courageous. Real courage means facing what you fear and overcoming it (Lewis, 1998). It means being able to ride a bike again after you have had a fall. It means being able to say what you believe in class. It means getting your immunity shot. It means going into a dark room.

We may feel fearful starting a new school, or going on stage for the first time, or going into an exam. But we gather our courage and do all these things. Sometimes children are afraid of imaginative things. They imagine there is a witch under their bed and are afraid. Courage means that you go ahead and do something you are afraid of whether real or imagined. What needs to be done may be fearful or difficult; courage is to be able to do it if it is the right thing to do.

When we overcome our fear, we get self-confidence and we can do the things we want to do. On the other hand, courage does not mean taking dangerous risks. Driving a car without a licence or driving over speed limits is not courage.

Fear can be of help sometimes. We fear walking in the middle of the road. This saves us from being run over. When swimming, we may be afraid of going beyond the beach limits. This will save us from getting hit by a speedboat (Labbé & Puech, 2008). This does not mean we should be afraid of swimming or of water.

How to Help Children Learn Courage

Fear is a feeling like love or anger. Therefore, one should never make fun of children's feeling of fear. The teacher should be able to help the children get over their fear without making them feel ashamed.

1. To help children learn courage, we need to praise their every little courageous act. If a child tells the truth when he has done something wrong, this shows he is displaying courage and needs to be praised. The wrongdoing can be dealt with separately later.
2. We should let children be active and not be too protective. When children are with friends and they play games and are active, they develop self-confidence and courage (Yazgan, 2009). So, parents should give their children the right to move and to be active.
3. If children make an attempt to overcome their fears by doing what really frightens them, they should be praised even if they fail so that it motivates them to try again.

Goodness and Kindness

What is the actual definition of good? *Oxford English Dictionary* defines it as 'anything that has the right or desired qualities'. So, a good thing is something that has qualities that are desirable. A good person then is someone who has qualities that are appreciated and liked. However, goodness is a little different. Any positive act carried out without thinking of a return is called goodness. If a child does a deed without expecting something in return, without expecting praise from the people around him, but just because he feels that it is the right thing to do, we can call this goodness. If a child is acting simply because he likes to make others happy, then we can say that he/she has internalised this value. This child is sad and unhappy when he sees others make fun of a child. He/she will show interest and may interfere. A child who has internalised this value is also good to animals and will disapprove of those who are not.

Can We Teach Goodness?

In our world, today, everything is valued by money. In our world, there are many examples of bad behaviour and bad deeds. So, we cannot expect children to become good on their own. We need to teach goodness and get the children to internalise this value. How are we going to do this? Borba (2001) gives some hints:

1. We need to be an example. (We have said this time and again but children learn best by seeing a role model.) Many adults act without thinking that they are doing good. It comes naturally because we have internalised this value. So we need to verbalise. We can say that being able to help someone makes us happy. We can also recount a good thing that we encountered and how someone helped us.

2. Explain the value to the child. Being good means thinking about others because they also have needs. To help others makes us happy. It may be our turn next. We want the people around us to be happy too. We want to live with people who are happy and good.

3. We must expect the child to be good. A child develops in the direction of our expectations. Do not aim at the child. Aim at the behaviour. Instead of saying, 'What a bad boy you are! Why do you make fun of your friend?' You can say, 'Making fun of your friend because he wears glasses is not a good behaviour. You made him unhappy.' In this way we show him that we accept him but not his behaviour. We can ask him to put himself in the other child's place. 'If you need glasses in the future would you like it if they made fun of you?' So maybe he can apologise and be friends again.

What about bad behaviour? Needless to say, we need good role models at home and in school. There are other things you can do. Do not say that the child is 'bad' or 'good for nothing'. Do not say things like 'You are lazy, bad or clumsy', even as a joke. Sometimes, we say things like 'You are going to be late again, you lazy boy!', 'Clumsy girl, you spilled all the paint again!' These will make the child lose self-esteem and self-confidence. The child will come to believe he/she is like that.

Teasing

To help the children who are 'being made fun of', we can show them ways in which they can protect themselves.

1. One way to stop harassment is to ignore what is said. Usually making fun of a child is to make her/him mad. So not heeding may stop it.
2. The child can say, 'Stop it! I don't want to listen to you.'
3. The child can say, 'You say I am stupid. Why am I stupid?'
4. The child can explain his/her view: 'Yes, my eyesight is bad, but with glasses I can see everything.'

Each case needs a different approach and the child will need help to resolve it. Sometimes an activity may help. The teacher asks the children the bad words they have said. She writes them down. She also asks for the kind of things that were said to make fun of someone. She also writes them down. She does this every day and keeps the papers in a box. Finally, on Friday the children close the box and bury it in the yard. So now the bad is buried and they will not say those things again.

Responsibility

Responsibility is a word children hear but do not really appreciate its meaning. It is doing your job. It is doing your part. It is doing your work. The teacher can start with the responsibility of the teacher. The teacher reads stories to the children, teaches them songs. Teachers of older children teach them numbers and letters. What happens if the teacher does not teach the children how to read and how to write? They won't learn anything. What is the responsibility of the children? Their job is to try to learn what the teacher is teaching. Paying attention and doing homework is part of the learners' responsibility. If they do not do their part, they will be ignorant. Children can be made aware of their responsibility towards their school. They should keep it clean to find it clean the next day. They should pick up the toys at tidy-up time so that the next day everything is in place.

Next, the teacher can talk about families and what each person in the household does and what happens if they don't. There are many examples. Playing with a sibling while mother prepares dinner is carrying a responsibility. When a child helps at home or in school, does this make him/her happy? Does helping make the child feel grown up? Is it a good feeling?

We can also remind them that they are responsible towards animals. There are also consequences of responsibility. Those who have a dog must walk him every morning and evening. What happens if we don't? Animals need to be fed. What happens if we don't feed them? What other responsibilities are there? We are responsible for laws and regulations. What happens if we do not stop at red light? What happens if we do not use our safety belt in the car?

Children can be asked to tell the responsibility of different jobs people have. What is the responsibility of a fireman, a doctor, a pilot, a teacher, a nurse, a farmer, a bus driver? And what happens when they do not do their job?

We can also explain to children who are jealous of their siblings that mother is responsible for the baby. For instance, when the mother is reading a story to the child and the baby cries, the mother leaves the child and attends to the baby because she is responsible for the baby as well as the older child. She needs to feed him or clean him so that his need is also satisfied. If she does not go, the baby may suffer and become ill.

Responsibility can be shared. At home, father can help with the baby. At school, tidy-up time is a good example of shared responsibility.

Justice and Fairness

What do we mean by justice? For adults it is easy to define. It means being just, not taking sides, obeying rules, acting equally and showing no favour for any group or person regarding their race, religion, language, class or gender.

Children learn well with examples, so we must act fairly towards them as well. We should ask ourselves as parents or as teachers if we are approaching children equally. Or are we making exceptions? We should also ask ourselves if the rules we make are just. Are there reasons for making those rules? Are the rules made so the children can obey them? Are we ready to compromise when necessary? As adults do we listen to both sides? When we make a mistake, do we apologise? If we are fair on these issues, then we can ask the children to be just.

If they are not fair, tell them, and tell them why. Expect them to be just and honest. They should be aware of this expectation. A research done by Borba (2001) shows that parents expect this kind of behaviour from their children. But we should keep in mind that they are children and our expectations should be in accordance with their age, depending on how much they can understand and how much they can do. Each child is unique. Do not compare children or their behaviour. Each child should be guided according to his/her capacity.

Guidelines

1. Because children at this age are egocentric, it is hard for them to see with someone else's eyes. Help them to put themselves in another person's place.
2. Encourage sharing. Tell the children that their friends are happy when they share their toys with them.
3. Teach them to say 'sorry'. You should also say, 'I am sorry. I did not mean to raise my voice ...' if, indeed, you have shouted at one point.
4. When two or more children start a fight screaming 'This is not just!', first try to calm them down. Then you can explain: 'Your friend did not wait his turn. Maybe you are angry because of that.' (If the problem is something else, they will immediately shout it out.) Then listen to both sides. Then put the problem in clear language and ask them how it can be solved. Do not take sides.

Do not let them go without a resolution. Most importantly, get them to see the other's point of view.

5. Sometimes, the real reason cannot be seen. Then it is up to the teacher to find the real reason behind the problem. Does one child cleverly find a way to come clean all the time? Or is one child creating a problem to get your attention? Are you more lenient with one child and the other cannot support this? There can be a number of other problems not seen on the surface.

When explaining fairness to children, 'tell them':

1. Not to take sides even if it is a friend who pulled a toy from another child's hand. This is wrong and he/she should be told.
2. Obeying rules is important. For example, to run and scream in the classroom is not allowed because it disturbs others.
3. Not to cheat. When a child discovers he/she is going to lose the game, he/she should not stop playing or cheat to win.
4. To respect the rights of others. Not to go to the front of the line by pushing others but to wait one's turn.
5. Not to blame others. Not to say 'He/she did it' for something he/she himself/herself has done; not to say 'He started it' for a fight that he/she began.
6. To be open-minded, that is, try to understand your friend. This you can do if you listen.
7. To behave equally with all friends. Do not exclude someone because he/she is a boy or a girl. Not to exclude someone because he/she is from another group or place.
8. To share. Toys that are in school are there to share with others. At home if there is a special toy you do not wish to share, remove it before your friend arrives.

Sometimes it is not a fair share. When we get the smallest piece from a cake, we say, 'This is not fair.' Also when it is our birthday, we want the biggest piece. Sharing may not always be equal (Labbé & Puech, 2006). For instance, an elephant and a bird do not get equal share of water because an elephant is so big it needs more. There is a golden rule about sharing. If one child is cutting the cake, the first choice goes to the other child. If you are choosing the game, then your friend starts it. You can always count, or throw a coin to decide who does what.

9. To help others. If someone is in difficulty, you can share by helping.

10. Like adults, children have rights. The UN Convention on the Rights of the Child which was adopted in 1989 is the first legally binding international instrument to protect children's rights. It brings respect for children regardless of race, colour, gender, language, religion, opinions, origins, wealth, birth status or ability. For example,

    (a) Each and every child should have a name. To explain this, creative drama would be wonderful (Yılmaz & Alibeyoğlu, 2010). If you did not have a name, how would people call you? How would we know who did what? If everyone had the same name, how could we call the person we want? How could we tell people apart? Another topic for drama would be each person having four or five names and everyone using another one of those names. This would be confusing for the child who had many names.

    (b) Each and every child has a right to go to school.

    (c) Each and every child has a right to live.

    (d) Each and every child has a right to be protected.

    (e) Each and every child has a right to play.

These are some of children's rights that preschool children will be able to understand. Drama is the best way to explain these rights and this 'Justice and Fairness Unit' is the best place to work with these ideas.

Friendship

Friendship is a little different from the values we have been talking about. Even though children may shout 'This is not fair', they seldom know what fairness is or what justice means. But friendship is different. Most children have an idea of what a friend and friendship means. A friend is someone you love and respect. A friend is someone with whom you have mutual affection. So, friendship is to build a sincere relationship with someone. For children, it simply means to have a good time together with somebody.

What Makes It a Value?

It is a value because it is helping and sharing without thinking of a gain. You help a friend because you like him/her and wish him/her well. In a friendship, love is essential. One also feels respect for a friend. You accept your friend as he/she is. You want your friendship to continue. Friendship is loyalty as well (Bukowski, Newcomb & Hartup, 1996). As you can see, all these concepts are values.

For children, friendship means that they are sensitive to the feelings, needs and problems of another person. Children behave thoughtfully with their friends because they love them and value them. So, you have an ethical sensitivity on the part of the child (Dunn, 2004). If a child as young as a preschooler can put himself/herself in the shoes of another, then he/she is being compassionate. This is important because preschool children consider themselves the most important being. To be able to show compassion means sharing sorrow as well (Wilson, 1993). This is a great step in socialisation. They learn how to behave in a society through friendship.

It is important to explain to the children that friendship is really sharing:

1. Sharing time
2. Sharing fun
3. Sharing feelings
4. Sharing thoughts
5. Sharing food
6. Sharing toys

A good friend is someone who is able to share, who is able to see the friend's needs and behave accordingly. Research shows that if children are given responsibilities, then they become more sensitive to the conditions of others, are more thoughtful and more compassionate (Eyre & Eyre, 1993). Friends make children happy. One of the important factors that bring about depression in children is being excluded from a group

(Frankel & Myatt, 2003). In order to avoid such an event, we can help children with tips in making friends:

1. *Listening*: To listen to what their friend is saying. To ask questions and develop a conversation is important.
2. *Sharing*: Not just a cookie, but sharing a conversation. If only one person speaks, that is not a conversation.
3. *Helping*: Helping the other person is part of friendship.
4. *Sensitivity*: Trying to understand the thoughts and feelings of the other person always helps friendships.
5. *Borrowing and returning*: Friends borrow things such as pencils, toys, even T-shirts. It is important to return them. A ball should not be the means to end a friendship.

When explaining friendship, it is easier if the teacher can give examples. Ask them why they like their friends. Then it will be possible to talk about 'liking', 'sharing' and 'helping'.

Peacefulness

Peacefulness, calmness, serenity all mean being at peace with yourself. It means that inside us we have a good feeling. Eyre and Eyre (1993) use the term peaceability meaning understanding, calmness, patience, control and accommodation. In their book, they say that when we try to understand, we seldom lose our temper. When we are calm, we do not want to fight. This does not mean that everyone is of the same opinion. We are bound to encounter different opinions, and problems. The important thing is to be able to control our anger and solve these in a peaceful way, without fighting. In the same book, they recount a mother hitting a child because the child hit his younger sister. But we know this act does not teach the child not to hit.

Sometimes adults lose control of their lives. We fail a test, or we lose our job and feel angry. When we feel angry, we feel like taking it out on the other people around us. But, of course, the best thing is to calm down and try to find a solution to our problem. When children are angry, they need to get rid of the energy within them. It helps to run, hit a ball, jump up and down, or ride a tricycle. When children are calm, and at peace with themselves, they feel secure and safe.

A fight is between at least two people. Coming to an understanding is for the benefit of both. Sometimes, a resolution is found. Otherwise, shaking hands and saying, 'We can each think the way we want but let us not fight over this' can be a solution in itself.

What Makes Peacefulness a Value

Peacefulness makes us and the people around us free of tension. When we feel peaceful, we also make people around us calm. If we can control anger and be peaceful, then we can teach this technique to others and they can use it all their lives.

Self-Control
Peacefulness does not happen by itself. We must make an effort to attain it. It takes time and effort to learn to control anger, to be able to stay calm, to be ready for a peaceful solution and to keep all this in mind.

Role Model
Needless to say, while teaching peacefulness, the adults should stay calm and collected. As we said many times, role modelling is the best way to teach values. For example, when the children are shouting, do not shout in order to be heard. Try a whisper. You will see that the children will start to whisper also.

Ego Message
Instead of blaming the other person, you can tell him/her how you feel. Can children learn and use this technique? Maybe they can learn. Instead of saying, 'It was my turn but he took the bike. He is bad and acts wrong. The child could say, 'I feel very angry when it is my turn and someone else takes the bike. I think it is not fair.' To be able to do this, the child should be able to decipher his feelings. It is difficult for preschoolers, but it is worth a try.

Honesty

For this value, I am going to give examples of concrete materials to use.

Being honest is first of all being truthful. To tell the truth means telling everything as it really happened, and telling it in such a way that everyone understands what you mean. Telling the truth also means telling the whole truth, the whole incident. If we don't tell all, if we omit something, we may mislead others' understanding of the event, for example, 'John hit Jim; but I told him to do it.' If we say only the first part of this sentence, we are telling a lie because with only the first part we are putting all the blame on John.

Honesty is also keeping your word when you promise something. If we do not keep our promise, that means we are lying when we make the promise. May we remind parents and teachers that if you make a promise to the child and do not keep it, you become a liar in the eyes of the child. For example, if a mother says, 'I'll be right back' and leaves for work, and does not come until evening, then the child is not going to believe her again. A teacher may say, 'Let us pick up the toys and then we can go out to play.' And when the room is tidy, if she does not take the children out, she will lose their trust.

When a teacher knows a child is lying, usually the reaction is, 'Don't lie to me.' However, it is better to say, 'Now tell me the whole story. Tell me the truth.' Or better still, 'I think maybe the real story is a little different from the way you are telling it.' Sometimes even a puppet may help. The teacher can say, 'Now the puppet is going to tell the whole story honestly, straight out.'

It Is Important to Give Examples When We Are Explaining Honesty

1. Jane and Joe are playing in the house and they break a vase accidentally. What must they do?
2. Mary puts her bag on the table where there are some clay figures the other children made that morning. Her bag flattens one of the figures. Should she say she was the one who did it?

Next Is the Open-Ended Story

Selin and Selim are twins. They go to school together and play together. One day Selim finds a chocolate bar in his school bag. Selin says that it must be from the first day of school and must be stale by now. 'Let us not eat it' she says. At that moment a friend comes along and seeing the chocolate asks for a piece. Selim gives the whole bar without telling him it is stale.

The teacher can work with this text about saying the whole truth and truth in general.

Games

1. Children sit in a circle. The teacher sits with the children. She does something like opening a book. She says, 'I opened a book. Am I telling the truth? Children answer. She picks up a pencil and says, 'I picked up a doll. Am I telling the truth? Children answer.

    When children are familiar with this game, she can ask a child to come and lead the game. For older children, she can ask things they know (Eyre & Eyre, 1993):

    i.   The sky is green.
    ii. Ants are bigger than horses.
    iii. We see with our eyes.
    iv. We hear with our nose.
    v.   This is my hand (shows her hand).
    vi. This is my foot (shows her head).

2. This is exactly like 'Simon Says'. Similarly, the teacher tells the children to do the actions she is doing when she says 'truth' and not to move when she says 'lie'.
3. The teacher prepares a list of things thinking of the things the children like and dislike:

    i. I love my mom.
    ii. I fight with my brother.

iii. I hate broccoli.

iv. I love ice cream.

v. I don't like playing with my younger sister.

vi. I like drawing pictures.

Children sit in a circle with their teacher with colourful blocks in the middle. As the teacher reads the list, she wants the children to pick up a block if they think the statement is true. At the end the teacher can ask:

i.   When did you pick up a block? Why?

ii. Was there a time when you were unsure? Why?

iii. Was there a time when you should have picked up a block and did not? Why?

A child will know that fighting with a sibling is not a good thing so he/she does not pick up a block even though he/she fights occasionally.

Right–Wrong and True–False

We know that young children may not differentiate a 'lie' from a 'wrong'. We may say something that is not 'right', that is 'wrong'. But if we do not know, if we are not aware that it is not right, then it is not a lie. We simply call that 'wrong'. A lie is told deliberately. We know we are not telling the truth. We should explain this to the children.

(I would like to make a comment here. Children may not say the truth simply because they want it to be otherwise. A child who wants her mother to buy her a doll may say, 'My mother bought me a doll.' This is not a deliberate lie. This is wishful thinking.)

The teacher may ask the children why it is so important to tell the truth and help them find the answers below:

1. It stops others getting punished.
2. It is better to tell the truth than lying because it prevents what may happen if you are caught lying.

3. If you tell a lie, then you have to continue lying.
4. People trust those who tell the truth.
5. People like those who tell the truth.
6. You feel good when you tell the truth.

Note

- The story for this unit is an extract from Pinocchio.
- The activity for this unit is making a finger puppet of Pinocchio.
- The tale is the story of the 'Lion and the Fox'.

The song (I am including an English poem instead of translating the Turkish one) is:

The Cuckoo[1]

The Cuckoo is a merry bird,
She sings as she flies;
She brings us good tidings,
And tells us no lies.

Conclusion

I have tried to make the teaching of ethical values to preschool children not like a lesson but in the context of everyday events. I used concrete examples because young children cannot form abstract concepts. I wrote open-ended stories so that teachers could discuss these values with the children. Adding songs, games, activities, drama and tales will reinforce what the teacher is explaining and will make it easy for the children to retain the value the teacher is talking about.

Research shows that children internalise values early. So, it is important to familiarise them with these values in preschool years, if we want them

---

[1] Opie and Opie (1967).

to grow up to be conscientious individuals because, I believe, citizens who abide with ethical values make a society function well.

References

Borba, M. (2001). *Building moral intelligence*. San Francisco, California: Jossey Bass.

Bukowski, W. M., Newcomb, A. F. & Hartup, W. W. (1996). *The company they keep*. Cambridge, UK: Cambridge University Press.

Dunn, J. (2004). *Children's friendships*. Malden, Massachusets: Blackwell.

Eyre, L. & Eyre, R. (1993). *Teaching your children values*. New York: Simon & Schuster.

Frankel, F. H. & Myatt, R. (2003). *Children's friendship training*. New York: Psychology Press.

Grusec, E. J. & Kuczynski, L. (1997). *Parenting and children's internalization of values*. New York: Wiley.

Labbé, B. & Puech, M. (2006). *İyi ve kötü* (The good and the bad) [Translation from French by Azade Aslan]. İstanbul: Günışığı Kitaplığı.

Lewis, B. A. (1998). *What do you stand for?* Minneapolis, Minnesota: Free Spirit Publishing.

Nucci, L. (2000). *Nice is not enough*. Chicago, Illinois: University of Chicago Press.

Önder, A. (2003). *Okul öncesi çocukları için eğitici drama uygulamaları* (Educational drama for pre-school children). Istanbul: Morpa Kültür Yayınları.

Opie, I. & Opie, P. (1967). *The Oxford nursery rhyme book*. Oxford: Clarendon Press.

Raths, L., Harmin, M. & Simon, S. (1978). *Values and teaching*. Columbus, Ohio: Charles E. Merrill.

Smith, C. A. (1993). *The peaceful classroom*. Louisville, South Carolina: Gryphon House.

Wilson, J. Q. (1993). *Moral sense*. New York: The Free Press.

Yazgan, Y. (2009). *Düşe kalka büyümek* (Growing up with riks). Istanbul: Doğan Egmont.

Yılmaz, N. & Alibeyoğlu, M. C. (2010). *Haklarımı oynayarak öğreniyorum*: Çocuk hakları üzerine bir çalışma. Uluslararası Eğitimde Yaratıcı Drama Kongresine sunulan bildiri (I learn my rights by playing). Paper presented at the National Creative Drama Congress, Istanbul.

Section III

Educational Frameworks, Curricula and Models

7

Theory and Practice of Inclusive Education in Hungary

Agnes N. Toth

Hungary as a Middle-East European Country

Hungary is a relatively small country in the middle-eastern part of Europe sharing its borders with Austria, Slovak Republic, the Ukraine, Romania, Serbia, Croatia and Slovenia. Its population is nearly 10 million. A quarter of the population lives in the capital city, Budapest.

Hungarian membership of the European Union dates back to 2004. The most remarkable historical event of the country was the changing of the regime in 1989 when the impact of the Soviet policy including the philosophy of education came to an end.

> The new constitution paid tribute to the memory of the Revolution of 1956 by becoming effective on October 23, 1989 and Mátyás Szűrös, as a temporary president of the Parliament proclaimed the establishment of the Hungarian Republic from the balcony of the Houses of Parliament. (Bayer, 1996, p. 181)

Due to its history, Hungary is regarded as a post-communist state with all the achievements and shortcomings in its economy and society.

Education System and Its Traditions

Before changing the political regime, Hungary was almost exclusively affected by the Soviet and eastern European communist countries whose impact was profound on the Hungarian education system as well. Hungary had a traditionally separated schooling system for mainstream and disabled children due to the diagnosis-based model of special needs pedagogy. Vygotsky was one of the most popular scientists in Moscow who developed 'an area of scientific scholarship devoted to problems of diagnosing, educating and rehabilitating·children with physical and mental handicap (known as "defects")' (Knox, 1989, as cited in Ainscow & Memmenasha, 1998, p. 16).

The current structure of education has not changed significantly since 1989 except for secondary vocational education which was formulated from a short (three-year-long) to a regular (four-year-long) variety (see Figure 7.1). The Act of 1993 (Section No. LXXIX) introduced matriculation after finishing vocational studies.

The Act of 1993 (No. LXXIX) was determinative from the aspect of special education. Different groups of disabilities (such as sensory disability, physical disability, speaking disability, mental disability, autism and 'other disabilities') were categorised in the term 'disability', which was consequently used instead of 'special needs'.

> In 1980 the WHO (World Health Organization) published the ICIDH (International Classification of Functioning, Disability and Health) for field trial purposes, which provided a scientific model of disability as well as a clarification of terminology for clinical use, data collection and research. Since the concepts of 'handicap' and 'disablement' are different, agreement between the perceptions of an individual's handicap and the individual's disability described merely by a medical classification, cannot be expected. (Bornman, 2004, p. 183)

A category called 'other disabilities', which was introduced by the act mentioned above, refers to children with learning difficulties and other disorders of psychological development, for example, in sub-skills and learning disorders in school performance. The regulation made schools interested in opening their doors in front of disabled children, thanks to the extra financial support offered to them.

Figure 7.1

Current System of Education

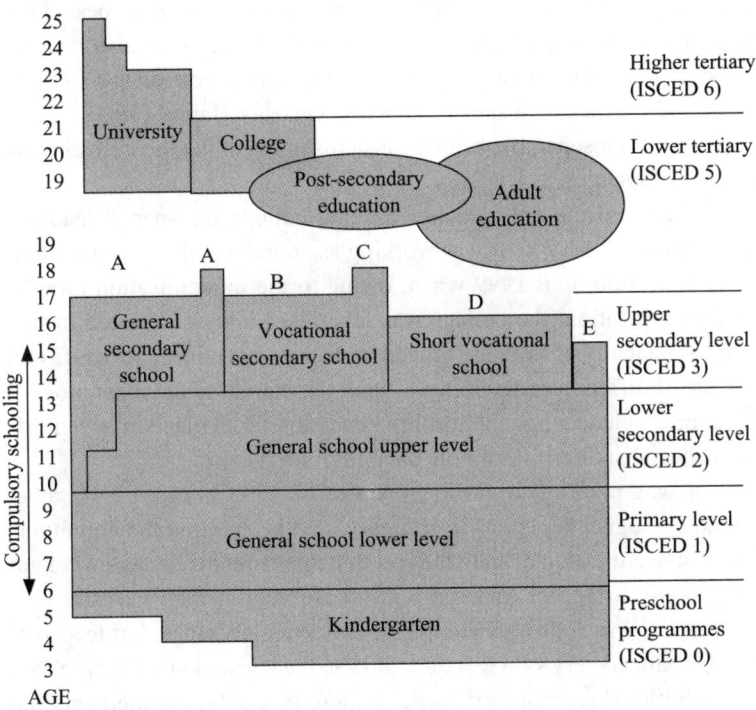

A: Matriculation exam (school-leaving exam)
B: Matriculation exam and vocational qualification
C: Technician's certificate
D: Skilled worker's qualification
E: Lower level vocational qualification given by special short vocational school

Source: National Centre of Career Information (2002).

Disabled students can apply for two kinds of financial support. They may receive financial support on the one hand as a person with disability and on the other hand as a student. General financial disability supports are family allowance, temporary invalidity annuity, regular social allowance, public medical service, transportation allowance, etc. (Gyulavári, 2010, p. 2)

The statistical number of disabled children in Hungarian schools increased considerably after 1996 as a result of an opportunity to receive extra financial support (Csépe, 2008).

Hungarian special education has brought about a number of significant achievements all over Europe. The first separated school for deaf students was established by András Cházár in 1802 in Vác, near Budapest. That date is also recognised as the year of establishment of special education in Hungary. Another outstanding figure of special education is a medical doctor and teacher of disabled students, Gusztáv Bárczi (1890–1964), whose name is inseparable from the establishment of the theoretical basis of special education in Hungary.

The first and the only teacher training college for special teachers was established in 1906. It was working as an independent institution of higher education until 1999 when, owing to the modernisation process in higher education, the college was integrated into and existed in that period as a faculty of Eötvös Lorand University. Its training structure and contents of different programmes follow the claims of the most modern educational science. Special teacher education takes place in seven different specialisations to promote disability intervention.

As it was mentioned earlier, the Act of 1993 is one of the most remarkable legislation steps in Hungary, that is, creating the conditions of inclusive education despite the fact that mainstream teachers were not totally ready to accept children with disabilities in their classes. That arrangement was followed by several in-service trainings, but teachers' attitude changed very slowly. Later, in 1996 the legislation was completed by an additional requirement; to put it more precisely, disabled children in their seventh–eighth grades in primary schools were not allowed to be taught in 'combined classes'. To make it clearer, in Hungarian villages, there was a schooling tradition that if the number of disabled children in a grade was less than the necessary to create an independent class at a given grade, then different grades were united into one class and taught by one teacher. The maximum number of grades in a combined class was 3. Since 1996, the seventh–eighth grades have not been allowed to be taught together with other grades in order to prepare them for their special vocational studies. Headmasters of village schools understood the importance of the regulation and found a less costly solution. 'Private student status' was recommended for those students, but the status had to be required by parents. It meant that the school did not have an obligation towards the children except to provide them with the possibility to pass their exams in every half an academic year. This provision was in practice for a year only as the legislator recognised the disadvantage of the disabled children caused by the law.

The following important regulation was the introduction of the National Curriculum Guidelines for Disabled Students in 1997. Different areas of public education from early childhood education (ECE) to secondary school education were described for each category of disability in the document, including subjects and their criteria. Teachers were happy to accept the law because they needed central curriculum standards to create their syllabuses; hence, they were strongly required to create their local curricula on the base of the newly introduced National Core Curricula. They felt they were not prepared for those tasks which caused uncertainty.

According to the National Core Programme of Kindergarten Education, published a year earlier (1996), Hungarian preschool (kindergarten) time-tables were organised to look through the academic year. It recommended kindergartens not to segregate children with special needs, a practice that has its traditions in the country's early education institutions. ECE is strongly connected to the public education; namely, institutes usually provide services for families having different-aged small children in order that they can participate in the labour market. These organisations gener-ally are managed by school principals in given village.

The same legislation defines the minimum opening hours of such institutes as 10 hours. However, children usually arrive at kindergartens at 8 a.m. and leave for home at 3 p.m. Students have three daily meals: breakfast, lunch and afternoon tea. They also have a two- or two-and-a-half-hours' rest time ensuring afternoon sleeping. In 2003, Public Education Act of 1993 (No. LXXIX) was modified and completed with some new elements. For instance, the previous potential of integration became an obligation for each school, except for children with a severe disability who cannot be taught together with their mainstream peers.

In Hungary, as written in National Action Plan (2004), the proportion of children with special educational needs (learning disabilities) is 5.3% while the figure for the European Union is 2.5–3%. The other significant problem in addition to this exceptionally high rate is the overrepresentation of Roma children. Nearly 20% of Roma students are qualified as having special educational needs, while the rate for non-Roma students is only 2%. It often happens that children are redirected to special-needs schools simply because their social circumstances are poor and as a result they are not yet mature enough for school, or because they perform poorly on culturally-based tests. In 2003, a reform of the current system of defining students with special educational needs was initiated which focused on the issue how to prevent social disadvantages directly translated as special educational needs. The Act on Public Education included a new term 'special needs' to replace the term 'disability', previously used to label children. The goal of a project called 'Out of the Back Row' is to reduce the number of students who are unreasonably labelled as disabled and to return them to schools and classes with general curricula. As of September 2004, local self-governments will receive enhanced capitation grant for children thus returned to the mainstream education. The [...] central programme contains the resources intended to standardise the non-culture-biased tests that are relevant to the programme. At present about 3,000 children a year begin the first grade labelled as mildly disabled. The target of the programme is to reduce that number by two-third. (National Action Plan on Social Inclusion, 2004–2006, pp. 34–35)

In the academic year of 2007–2008, the Act on Public Education (No. LXXIX) was modified with respect to the definition of the target group, and in the 14/1994 Ministerial decree on qualification obligations and pedagogical special services regulated the operation of the expert committees. The background of the public education–political decision was a continuous increase in the number of children, students with special educational needs (SEN), more specifically, those in need of special education due to psychological development disturbances and the significantly differing rate in different counties. Based on the evaluations:

1. There was a revision of learners involved based on strict criteria.
2. The need for special education was terminated if the severe and long-lasting recognised disorder of functioning or behavioural development were not justified.
3. If the severe and long-lasting disorder of functioning or behavioural development were recognised, but were not due to organic reasons, and the student participated in corrective teaching–education in a special class, faculty or school, subsequent assessment indicated that the student in the following academic year can participate in general, that is, in integrated education. This assessment serves to hinder unreasonable segregation (European Agency for Development in Special Needs Education, 2010, p. 28).

The latest change in legislation took place in 2010 when the diagnosis process was described by a ministerial decree (4/2010). The arrangement, following the common European classification of special needs, regulated the diagnostic protocol of Special Experts' Teams (Expert and Rehabilitation Committee for Examining Learning Abilities TKVSZRB) in different regions of Hungary. Identifying special needs in Hungary takes place at two different levels. The first level is an Educational Advisory Team (*Nevelési Tanácsadó*), which identifies psychological development disturbances, such as learning difficulties or behavioural disorders. This team includes special teachers, psychologists and therapists. If a severe and long-lasting disorder (disability) is recognised by the advisory team, the child is forwarded to the second level, called Expert and Rehabilitation Committee for Examining Learning Abilities (TKVSZRB) and Rehabilitation. Members of the committee are special teachers, medical doctors, paediatric neurologists, psychologists, etc. The latter has competence to identify all the disabilities and provide help for schooling. Parents are involved in the examination process and entitled to ask for an appeal against the decision.

Theory and Praxis of Inclusive Education Inside and Beyond Europe

The inclusion of people with disabilities in education is sometimes described as a strategy of modern education science and an education scenario in which every teacher and administrative staff knows their tasks, whereas in Hungary, this just does not seem to work out smoothly. When attempting to achieve the total inclusion of people with disabilities in society and/or in education, it seems to be not quite adequate in spite of the best of our intentions. As Csépe (2008) writes, in Hungary there is a traditional diagnosis-based schooling model for disabled children and this model causes several difficulties in education praxis. Just for instance, diagnostic process is not uniform in the country due to different protocols applied by different teams.

According to the estimation of United Nations Educational Scientific and Cultural Organisation (UNESCO, 2005), by 2015, all children should be able to enjoy a full course of elementary education. However, without the inclusion of children with disabilities, this goal cannot be achieved. The scope of this task is demonstrated by the fact that out of the 115 million children worldwide who are excluded from education, at least 40 million are disabled. Of all the disabled children in developing countries, only 2–10 per cent attend school (UNESCO, 2005).

Present education policy in Hungary focuses mainly on school management and the economic status of institutions, but the real troubles of inclusive education become visible in the classrooms (Némethné et al., 2008).

> While focusing on the quality of education and as seen in international comparative research on teaching in inclusive classes, students with or without special needs are still being ignored. It also seems that teachers' difficulties are often ignored. This is understandable if we consider that students' key competences are also in the centre of professional education since the 1990s in Europe. We must think about a fresh view about the basic skills and abilities that should be developed at school, a modern concept must be formulated and in the future, this could constitute a common basis for reforming European education. A lot of different kinds of schools are available for skills development. Each of them takes a stand somehow on their own practice and methods and though most of them are linked to a school of thought, in fact they focus on developing key competences in their educational practice. (Hanák, 2008, p. 12)

> According to the latest data published by UNESCO (2005), efficiency of Hungarian schools on development of pupils' key competences is at the absolute medium level among the 66 compared countries. Moreover, European statistics show that in Hungary, only about fifty per cent of children with special educational needs are educated in fully inclusive settings. (European Agency for Development in Special Needs Education, 2010, p. 30)

Inclusion is still an 'under-theorised' area of education science (Topping & Maloney, 2005, p. 5). Scientists in Hungary usually talk about inclusion from various aspects: ethics, sociology, philosophy and economy. Unfortunately, mainstream education practice still does not use a full-fledged definition as a generally adopted scientific theory from the anthropology, psychology, sociology or education science side. Inclusive education is described almost exclusively from the point of view of special education, and there are only a few publications by researchers being not representative of the special education. It seems that this is a matter only for special education (Némethné et al., 2008). Educational integration requires schools to be organised for all. Every child should be educated without a stigma or label and should be developed individually (Réthy, 2002).

According to the definition that inclusion is a humane solution in which each country is presented with the challenges behind the inclusion movement, most European nations deal with SEN in different ways due to their educational traditions.

Northern and Western European countries such as Sweden, Denmark, Norway, as well as United Kingdom, Spain and France have more experience and longer traditions in inclusive education than central and eastern European countries. Several of them have had national legislation on inclusive education since the 1970s, as documented in Italy and Sweden. The Swedish policy of inclusive education and the Italian policy envisage individual development for each pupil in accordance with their needs. In Italy, there is a currently general agreement in identifying five large areas where effective inclusion strategies may work better: the link between individualised programming and the class curriculum; classmates and schoolmates involvement; integrating behavioural strategies into the regular learning activities and educational relationships; meta-cognitive teaching and learning; and information communication technology (Ianes, 2009).

> More than 30 years after the entry into force of Law no. 517/1977, nowadays the integration of students with disabilities is an evolving process, which has already brought significant innovations to Italian schools towards a more inclusive system; however, some critical issues still need to be addressed. (D'Anna, Pastena, D'Alessio & Gomez Paloma, 2013)

Just like other Nordic countries, *Norway* has been focusing on compulsory education and social inclusion far earlier than Eastern European countries. A remarkable change in schooling was brought about in the mid-1970s when the scheme 'School for All' was introduced. The real breakthrough happened only in 1996 when inclusion was defined in the new National Curriculum as participation in the academic, social and cultural community of the school (Feyerer, 2005). In this context, it should be mentioned that while the OECD (Organisation for Economic Cooperation and Development) countries spend an average of 5–5.8 per cent of their gross domestic product (GDP) on education, Norway spends 6.2 per cent of its GDP. The Norwegian school system is quite comprehensive. There is no difference in the schooling provided for mainstream students or for students with special needs (Boarini, 2009).

The *Danish* approach demonstrates teaching as a 'pedagogical–psychological counselling service' since the early 1960s. The segregation of pupils with special needs was abolished in 1981 (Réthy, 2002). The number of students with special needs attending mainstream classes increased remarkably at first, but a few years later it fell again. 'In the academic years 2005–06, 2.1% of the pupils in primary and lower secondary school were supported within the framework of the *folkeskole* [primary school], while 0.7% of the pupils attended a special school, thus segregated from mainstream education' (Eurydice, 2006, p. 6).

In spite of the initial uncertainty caused by the firm belief of parents and teachers regarding the dual system of mainstream and special schools, by the 1990s the Scandinavian principle 'School for All' was included in the Dutch legislation (Pijl & Meijer, 1999). Conceptual opportunity of inclusive education was given in the Netherlands, but the teaching practice depends on alternatives in schools (Réthy, 2002).

Social and educational inclusion craggily appeared in the education policy of the 1970s in the *United Kingdom* and determined the tasks for the coming decades such as legislation since 1981 in the United Kingdom (ibid.). According to the British theory, social inclusion may not be achieved without integrative education. Inclusion is not merely a school-based idea of acceptance; it overgrows the frames of education, and it is a part of human rights. We should not identify inclusion with assimilation knowing that assimilation means only giving place to children with special needs but still does not mean equal opportunities for all (Thomas & Davies, 1999).

Inclusive education is well achieved in early childhood in present-day *German* schools, because the right to select a school for their children is given to the parents. But, this advantage is still not totally observed as several civil organisations disapprove it. Integration was involved in some of the newly designed courses as a part of the changes in teacher training, and the conversation began between mainstream and special schools (Bick, 2008).

Special education receives guaranteed funding in *France* so that each school can provide this service for students with special needs, as required by law since 2005.

> The law of 2005 stipulates that all pupils have the right to be registered with a mainstream school as their base institution, even if they attend a special school because of their disability. This is described as their 'learning path' and learning continuity. The law tries to address the problem of dispersal of structures by introducing new actors in new structures for coordination purposes. (Zay, 2009, p. 109)

Inclusive education, together with the right of parents to choose a school for their child, first appeared in *Austrian* legislation in 1993. The number of students in inclusive classes increased significantly between 1989 and 2002. Behind this fact there were other factors, namely, the quick growth of the number of inclusive classes from 4 to 412 over the course of 15 years in Upper Austria (Feyerer, 2005).

'The policy of integration is currently being developed in *Romania*. Most children (36,729) with special educational needs attend special schools. The structure of special education in these schools is very similar to that of mainstream education' (Eurybase, 2001, p. 3).

As a new member of the European Union (EU), *Bulgaria* also has a national policy shift towards an inclusive society, but this evidence appears mainly in the theoretical literature of special education in the late 1990s (Tzokova & Dobrev, 2013). Recently, Bulgaria has adopted a national programme for the next decade focusing on inclusive education in the school system. The Centre for the Educational Integration of Children and Students (CIE) was set up to handle this aspect of human rights (Valtchev, 2008).

According to the literature of special education, 10–14 per cent of the student population had SEN in *Turkey* in the 1990s. However, there are some doubts in educational policy and practice about the quantity and the quality of the special support provided for pupils with SEN and about the cooperation between special and mainstream schools. 'The right to equal educational opportunity is routinely accepted as a general principle, but is widely ignored in practice' (Sari, 2000, Conclusion section, para 8).

Inclusion in society, policies and education is quite a new theory, intensified in the past 20 years in central and eastern European countries such as Slovakia, the Czech Republic, Hungary and Romania. Some doubts are perceived in the phrasing even today. The notion of 'inclusive education' relates to the social acceptance of disadvantaged people, to ethnic minorities and also to people with disabilities. Groups of ethnic minorities, for example, gypsies and socially disadvantaged people, have practically never had a separated school system. Students with disabilities really need this new concept because their separated schooling has had such traditions for centuries in the central and eastern parts of Europe like in Hungary.

Inclusive Education in Hungary

Students' rights to be educated in mainstream schools have been legislated in *Hungary* since 1993, but the social tolerance, including teachers' inclusive approach towards the SEN students, has been changing very slowly. Currently, a modern support system is in place to look after a child's individual needs. Since the missing diagnostic protocol has described a student with special needs is educated in the following settings: an inclusive mainstream class, a special class in a mainstream school or in a special school. The student's placement depends on the suggestion of an expert team which has members such as a psychologist, a neurologist and special teachers. The Experts Committee (TKVSZRB) is well informed about the possibilities of the given family and schools as well as of its local area of operation. The number of children with SEN placed in special schools and special classes has been shrinking since 2003 when the previous education law (LXXIX/1993) was modified.

This legislation made it possible for several special schools in Hungary to change their profiles only to become a 'solid methodical institute' to help inclusive education in mainstream schools (EGYMI: Egységes Gyógypedagógiai Módszertani Központ; Centre for a Single Methodology in Special Education). It is necessary to change Hungary's diagnosis-based schooling model for a modern education needs-based model, but the latest legislation (of 2007) did not result in a clear situation regarding the education profession and the relevant financial support. Two categories of SEN were introduced by the law of 2007, namely, group 'a' and group 'b'. 'SEN-a' means a student's SEN are traced back to organic causes, while symptoms of the 'SEN-b' group are not. This arrangement is an issue of practice which has been adopted by schools to receive more funding for the increasing number of students with special needs (Csépe, 2008). Some uncertainty can be traced in the terminology of SEN in school practice. Most troubles were caused by the distinction between learning disability and mild mental retardation. Four different categories were used previously to indicate the various degrees of difficulties: learning troubles, learning disorders, learning disabilities and mental retardation (Mesterházi, 1998). According to the Act of Public Education of 2003 (No. LXXIX/2003), categories of learning troubles are the following: learning and behavioural difficulties, permanent and severe learning difficulties (dyslexia, dysgraphia and hyperactivity), mild and moderate mental retardation. While there was a terminological uncertainty in schooling, parents were advised and financially helped to take their children into kindergartens.

> Kindergarten subsidy: is granted from January 2009 twice a year to families with multiply disadvantaged small children aged 3 or 4 who are enrolled to kindergarten, provided that the children attend the kindergarten regularly.
> Extension of places at kindergarten: The number of places at kindergarten is extended under the scheme of the infrastructure development within the Regional Operational Programme. (Ministry of National Resources, 2011, p. 6)

Moreover, since the 1980s it has been obligatory for parents to send their children to kindergarten in the last year before starting primary school. The newest Act of Public Education (No. CXC. 20 December 2011) makes it obligatory for children to attend kindergarten not only from the age of 5, but already from the age of 3 (Act of Public Education No. CXC. 20 December 2011).

Experts dealing with this age group do not talk about inclusion related to ECE since most psychological development disorders cannot be tested distinctly due to the significant differences among children at this age.

The inclusion of students with a disability as a teaching strategy appeared in Hungarian schools only after the changing of the political system in 1989 (Csépe, 2008). We had some pilot schools in the early 1980s to deal with inclusive education, but their results did not receive wide publicity. The first laws after changing the political system were permissive and allowed integration, but teachers were neither trained nor experienced. That was the main reason why many teachers disapproved of the idea of integrating these students into mainstream schools. Accordingly, our segregated educational system existed for the very few, even with inclusive education spreading over Europe. Laws adopted in the past few years not only provided the opportunity of educational integration but also stipulated obligations for mainstream schools (Act of Public Education, No. LXI/2003, No. LXXIX/1993).

The integrated educational policy was laid down in the Act on equal treatment and equal opportunity from January 2004, which bans discrimination in schools. In line with this legislative framework, to prevent disadvantaged and Roma students from dropping out of school and to reduce current school segregation practice, as of September 2003, a programme of integrated education was established in Grades 1 and 5 of primary schools and in Grade 9 of secondary education. The programme involved the introduction of integration training in the grades given and 'fostering talent' programmes in the other grades, with state capitation grant (National Action Plan on Social Inclusion, 2004–2006, p. ix).

Regarding regulation, students with learning disabilities or mild mental disabilities do not have to go to special schools or classes since 2003. Unless recommended otherwise by the special teachers' team, students with a learning disability are supposed to go to mainstream classes.

> In this case schools play a double role. On the one hand they have to find the qualities in pupils which could be changed and have to do so in the most appropriate time during the pupils' sensitive periods. On the other hand schools have to find ways of handling the qualities which cannot be modified by the school. (Gáspár, 2003, p. 147)

We must put our fingers on or apply new teaching strategies or methods when we have already far too many descriptions focusing on the various aspects of inclusion, but we still lack a complex definition accepted by all the branches of relevant sciences. We know what inclusive education does not mean, but still do not know what it does. Theoretical and practical scientists in Hungary must deal with this issue as much as it deserves.

Some primary schools in Hungary have experience in different models in teaching strategies involving the so-called 'cooperating–teaching' method, while others offered their students with SEN extra-curricular classes given by special teachers. A student with a learning disability must receive a minimum of 15 per cent extra time in compensation for his/her learning abilities, guided by a special education teacher. This means that if a school undertakes to educate students with SEN in a peer group, it must guarantee this service. Such schools with an inclusive approach towards students with SEN must maintain professional ties with a special education teacher and every mainstream teacher should have the opportunity to consult the special teacher as often as needed.

It seemed to be an absolutely new idea in schools; so, many of the mainstream teachers did welcome it, though they had some misgivings about inclusive class teaching. The knowledge-centred Hungarian schools of the 1980s should have been transformed in a number of ways, for example, placing their focus on key competences instead of the earlier factual-knowledge teaching; their methodological culture should have been renewed to accept modern co-teaching techniques instead of their much-favoured frontal methods; their race–pedagogical approach should have been replaced by the idea of individual development or cooperative learning strategy and, last but not least, teachers will have to make efforts to teach heterogeneous groups of students. In addition to new challenges, Hungarian teachers had to make themselves ready for a new system of administration and teaching plans such as curriculum editing and research-based education, providing qualitative evaluation of their students' knowledge or the implementation of new teaching technologies, for example, computer-based teaching (Kárpáti, 2008).

Teachers' Attitudes towards Inclusion in Hungary

Underlining the exclusivity of compulsory public education definitely does not help to promote the desire to meet SEN. Catering for individual needs can be successful only and exclusively if we are able to ensure an individual opportunity to participate in life-long-learning programmes as well (Csépe, 2008).

Our survey excludes data on the attitudes of kindergarten teachers since separation has never been an issue in Hungarian kindergartens. Inclusion is a fairly traditional strategy of education in early childhood because there have been only a few institutes for young children with special needs and they only cater for the severely disabled. In contrast, the differentiation in school system caused more difficulties for spreading inclusive approach in schools in our country.

As it follows logically from the fact above, we have been inspired to assume that teachers were impressed by those new challenges and the effect is identifiable in their attitudes towards the integration of children with special needs (Némethné et al., 2008). As a starting point, we tried to evince how teachers' attitudes towards special needs have been changing during the past two decades in Hungary. It was expected that teachers would aim to learn more about students with SEN, and that they would be ready to teach students with SEN together with other students in their mainstream classes because they understand the importance of the new paradigm in education. Given the fact that the first groups of students with SEN educated in inclusive schools have already entered secondary schools, it was also assumed that there would be no differences between the attitudes of mainstream teachers in primary and secondary schools. That is why opinions were compared in the frame of a survey.[1]

To ascertain answers to the questions raised earlier, 10 schools were selected in three different counties of the Western Transdanubian Region in Hungary. These included 5 primary schools in towns and villages and 5 secondary schools in towns. All of them identify themselves as inclusive institutions in their documents of establishment. That was a part of a survey in 2007. The sample was quite small (170 mainstream teachers) and the schools were selected randomly. Representativeness of this study was not ensured, but it was supposed that our findings were in line with a representative research's results. Due to the small size of the sample, it was impossible to have generalised conclusions, and applied to larger populations like a nation or so. All the teachers were requested to answer the survey at their respected schools.

The findings of the survey show that teachers' attitudes towards inclusion are influenced by a number of factors ranging from teacher preparedness, gender influences, teacher attitudes and perceptions, years of teaching experience, past experiences working with special needs students and the availability of support services (Avramidis & Norwich, 2002). As we

---

[1] In a previous research, students in teacher training at our university expressed the opinion that integration means difficult tasks for teachers at schools. However, 58 per cent of them said they would not have any problems with inclusion of SEN in their classrooms.

know from our earlier experience, teachers generally do not have enough theoretical knowledge about SEN because of their inadequate education in this field. Studies on special needs were published only in specific subjects as part of Hungarian teacher training but the whole of the teacher training should be transformed by getting information about individual needs which require interdisciplinary collaboration (Csépe, 2008).

Hungarian mainstream teachers did not learn about the typology of disabilities at universities earlier because we had a separated teacher education system to train teachers for special needs. As a result, their knowledge should have been completed by self-study. On the other hand, it is known in Hungary that there is a strong requirement for teachers' continuing education (Government Decree 277/1997 XII. 22). 'Teachers are required to complete 120 hours of in-service training every seven years, whether they incorporate their new skills and knowledge into their teaching is up to individual preferences' (Kárpáti, 2008, p. 19).

Our results indeed confirmed this necessity. Only 62 per cent of responders could define the categories correctly. It was shocking that one in three of them did not recognise disability as a very special deficiency. The coefficient of standard deviation was quite high (sd = 22) among the different teacher groups of public education (Némethné, 2009).

One of the main problems is that teachers confuse notions such as learning difficulties, learning disorders, learning disabilities and mild mental disabilities. Some of them define learning disabilities as a mental handicap and suggest that students with those syndromes should be placed and taught by special teachers in separate classes.[2] Ammah and Hodge (2005) studied attitudes and practices in teaching and they found that teachers do not believe that they are adequately prepared for inclusive education. Our finding is similar; mainstream teachers disapprove their special preparation for teaching in inclusive classes at their high schools and universities. This confusion is partly understandable considering the possible translation disharmony in English–Hungarian terminology, as

[2] Only an incidental note. Some differences are also discovered in denominations of different education stages in different countries. For instance, an institute of early childhood education is called kindergarten, 'preschool' or 'infant school' in different European countries. Presumably, languages mirror the dominant activity (teaching, schooling before school) in these institutes.

Table 7.1

Terminological Differences

American Terminology	Hungarian Terminology
Mild intellectual disability	Tanulási akadályozottság
Mild cognitive disability	Learning disability
Mild mental retardation	(Mild mental retardation group)
Learning disability	
Learning disorder	Tanulási zavar
Learning difficulty	(Learning disorder)

Source: Fejes and Szenczi (2010).

Fejes and Szenczi (2010) observed such differences between American and Hungarian terminology (see Table 7.1).

This terminological confusion causes problems in education practice and the widespread implementation of inclusive education. According to the British Institute of Learning Disabilities (n.d.) definition: 'IQ is one way of classifying learning disability,

- 50–70 Mild learning disability
- 35–50 Moderate learning disability
- 20–35 Severe learning disability
- Below 20 profound learning disability' (p. 3)

In the previous legislation, Hungarian marking of the groups with IQ 50–70 refers to 'mild mental disability' and groups having IQ over 70–85 are referred to 'learning disability'. This difference derives from the disharmony that we experienced between denomination in professional literature and the statutory language.

Given the right of students with disabilities to learn together with others, integration is becoming more and more common in regular schools. Although our research was not a nationwide representation and focused on the region of our university, still, it provided quite illuminating results. No more than half of the responding teachers at the Western Hungarian mainstream schools said that they were informed about the terminology of special needs or about the methodology of inclusive education, but it is known that this is not a feasibly extended inclusion all over the country. As a nationwide foreign project showed (Campbell, Gilmore & Cuskelly, 2003), teachers with more positive views of inclusion had more confidence in their abilities and competences to support students in inclusive settings and to adapt classroom materials and procedures to accommodate their needs.

We suppose new educational challenges could not really affect the attitude of teachers towards inclusive education in the 10 schools involved in the survey. Avramidis, Bayliss and Burden (2000) also found that teachers who had been implementing inclusive programmes for some years held significantly more positive attitudes than the rest of the sample who had apparently little or no such experience. Others had established this earlier; inclusion needs to be pursued in a thoughtful manner not only by teachers, but also by other professionals, administrators and parents (Giangreco, Baumgart & Doyle, 1995; Waligore, 2002). These findings suggest the same conclusion to both researchers and the Hungarian decision-makers, namely, that inclusion is far more than merely yet another education philosophy and should be regarded as a way of acting together, involving all players.

However, it is not enough to prescribe something for schools such as integration without providing them with the necessary means and/ or guidance. We found that a lot of teachers still have negative attitudes towards disabled students' integration probably because of their classical 'achievement-orientated' or 'competition-based' teaching practice. It was experienced that secondary school teachers do not or hardly use any modern methods of competence-based teaching such as cooperative, individual and project learning programmes. Accordingly, we are looking forward to the outcome of the two-level teacher education which should ease these troubles, coming from the lack of the classical system. Yet, the standards of Hungarian teacher training at the various universities should be revised (Kárpáti, 2008).

In addition, one in every five of secondary school teachers would accept students with special needs neither in schools nor in their own classes, contrary to elementary school teachers whose significant proportion would undertake to teach disabled students together with the others, either in school or in their classes. It must be pointed out that the secondary school teachers' approach should be changed as soon as possible before a large number of students with SEN appear at the secondary school level in the next five years. This poses a major problem considering the outcome of the survey indicating the reluctance of secondary school teachers to enrol for in-service trainings. It seems, however, that the actual application of their newly acquired skills is hard to measure. 'Even if we could measure this, then the way to do so would require measuring the extent to which the newly acquired skills are put into classroom practice' (Kárpáti, 2008, p. 210).

Mainstream teachers in Western Hungary with experience in integrative pedagogy are hanging on to the limited range of their teaching methodology, their teaching tools and limited knowledge about the organisation of learning and classroom management, as well as SEN terminology. They clearly believe that only because 15 or 20 years ago they did not have the opportunity to be taught about children with SEN in their professional training at colleges or universities, they, in turn, can use this as an excuse for their shortcomings and deficiencies in teaching. The issue of limited teaching tools is a matter for the management of the school or its maintainer to think about.

Unfortunately, our respondents in Western Hungary generally think negatively of postgraduate or in-service training courses. There might be all sorts of reasons for this, for example, trainings that are too long and have unrealistic theoretical content. Sometimes, a lecturer may not be the right person to guide the teachers and manage the courses. Experience shows that our department (Department of Education) should develop post-graduate training courses for practising teachers, but also pay more attention to the teachers' learning needs. Consequently, trainings must be short and practice-orientated and lecturers must be selected according to their presentation skills and their teaching and research experience. The research results seem to suggest that distance and/or e-learning must be offered to teachers. Our conclusion is in full harmony with the findings by Kárpáti (2008), who points out that further training course development for teachers should have a much closer relationship with the formal institutions of teacher training than they do now (Csapó, 2007). Our greatest challenge is that Hungarian teacher training should be transformed into research-based training programmes, ensuring more emphasis on research methods as a part of university/college teacher training.

Implications

Inclusive education is a new challenge in Hungarian education policy as well as in society and education science. Due to the effects of foreign research results, it seems that the development of education science in several orders of magnitude is faster than that of the policy and of the society. A lot should be done in this field including the change of social approach. Mainstream Hungarian school teachers should be more aware of the theory and practice of inclusive pedagogy on the one hand, and more confident to use their teaching competences.

The other difficulties are methodological and curricular ones; personal development, group dynamics, planning and management should be subject to more ongoing research. This is an important aspect for the development of teacher training at our university, which has just undergone a renewed procedure of accreditation. Unfortunately, this had not been preceded by broad research on the inclusion of students with SEN. New teaching methods should be elaborated and evaluated according to their efficiency for renewing our pedagogical culture. When introducing the new methods and techniques, it is indispensable to abandon the classical frontal class management (Csapó, 2008). This statement is also reasoned by the words of Gyulavári (2010) who said:

> General teacher training does not include the treatment of people with disabilities. To be able to treat these persons, teachers must complete a special pedagogical training which is available at two universities. Universities must establish a committee on equal rights to promote adequate education and the equal rights of disabled students. Each institution has to employ a coordinator of disability affairs to help disabled students. The schools with integrated education receive higher amounts of normative support from the government (€450 per person, per year), which is dispensed by the coordinator of disability affairs. The Government may order preferential treatment for disadvantaged student groups and disabled applicants. (p. 2)

Knowing how teachers' attitudes affect the students, their service is an essential ingredient to improve their teaching. Regarding that, the teaching profession is mainly based on personal aptitude, so the views on teaching activities of teachers are organised around their professional knowledge (Köcséné, 2007). We firmly believe that identifying, redirecting and changing attitudes of our future educators are a huge step forward in a process that we hope to initiate, ultimately resulting in improved outcomes for all the students with disabilities.

> Preparing mainstream teachers for dealing with special needs children brings up significant questions such as: What kind of teachers should we train? What kind of licences and rights should inclusive teachers be given? What do we mean by teacher versatility? Should versatility be required of every teacher? (Barton, 2000, p. 61)

We try to answer the questions above by analysing our curricula and training programmes. These new tasks and achievements are highlighted in our new programmes to make sure that the future teachers leaving our institute are able to fulfil the requirements of public education in every aspect.

References

Ainscow, M. & Memmenasha, H.-G. (1998). The education of children with special needs: Barriers and opportunities in Central and Eastern Europe. *Innocenti Occasional Papers, Economic and Social Policy Series* (Vol. 67). Florence, Italy: UNICEF International Child Development Centre.

Ammah, J. O. A. & Hodge, S. R. (2005). Secondary physical education teachers' beliefs and practices in teaching students with severe disabilities: A descriptive analysis. *High School Journal, 89*(2), 40–54.

Avramidis, E., Bayliss, P. & Burden, R. (2000). A survey into mainstream teachers' attitudes towards the inclusion of children with special educational needs in the ordinary school in one local authority. *Educational Psychology, 20*(2), 193, 201, 207.

Avramidis, E. & Norwich, B. (2002). Teachers' attitudes towards integration and inclusion: A review of the literature. *European Journal of Special Needs Education, 17*(2), 129–147.

Barton, L. (2000). Market ideologies, education and the challenge for inclusion. In H. Daniels & P. Garner (Eds), *Inclusive education* (pp. 62–78). London: Kogan Page and Sterling, Virginia: Stylus Publishing.

Bayer, J. (1996). The process of political system change in Hungary. In F. Glatz (Ed.), *Innerhalb der Europäischen Union* (Vol. 22, pp. 171–185). Band: Begegnungen Schriftenreihe des Europa Institutes Budapest.

Bick, H.-W. (2008, November). *School system in Germany.* Paper presented at the Study Visit Conference, Dublin.

Boarini, R. (2009). *Making the most of Norwegian schools.* OECD Economics Department Working Paper No. 661, pp. 1–50. Paris: OECD.

Bornman, J. (2004). The World Health Organisation's terminology and classification: Application to severe disability. *Disability and Rehabilitation, 26*(3), 182–188.

British Institute of Learning Disabilities. (n.d.). *Factsheet—learning disabilities.* Retrieved from http://impactofspecialneeds.weebly.com/uploads/3/4/1/9/3419723/factsheet_learning_disabilities.pdf (accessed 17 December 2012).

Campbell, J., Gilmore, L. & Cuskelly, M. (2003). Changing student teachers' attitudes towards disability and inclusion. *Journal of Intellectual & Developmental Disability, 28*(4), 369–379.

Csapó, B. (2007). A tanári tudás szerepe az oktatási rendszer fejlesztésében (Role of teachers' knowledge in developing of educational system). *Új Pedagógiai Szemle* (3–4), 11–23.

———. (2008). A tanulás és tanítás tudományos megalapozása (The underlying scientific basis of teaching and learning). In K. Fazekas, J. Küllő & J. Varga (Eds), *Zöld könyv a magyar közoktatás megújításáért* (*Green paper for the renewal of Hungarian compulsory education*) (pp. 223–224). Budapest: Ecostat.

Csépe, V. (2008). A különleges oktatást, nevelést és rehabilitációs célú fejlesztést igénylő [SNI] gyermekek ellátásának gyakorlata és a szükséges teendők (Current practice and the future agenda of special educational needs). In K. Fazekas, J. Küllő & J. Varga (Eds), *Zöld könyv a magyar közoktatás megújításáért* (*Green paper for the renewal of Hungarian compulsory education*) (pp. 139–165). Budapest: Ecostat.

D'Anna, C., Pastena, N., D'Alessiol, A. & Gomez Paloma, F. (2013). Physical education in the primary school. Educational pathways to personal and social autonomy to the best quality of life. *International Conference on Education and New Developments*, Lisbon, Portugal, 1–3 June. World Institute for Advanced Research and Science (WIARS), Lisbona Mafalda Carmo, pp. 242–246.

Dutch Coalition on Disability and Development (DCDD). (2006). *All equal, all different inclusive education. Towards an inclusive policy: A DCDD publication series about integrating disability in policy and practice.* Retrieved from http://www.eenet.org.uk/theory_practice/DCDD%20All%20Equal%20All%20Different.pdf (accessed 16 February 2009).

European Agency for Development in Special Needs Education. (2010). *Special needs education, country data, 28.* Retrieved from http://www.european-agency.org/publications/ereports/special-needs-education-country-data-2010/SNE-Country-Data-2010.pdf (accessed 17 December 2012).

Eurybase. (2001). *Summary sheets on education systems in Europe.* Retrieved from http://www.see-educoop.net/education_in/pdf/eurypres-rom-misc-t05. pdf (accessed 2 November 2012).

Eurydice. (2006, September). *National summary sheets on education systems in Europe and ongoing reforms* (p. 6). Retrieved from http://eng.uvm.dk/ Education/~/media/UVM/Filer/English/PDF/081110_summary_sheet_on_ danish_education_system.ashx (accessed 17 December 2012).

Fejes, J. B. & Szenczi, B. (2010). Tanulási korlátok a magyar és az amerikai szakirodalomban [Learning limits in Hungarian and American professional literature]. *Gyógypedagógiai Szemle [Journal of Special Pedagogy], 38*(4), 273–287.

Feyerer, E. (2005, 1–4 August). Inclusion in Norway. In E. Feyerer, L. Hayward, N. Hedge & K. Ness (Eds), *Towards an inclusive masters' curriculum in Europe.* Paper presented at the Inclusive and Supportive Education Congress (ISEC), Glasgow, Scotland.

Gáspár, M. (2003). *Stability and variability at the evolution of personality.* Budapest: Új Mandátum Kiadó.

Giangreco, M. F., Baumgart, D. & Doyle, M. B. (1995). How inclusion can facilitate teaching and learning. *Intervention in School and Clinic, 30*(5), 273–278.

Government Decree, 277/1997 (XII. 22). Budapest.

Gyulavári, T. (2010). ANED country report on equality of educational and training opportunities for young disabled people. *Academic Network of European Disability Experts* (ANED). doi: VT/2007/005.2.

Hanák, Zs. (2008). Program adaptations in the development of a competence based teachers' training in Hungary. *007 International Magazine for Education Science and Practice* (2): 12–18.

Ianes, D. (2009). *The Italian model for the inclusion and integration of students with special needs: Some issues.* Retrieved from http://www.darioianes.it/ focus4a.htm (accessed 2 November 2012).

Kárpáti, A. (2008). Tanárképzés és továbbképzés (Teacher education and training). In K. Fazekas, J. Küllő & J. Varga (Eds), *Green paper for the renewal of Hungarian compulsory education (Zöld könyv a magyar közoktatás megújításáért)* (pp. 193–217). Budapest: Ecostat.

Köcséné, S. I. (2007). Milyen tanár leszek? (What a teacher I will become?)— Hallgatók vallanak magukról, a tanári hivatásról (Candidate teachers' imagination of the teaching profession). In I. Falus (Ed.), *A tanárrá válás folyamata [Becoming a teacher]* (pp. 121–155). Budapest: Gondolat Kiadó.

Mesterházi, Zs. (1998). *Tanulásban akadályozott gyermekek nevelése az általános iskolában (Schools-based education of students with learning difficulties).* Budapest: Bárczi Gusztáv Gyógypedagógiai Tanárképző Főiskola (Bárczi Gusztáv College of Special Education).

Ministerial Decree on Pedagogical Services 4/2010. (I. 19.). Budapest.

Ministry of National Resources. (2011). *2011 National report on the implementation of the strategic framework for European cooperation in education and training (ET2020)*. Retrieved from http://ec.europa.eu/education/lifelong-learning-policy/doc/natreport11/hungary_en.pdfhttp://ec.europa.eu/education/lifelong-learning-policy/doc/natreport11/hungary_en.pdf (accessed 17 December 2012).

National Action Plan on Social Inclusion. (2004–2006). Retrieved from http://www.google.hu/url?sa=t&rct=j&q=&esrc=s&source=web&cd=1&sqi=2&ved=0CCAQFjAA&url=http%3A%2F%2Fwww.szmm.gov.hu%2Fdownload.php%3Fctag%3Ddownload%26docID%3D14303&ei=VuOTUPfQBNHSsgbWpoHwAw&usg=AFQjCNGTP1TQJaWPc3ZSWdXyx-NqDSmGVg&sig2=tNqlnSs_dmXsuCtd5PyhAA (accessed 17 December 2012).

National Centre of Career Information. (2002). *The education system of Hungary*. Retrieved from http://www.npk.hu/public/kiadvanyaink/2002/2002_2.pdf (accessed 17 December 2012).

National Core Programme of Kindergarten Education. (1996). 137/1996. (VIII. 28.)

Némethné, T. Á. (2009). Tanári attitűdök és inkluzív nevelés [Teachers' attitudes and inclusive education]. *Magyar Pedagógia, 109*(2), 105–120.

Némethné, T. Á. et al. (2008). Inklúzió, ahogy mi csináljuk (Inclusion, as we do it). *Fejlesztő Pedagógia* (6), 17–31.

OECD. (2010). PISA 2009 Database. Retrieved from http://dx.doi.org/10.1787/888932343342

Pijl, S. J. & Meijer, C. (1999). The Netherlands: Supporting integration by re-directing cash-flows. In H. Daniels & P. Garner (Eds), *Inclusive education* (pp. 215–237). London: Kogan Page.

Réthy, E. (2002). Integrációs törekvések Európában (Integration attempts in Europe). In I. Bábosik & A. Kárpáti (Eds), *Összehasonlító Pedagógia* (pp. 314–332). Budapest: Books in Print.

Sari, H. (2000, 24–28 July). *Development of special education provision in Turkey: From the inclusive perspective*. Paper presented at the International Special Education Congress (ISEC 2000), University of Manchester.

Thomas, G. & Davies, D. J. (1999). England and Wales: Competition and control—or stakeholding and inclusion. In H. Daniels & P. Garner (Eds), *Inclusive education* (pp. 64–72). London: Kogan Page.

Topping, K. & Maloney, S. (2005). *The Routledge Falmer reader in inclusive education*. London: Routledge Falmer.

Tzokova, D. & Dobrev, Z. (2013). Gypsy children and changing social concepts. In H. Daniels & P. Garner (Eds), *Inclusive education* (pp. 138–148). London: Routledge.

UNESCO Institute for Statistics. 2005. *Children Out of School. Measuring Exclusion from Primary Education*. pp. 3-4. Retrieved from http://www.uis.unesco.org/Library/Documents/oosc05-en.pdf (accessed 25 September 2014).

Valtchev, D. V. (2008, 25–28 November). *Inclusive education: The way of the future*. Paper presented at the International Conference on Education, Geneva, Switzerland (pp. 25–28). France: United Nations Educational, Scientific and Cultural Organization (UNESCO).

Waligore, L. R. (2002, 9 May). Teachers' attitudes toward inclusion: What did they say? (Master's thesis). Rowan University, Glassboro, New Jersey (by Dr Joy Xin, Master of Arts in Special Education).

Zay, D. (2009). *Inclusion and education in European countries* (Final report no. 4). Retrieved from http://ec.europa.eu/education/more-information/doc/inclusion/france_en.pdf (accessed 17 December 2012).

8

Multicultural Umbrella Model: Six Cs for Successful Integration

Jean-Baptiste Quillien, Gabriela M. Theis and Veronica R. Quillien

The need for interculturalism in diverse educational settings is increasing as the world is becoming more and more global. People are crossing cultures, and as a result cultural boundaries are shifting. If the role of education is to prepare future generations to become productive members of society, it is critical that inclusive strategies to facilitate cultural awareness be implemented. In this chapter, we consider a multicultural approach to the inclusion process in an educational setting. In fact, we argue that to effectively implement inclusion in a diverse population, policy makers and educators must take into account cultural differences. The insufficient Golden Rule, 'Do unto others as you would like done unto you', only implies sympathetic behaviour. The Platinum Rule (Bennett, 1998a), 'Do unto others as they would like done unto them', is a mindful approach that acknowledges intercultural differences and incorporates culturally sensitive behaviours. The need to consider the Platinum Rule is not limited to the educational practice itself. It should also help policy makers to improve and modify early education and education in general while favouring cultural competence. In fact, some argue that we witness a Western hegemonic view of early education (Dahlberg, Moss & Pence, 1999). This Western perspective, about early childhood education, imposed on the rest of the world is an illustration of the Golden Rule. This is the reason why the Platinum Rule is central to the implementation of educational policies as well as educational practices in the classroom. Policy makers and teachers should be concerned by the ethnocentric threat.

Studies have posited the positive outcome of early education in terms of cognitive and academic abilities in the short and long term (Bryant & Maxwell, 1997; Campbell, Pungello, Miller-Johnson, Burchinal & Ramey, 2001). The initial years of education are particularly critical for students' social achievement (Yoshikawa, 1995). It is fundamental to promote effective inclusion for minorities during their first year of school. This chapter is not exclusively aimed towards early education; however, the implementation and material developed are guiding teachers and policy makers to promote early effective inclusion.

Effective inclusion is a central concept in this study. The educational achievement gap in the United States (Ladson-Billings, 2006), or the high rates of unemployment in populations issued from immigration in France and other European countries (Collegia, 2012), are examples of ineffective inclusion in education. The purpose of this chapter is not to discuss the practices that are not working, but rather to illustrate with a case study—The Metamorphosis Project® (MP)—the application of a theoretical framework, the 'Multicultural Umbrella Model' (MUM), in order to include diverse populations in education and in society at large.

Theoretical Framework

The process of learning another language is a process we have personally experienced as co-writers of this chapter. Such shared events are second/third language learning, migration to new countries, acculturation, intercultural marriage and exposition to different educational systems. To support our practices and perspectives in regards to educational inclusion, we will draw on a modified version of The Five Cs framework for language learning (National Standards in Foreign Language Education Project, 1999).

The Five Cs framework incorporates five keys to successfully teach world languages. The content of the instruction is based on Communication, Cultures, Connections, Comparisons and Communities. To this approach, we are adding Collaboration to bring another dimension and refine the existing theoretical framework in terms of inclusion. We will redefine the Cs in order to promote inclusion in the multicultural classroom.

This chapter is organised as follows. The first section discusses about the theoretical background. In the second section, a case study of a meta-morphosis project has been given, which has further been categorised into two sections: (a) the organisation as an entity and (b) individual perspective.

Theoretical Background

The MUM is defined as 'The six Cs for success'. It is the result of the authors' experience and discussions about diversity, cross-cultural bound-aries and education. This interdisciplinary model merges the authors' diverse backgrounds and their fields of interests in anthropology, edu-cation, intercultural relations, psychology, multicultural education and linguistics.

This model is designed to help educators and policy makers to imple-ment efficient inclusion in the context of multicultural education. It will assist policy makers, researchers and educators to raise pertinent questions about their attitudes and decisions towards inclusion in the context of multicultural education. In this part, we will briefly explain the 'genesis' of the model, the importance of language and the role it plays in expressing cultural identity, and then what the MUM is will be described.

Genesis

Language learning, especially foreign language learning, and growing up in different cultures are common factors shared by the authors of this chapter. When considering diversity and multicultural education, the word 'culture' is probably the one that comes into the mind of many of us. Cultural identity is expressed and passed on to future generations through language (Schecter & Bayley, 1997).

Language is the vehicle of cultural identity. The transition seems natural between the importance of language to express and transmit culture, and the need for foreign language learning. Foreign language learning has been studied for many years. What is the best way to teach language? The National Standards in Foreign Language Education Project proposes five principles, the five Cs: Communication, Cultures, Connections, Comparisons and Communities. It is argued that those five principles are linked together and can be subdivided into standards. The aim of those standards is to help teachers optimise their lessons. The five Cs principles for foreign language acquisition have been claimed to be efficient in teaching foreign languages (National Standards in Foreign Language Education Project, 1999). The MUM developed in this chapter uses those five Cs with the addition of *Collaboration* to make them six. Based on the authors' multicultural educational experience, it is important to recognise those six Cs as being part of a comprehensive and effective model for including diverse population. This model is composed of three distinctive parts (see Figure 8.1):

Figure 8.1

The Multicultural Umbrella Model (MUM)

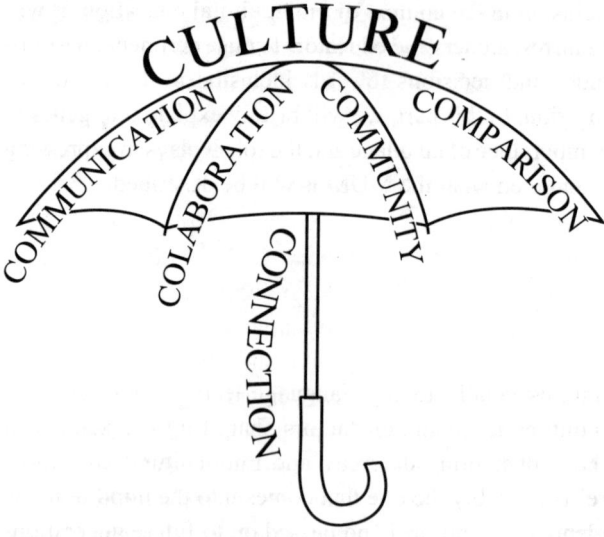

Source: Authors.

1. Fabric: Cultures
2. Hand crook: Connection
3. Stretchers: Community, Comparison, Communication and Collaboration

Multicultural Umbrella Model

Nowadays, education no longer takes place in a monocultural environment due to shifting boundaries such as multiple waves of immigration, cultural transiency, intercultural marriages and the Internet revolution (Friedman, 2005; Hall, 1998). Cultural institutions (created by individuals) and objective culture (music, dance, heroes, history, economic system) define the 'big C' culture, whereas, 'little c' culture is defined in terms of cultural behaviour (how individuals behave) and subjective culture (verbal behaviour, non-verbal behaviour, Communication style, cultural values) (Bennett, 1998b).

In this chapter, the environment is considered to be multicultural, and is composed of cultures in contact. It is in this context that Street's definition of Culture gives the flexibility and accuracy to explain the multicultural environment of educational settings today. He claims that the question is not so much what Culture is, but its product: 'Culture is an active process of meaning-making and contest over definition, including its own definition' (Street, 1993). Multicultural education is a moving target; therefore, Cultures should not be defined as 'nouns', but as 'verbs'.

Developmental psychologist Bronfenbrenner (1979) considers Culture as the macrosystem of his Ecological Theory. Culture influences and is influenced by everything surrounding the individual. The Ecological Theory illustrates the interplay between research and policy when considering child development. Culture is also central to the MUM model for the role it plays in the individual's environment.

The debate about multicultural education has been highlighted since the 1980s (Banks, 1998). Policy makers', educators' and researchers' ethnocentrism is often pointed out as being one of the major obstacles in integrating pupils issued from diverse population (Bhachu, 1984). Avoiding ethnocentrism and being interculturally competent is a process

(Hammer & Bennett, 2001). Intercultural competence can be defined as the junction between linguistic and communicative competence, intercultural knowledge and the features of personality in a given context (Hall, 1998; Ting-Toomey, 1999). In the context of multicultural education, intercultural sensitivity is the key to move away from ethnocentrism in order to reach an ethnorelative mindset (Bennett, 1998a). Ethnocentrism happens when someone judges or acts with someone else according to his/ her own standards. The Golden Rule, 'Do unto others as you would like to be done unto you', reflects an ethnocentric reaction. On the other hand, ethnorelativism is defined as the capacity to adapt to different standards by integrating them in order to function effectively in a multicultural environment (ibid.). The Platinum Rule illustrates an ethnorelative approach: 'Do unto others as they would like to be done unto them'. Empathy is the difference between the Golden Rule and the Platinum Rule. In order to proceed from the Golden Rule to the Platinum Rule, one needs to put oneself into someone else's shoes. To move away from ethnocentrism, one needs to see the world similarly as the person he/she is interacting with.

Efficient integration has to be defined in terms of intercultural sensitivity. The intercultural sensitivity of teachers, policy makers, programme directors, students and family is the key to efficient integration. When Cultures represent a multicultural environment, the second part of the model, Connection, depends upon intercultural sensitivity. If the nature of the connection is based on ethnocentrism, the inclusion will be weakened and the multicultural project may result in failure. On the other hand, if the quality of the connection is more ethnorelatively based, the inclusion of diverse populations in the educational project has greater chances to occur.

If the relationship between Cultures and individuals' Connections is the key to efficient inclusion, the tools to reach it are: Community, Comparison, Communication and Collaboration. Those four tools are critical to allow individuals to build ethnorelative Connection with Culture. Those four elements make the difference between efficient inclusion, following the Platinum Rule, and non-efficient, which is represented by ethnocentrism.

In the MUM, the metaphor of the umbrella helps the reader understand how the model works. The Cultures represent the fabric of the umbrella, a patchwork that illustrates the nature of the multicultural environment.

The hand crook is the symbol of the *Connection* between the individual and the Cultures. Finally, Community, Comparison, Communication and Collaboration are the stretchers of the umbrella. They are the change agents that will allow the umbrella to fully open and make it efficient in case of rain (i.e., the longer the stretchers, the better the expansion and the bigger the size of the umbrella). In other words, the organisation that would not use Community, Comparison, Communication and Collaboration appropriately in implementing its multicultural programme may have limited success. It would not be protected from an ethnocentric approach in the realm of including students with different backgrounds.

Definitions

Keywords often need to be defined in order to comprehend the larger mechanism in which they are involved. Understanding the six Cs is essential to manoeuvre within the MUM model.

1. *Culture*: Understanding the students' culture to make sure decision-making or policies are delivered and implemented effectively. Taking into consideration students' culture will allow students to develop an appreciation and ownership of implemented policies.
2. *Connection*: To be able to connect between staff, families and institutions to better educate and help students in the classroom. This connection happens through finding similarities between people and cultures. There are two levels of definitions for each of the four tools. The programme in which we want to implement the model can be seen as an entity. Secondly, the tool may have another signification for the individual participating in the programme.
3. *Community*: Outreach with businesses, families and institutions to collaborate with the programme in diverse capacities (help and recognise community help to get support, and understand individual differences) (Poplin, 1979).
4. *Collaboration*: Working collectively with the same goal between staff, families, institutions and communities. This collaboration

facilitates finding resources and appropriate tools to achieve success (it builds bonds, and deepens the level of understanding with people from different backgrounds).

5. *Comparison*: Stakeholders are encouraged to compare to find similarities and differences between students in order to include all students in policies and practice (reach an understanding, and it helps in the process of creating a third culture, the result of the cultures in contact).

6. *Communication*: Communication between universities, families and staff to provide students the appropriate service. (The use of eye contact and understanding high/low context culture help in the creation of a third culture.)

The programme as an entity has three objectives in order to function: promote its mission; recruit participants and staff; raise money. In order to facilitate efficient inclusion, policy makers need to keep in mind the MUM model.

The programme as an entity will promote its philosophy in the surrounding communities:

$$\text{Programme} \rightarrow \textit{Community}$$

In return, the community will sustain the programme:

$$\text{Programme} \leftarrow \textit{Community}$$

- Participants (Families → Students)
- Funds (Grantors → Money)
- Staff (Universities → Tutors)

This transaction represents the Collaboration between the programme and its Community. The promotion is done via effective Communication. Members of the Community (grantors/families/universities) will Compare the various programmes offered. Vice versa, the programme will Compare the different grantors, universities and families to identify the best matches for their mission.

The Metamorphosis Project: A Case Study

Entity

The history described below provides a basic understanding of the evolution of the MP. Quillien, along with other professional women of colour in the community, shared personal struggles and the realities of young women of colour in the Twin Ports of Duluth (Minnesota) and Superior (Wisconsin). Their common experience across cultures, generations and socioeconomic status led them to determine projected needs for the young women of colour of this community. Consequently, they identified what types of skills will be beneficial for potential success. At first, the goal was to create an instrumental change for young women of colour in the Twin Ports community, and they began a project within the Duluth Schools called The Metamorphosis Project. The MP revised its mission to serving all individuals. Since 2012, MP has been serving both boys and girls. In this chapter, the MP is presented as a case study during the year 2011–2012.

We are using the metamorphosis metaphor to provide a framework for the changes these young women will experience as a result of participating in the activities. The goal of the MP was to give butterflies, ages 8 through 16, the tools to redefine their lives by promoting high academic achievement. In calling them butterflies, we use the MP to work towards redesigning girls' success, envisioning the strength they have for life and encouraging them to invent guiding principles with utmost faith and confidence in their ability to become women of character through academic activities and group work.

The first programme was offered for the school year 2010–2011. The MP provided a grassroots movement by the community of colour, leading young girls into leadership development. In the first cohort, most students had low test scores, as well as academic and behavioural issues. The programme was a way for Quillien to give back to her community by helping students, mostly from low-income families, not unlike her own experience while attending school. In the summer of 2011, the Office of Education and Equity, from the school district, recommended the project seek grant funding.

Experientially, we gained insights on time management, evaluation and design of the programme, which evolved during Fall 2011. A new group of girls began new curricula designed to build a sense of unity and Community. The youth participated in activities teaching team building, leadership and responsibility to make choices and fill up a life skills 'knapsack' with tools for living. Quillien and Theis (project coordinators) utilised a research-based curriculum titled 'GirlsCircle', and focused on two units: (a) Honouring Our Diversity and (b) Friendship. Their goal that term was to promote self-esteem, self-efficacy, body image, social support and friendship.

Quillien then set out to establish the MP as a formal not-for-profit organisation. A Board of Directors was established, a business plan written, bylaws drafted and a formal curriculum implemented. The organisation received its non-profit status in February 2012. At the end of each session, the staff reviewed (Comparison) the outcomes to ensure that the needs of students in the community were met. As a result of the evaluations, the MP has adapted to build a stronger connection with its diverse communities.

The Metamorphosis Project

We will review the success of this agency in terms of including diverse populations utilising the six Cs as a theoretical framework. The goal is to show how all systems are interrelated and interact for the success of the agency. In this process, there will be two distinct evaluations:

1. We will look at this organisation from an individual perspective. This will involve programme staff, participating students and their parents and/or guardians.
2. We will look at the organisation from a concerted perspective. This will involve the Community (e.g., universities, after-school programmes, grantors and families).

The Board of Directors are responsible for the overall policies, direction of the organisation, and delegation of the responsibility of day-to-day operations to the staff and committees. The board receives no compensation.

The MP works in collaboration with the school district, more specifically with the Office of Education & Equity and the local middle school. The goal of this partnership is to ensure students' successful preparation and readiness for college. The MP aligns its goals on Community needs, as they relate to closing the achievement gap.

The purpose of the MP is to challenge the status quo and support academic endeavours by offering opportunities for success and experiencing different *cultures*. The MP believes in each girl's capacity to advance into womanhood and transform into an intellectual woman of character. Our mission is to encourage young girls to strengthen self-sustainability, transform into positive role models, nurture self-confidence, embrace self-esteem and transpire self-love. This programme is intended to provide additional support to students in order to assist them in increasing their level of academic achievement as well as in building a positive sense of school *connectedness*.

During this programme, students set goals and develop a structure for achieving those goals. They participate in team-building activities, which promote social bonds and school *connectedness*, develop organisational skills, learn effective study skills and receive support with their homework. These students receive assistance from the MP coordinators and trained tutors/mentors. Students also have the opportunity to participate in valuable experiences in the Community to support their academic and social growth. These experiences are open to MP students and their families.

The MP embeds within its programme the 40 building blocks of healthy development for youth, known as Developmental Assets. As stated by the Search Institute, '[I]t represents 40 common sense, positive experiences and qualities that help influence choices young people make and help them become caring, responsible, successful adults' (2012a). Their assets are organised within two clusters: external and internal assets. The external assets are support, empowerment, boundaries and expectations and constructive use of time (ibid.). The internal assets are commitment to learning, positive values, social competencies and positive identity (Search Institute, 2012b). The Search Institute has found that these assets have influence on adolescent behaviour and promote positive attitudes and actions. The MP uses the Developmental Assets Profile, a valid research-based instrument, to assess each participant's assets.

The MP's goal with these assets is to help young children grow up healthy, caring and responsible, and to increase the assets in our participants through weekly activities focused on social skills. The MP staff uses various strategies to effectively develop success among students served. In addition, the overall goal(s) of the organisation for the after-school programme are:

1. The promotion of higher academic success with the vision of closing the achievement gap
2. The development of leadership skills for students involved with the programme
3. The development of cohesive and healthy Community values for participating students

Promotion

The MP staff maintains contact with teachers and parents on a daily basis. A local after-school programme has the similar goal of promoting post-secondary education and has helped the MP by sharing ideas, information and materials to enrich the MP. A local organisation has also *connected* with the MP staff to promote the MP programme within the community. For example, the MP staff presented its programme at a local church. As a result, the programme is better known in the community and connected to the community at large.

Students are required to use in the community their leadership skills gained in the classroom. In order to promote the programme in the community during excursions, the girls wear their sweatshirts/t-shirts with the butterfly MP logo; they represent and promote the programme outside the community, for example, when actively participating in the hiring of the school district superintendent, while participating in cultural night at the local university, during our visit to the Duluth Superior Symphony Orchestra, fundraising at a department store. Students *connected* with the Community by answering questions about the MP logo and the programme.

The staff also promotes the MP in the Community through radio interviews, participation in local programming, articles in local newspapers and *collaborating* with local college students to develop the MP logo and a website. All those elements are the key to advertising the mission of the programme in the Twin Ports of Duluth Superior.

Recruitment

The programmatic approach is the result of input from key cultural informants from the school district. Integration specialists were identified for their specific positions based on their knowledge of the *cultures* and populations to be served. Also they have prior training and experience in working with children in behavioural settings, Community organisations and educational institutions.

A cadre of these key cultural informants determined that, on the basis of their experience and insight into the various Community problems, a strategic approach was required for many of the students in the current institutions. The school district educational institutions are the primary referral source for students to be recruited for this after-school programming approach at local middle school.

The MP receives secondary support from local universities. These institutions provide the MP with tutors/mentors through their education and social work programmes. Both of these institutions *connect* MP students to college awareness through visits to a series of cultural, social and educational events organised by the universities. They *collaborate* directly with key cultural informants who work for the school district as advocates for students of colour. A large number of MP students are from cultural informants' caseloads. They provide MP staff with information about particular issues each individual student is affected by, so that the staff are better able to tailor their services and provide individualised help to students.

The MP works in partnership with local organisations to cooperate and to provide excellent service to students. The Office of Education & Equity, of the school district, served as primary support until May 2012. For the 2012–2013 school year, local funders such as the Northland Foundation, Lloyd K. Johnson Foundation and the Minnesota Power Foundation supported the programme.

Coordinators

The MP staff is composed of people of colour with a great desire to make a difference in students' academic success. The MP coordinators ensure that all the staff match the students' population background. In addition, staff has to meet the qualifications required for the job. The MP board of directors also reviews academic progress regularly.

Tutors/Mentors

The MP recruits tutors/mentors from surrounding institutions. The selected tutors must meet a set of requirements. They are trained and they meet those requirements and expectations to be able to assist students. The tutors/mentors' responsibilities are to make sure our students are safe and receive quality support.

Speakers/Community Members

Since the MP serves a majority of students of colour, the programme invites community members and leaders from a diverse population to serve as positive role models. The goal of this exchange is to promote students' *connection* and understanding of their backgrounds and future endeavours. *Community* members come to the programme to share their experiences, their struggles and their personal/professional endeavours that led to their success. These speakers are required to be casual and flexible to answer students' questions. The desired approach with speakers is student-centred, which gives the opportunity to students to be in a leadership role. The programme has experienced a positive *connection* between speakers and students.

Funding

Grant/Organisations

The MP *connects* to local foundations through phone calls, meetings, emails or letters. As a result of that initial contact, they request a letter of intent. Once the funding organisations approve this letter, the MP submits a grant application. The foundations have guidelines or procedures according to which funding is granted. Therefore, they request a site visit to observe and confirm the content and intention of the funding request. The final stage is to grant the MP the funding based on the results of the above process.

Fundraising

The MP includes fundraising as an optional part of the curriculum. Students are expected to form teams and develop fundraising projects within the Duluth community. Students are required to brainstorm options for fundraising, and thus improve or demonstrate their leadership skills. These options come from the students' aspirations. Students lead and organise the different projects with staff assistance. These tasks provide students the opportunity to use critical thinking skills. They research, plan and develop local fundraising opportunities; in addition, they write an action plan to highlight the steps to accomplish their tasks. Once students finish their fundraising projects, they share their experience with the rest of the class, so other students learn as well.

Individual Perspective

The MP works in Collaboration with the school district, more specifically with the Office of Education & Equity and a local middle. The goal of this partnership is to ensure students' successful preparation and readiness for college.

It is under this direction that the MP partnered with a local middle school based on the opportunity, challenges and issues/needs it presented. The MP provides strong after-school academic programming to underserved school district students. Indeed, the MP staff are members of the community, productive citizens and role models students can relate to, and they provide developmental support to students participating in the MP.

Students attending the local middle school have little to no access to after-school programmes focusing on high academic achievement. Furthermore, there is a notion of relevance to their needs and circumstances as it relates to their cultural, ethnic and socioeconomic background. In addition, the programme participants have little to no role models in their lives to complement academic support. The composition of the student body participating in the MP programme was very diverse (Asians, Blacks, Hispanics, Natives, Whites).

Objectives under the Six Cs

The after-school academic programme has two strong goals: (a) help young children grow up healthy, caring and responsible; (b) increase the assets in our mentees through weekly activities focused on social skills. In order to reach those goals we committed to infuse the six Cs for success as a model of effective implementation to improve students' academic skills.

As an organisation working with at-risk students (Comparison), it was primordial that *culture* be the supporting base when *collaborating*, *communicating* and *connecting* with students, families, teachers and administration (Community). Staff of the MP uses various approaches to effectively develop success among the students served. The following objectives and strategies describe the methodology of the programming.

Objective 1: To Promote Higher Academic Success with the Vision of Closing the Achievement Gap

a. We provide Targeted Academic Instruction. This means that we meet with our families and explain to the parent(s), in the presence of the child, the goals of our programme. During that meeting, we stress the importance of frequent Communication, which, in turn, enhances parents' *connection* with the programme, follow-up and *compare* their child academic progress (grades, attendance, missing assignments) from one grading period to another.

Students learn in a small-group environment. We chose to have smaller groups to allow positive Communication and focusing on Collaboration (peer-to-peer learning; for example, a duo or trio working on similar math assignments). Such environment encourages *cultural* exchange among students, as they are learning, *comparing* and understanding their dissimilar classmates. During one social skills lesson, we discussed the use of stereotypes. The girls were surprised by their personal use of stereotype. One particular exchange, that of self-portrait and breaking stereotype, enabled them to conclude that it is not right to judge a book by its cover.

b. A highly trained staff of educators uses information from teachers and families to provide unique learning opportunities and target instruction. This highlights the importance of multicultural understanding. We work with the family as a unit; therefore, *communicating* with parents allows us to understand the home environment and use that information to *connect* with students. Vice versa, *collaborating* with teachers means sharing information. We can confirm that students have turned in homework, know how their day went and identify areas students need most help on. Detecting their academic struggles enabled us to target intervention and recruit specific mentors/tutors. The participants *communicate, collaborate* and *connect* to the college and Community mentors with whom they build strong, supportive relationships. These intercultural friendships inspire students to dream big and open their worldview.

c. Staff members hold high expectations for student growth. Students are called 'butterflies' to demonstrate The MP's belief in their change agent ability. This means we promote Communication between students and staff; as a result, students learn to become accountable and responsible for their education. It is the expectation of the programme that a student notify the staff with a written note from parents or guardians that she will not be able to attend a session on a given date. If a butterfly fails to provide a written excuse, she may be unable to participate in the month's academic reward activity. Those guidelines make it easier for participants to build a sense of belonging and *connection* to the programme; the guidelines motivate students to also connect to the school culture, understand the programme boundaries and develop healthy academic habits (homework, attendance). The point system put in place allows students to earn points to participate in the monthly reward activity, which students select based on the categories already established.

Objective 2: The Development of Leadership Skills for Students Participating in the Programme

a. Students will be given the opportunity to develop their personal leadership skills by actually managing projects and group functions, and participate in the planning of events. This represents an important role in building the developmental assets through *collaborative* efforts and *connection* with the Community. During one class session, the girls enquired (*compared*) why they never do fun things (by fun, they meant going to the water park, amusement park, etc.). We explained to them, in vain, that our limited budget does not allow us to expand to such activities. However, if they have ideas on how to raise money, we challenge them to develop something and we will assist them in accomplishing their goals. They concerted as a group and presented us with a few options such as packing groceries or selling a local department store's community event coupons. The next step was to call each company and identify the steps to attain their goal. The groceries packing gig fell through. They were able to sell community event coupons. At this point, they learned that gaining money is not an easy step and they understood why we can only do limited outings. The butterflies were able to raise $245. The girls donated the money they raised to the programme. This effort allowed them to bank on many developmental assets such as empowerment (Community values), support (positive Communication), constructive use of time (creative activities), social competencies (interpersonal competence) and positive identity (self-esteem and sense of purpose).

b. Students had a chance to assess the success of their efforts through a journaling effort, feedback to facilitators and discussion in small groups with peers. This positive approach always offers ways to improve our work with the butterflies. The girls often reflected on what we accomplished during the class and we encouraged them to also think of ways we can involve their parents. As a group, they wanted to thank their families for allowing them to participate in the programme and the Community for making the programme possible. They *collaboratively* worked together on developing a menu, which included courses and a traditional thanksgiving meal; in addition, they added different *cultural* elements to represent each girl's background.

c. Students had an opportunity to assess their performance as individuals within the team and through personal development activities. Our programme is girl-centred. This means all activities have to meet their academic, intellectual, personal and future needs. As the girls enter high school, we intentionally set up opportunities to ensure that they develop a commitment to learning, boundaries and expectations. With the help of our Community mentors and college tutors, we organised discussions about careers, college readiness and campus visits. We also *connected* butterflies to academic programmes such as Upward Bound that will help them gain all the skills to be prepared and make an informed decision about college.

Objective 3: The Development of Cohesive and Healthy Community Values for Students Involved

a. The MP is grounded as a service project and infuses service into its programmes to develop an ethic of civic engagement and responsibility among scholars. This means creating and sustaining a journey of community change, initiatives and asset-building. The students identified, connected and created relationships among community leaders dedicated to building assets with the purpose of working together over time and honouring the spirit of the Community. During the hiring of the new superintendent, the girls requested to attend the public forum. Their goal was to let the Community know that their voice mattered. They wanted to feel they have some influence over things that happen in their life, that is, they requested the candidates' profiles. The butterflies collaboratively worked together. They *compared* and sorted out the most qualified candidate. Through their questions, they supported the hiring of someone who has a *cultural* understanding of their struggle, who can *communicate* and *connect* with their concerns as students and influence the decision-making process. As a result, they developed their personal power. Going through this process helps them to be optimistic about their personal future as students of the district.

b. The MP exposes students to a wide range of educational enrichment experiences such as science, environmental studies, leadership, creative arts and health and nutrition. This means exposing butterflies to people of different racial, ethnic and *cultural* backgrounds in order for them to compare with their own cultural identity. The girls were invited to attend Cultural Night at a local university—they worked *collaboratively* with college students to decorate the dinner table (researched the countries represented at the university, identified fun facts and constructed different decorative objects). They recited Maya Angelou's 'Still I Rise' at Kwanzaa at a local university. One of their memorable moments was when they attended the Hispanic monthly meeting; they were startled to realise that black women can also speak other languages than English (Comparison).

Conclusion

As a result of the MP academic programming, we would like higher academic success with a future vision of closing the achievement gap in the school district. The butterflies strive to do well in school, for example, they complete their homework. Their active engagement to learning promotes early college readiness. Participants increase their leadership skills and empowerment by building assets during every class. The girls develop their community values. Each girl grows up healthy, caring and responsible while involved with the MP. Also, students will build leadership skills and empowerment by working on activities using the 40 developmental assets as a framework. In addition, students will gain Community values by being exposed to Community service programmes around the Duluth community. Lastly, the MP promotes post-secondary education by *connecting* students to college mentors and partnerships with local universities. To guarantee success, staff, board members, students, parents and the community will be involved in evaluating the programme. As a result of the evaluation, we will improve and/or expand services accordingly by creating support and planned programmatic efforts.

References

Banks, J. A. (1998). Multicultural education: Development, dimensions, and challenges. In M. J. Bennett (Ed.), *Basic concepts of intercultural communication: Selected readings* (pp. 69–84). Yarmouth, ME: Intercultural Press.

Bennett, M. J. (Ed.). (1998a). Overcoming the golden rule: Sympathy and empathy. In *Basic concepts of intercultural communication: Selected readings* (pp. 1–34). Yarmouth, ME: Intercultural Press.

———. (Ed.). (1998b). Intercultural communication: A current perspective. In *Basic concepts of intercultural communication: Selected readings* (pp. 191–214). Yarmouth, Maine: Intercultural Press.

Bhachu, P. (1984). Multicultural education: Parental views. *Journal of Ethnic and Migration Studies, 12*(1), 9–21.

Bronfenbrenner, U. (1979). Contexts of child rearing: Problems and prospects. *American Psychologist, 34*(10), 844.

Bryant, D. M., & Maxwell, K. (1997). The effectiveness of early intervention for disadvantaged children. In M. J. Guralnick (Ed.), *The effectiveness of early intervention* (pp. 23–46). Baltimore, MD: Brookes.

Campbell, F. A., Pungello, E. P., Miller-Johnson, S., Burchinal, M. & Ramey, C. T. (2001). The development of cognitive and academic abilities: Growth curves from an early childhood educational experiment. *Developmental Psychology, 37*(2), 231.

Collegia, J. (2012). *Le problème de la réussite scolaire des sans-papiers* [The issue of academic success in undocumented immigrants]. Paris, France: L'Harmattan.

Dahlberg, G., Moss, P. & Pence, A. (1999). *Beyond quality in early childhood education and care: Postmodern perspectives* (pp. 159–186). Levittown, PA: Taylor & Francis.

Friedman, T. (2005). *The world is flat.* New York: Farrar, Straus & Giroux.

Hall, E. T. (1998). The power of hidden differences. In M. J. Bennett (Ed.), *Basic concepts of intercultural communication: Selected readings* (pp. 53–67). Yarmouth, ME: Intercultural Press.

Hammer, M. R. & Bennett, M. J. (2001). *The intercultural development inventory (IDI) manual.* Portland, Oregon: Intercultural Communication Institute.

Ladson-Billings, G. (2006). From the achievement gap to the education debt: Understanding achievement in U.S. schools. *Educational Researcher*, *35*(7), 3–12.

National Standards in Foreign Language Education Project. (1999). *Standards for foreign language learning in the 21st century* (1st ed.). New York, NY: American Council on the Teaching of Foreign Language.

Poplin, D. (1979). *Communities: A survey of theories and methods of research* (2nd ed.). New York: Macmillan.

Schecter, S. R. & Bayley, R. (1997). Language socialization practices and cultural identity: Case studies of Mexican-descent families in California and Texas. *TESOL Quarterly*, *31*(3), 513–541.

Search Institute. (2012a). Development assets data file. Retrieved from http://www.search-institute.org/content/40-developmental-assets-adolescents-ages-12-18 (accessed 30 July 2012).

———. (2012b). Developmental assets data file. Retrieved from http://www.search-institute.org/introtoassets (accessed 30 July 2012).

Street, B. (1993). *Language and culture*. Tonawanda, NY: British Association for Applied Linguistics.

Ting-Toomey, S. (1999). *Communicating across cultures*. New York: Guilford.

Yoshikawa, H. (1995). Long-term effects of early childhood programs on social outcomes and delinquency. *The Future of Children*, *5*(3), 51–75.

Further Readings

Adler, N. J. & Gundersen, A. (2007). *International dimensions of organizational behavior* (5th ed.). Cincinnati, Ohio: South-Western.

Davis, B. (2007). *How to teach students who don't look like you*. Thousand Oaks, California: Corwin Press.

Gudykunst, W. B. & Ting-Toomey, S. (1988). *Culture and interpersonal communication*. Newbury Park, California: SAGE.

Hofstede, G. (2001). *Culture's consequences: Comparing values, behaviors, institutions, and organizations across nations* (2nd ed.). Thousand Oaks, California: SAGE.

Hovland, K. (2006). *Shared futures: Global learning and liberal education*. Washington, D.C.: Association of American Colleges and Universities.

Howard, G. (2007). *We can't teach what we don't know* (2nd ed.). New York: Teachers College Press.

Kolb, D. A. (1984). *Experiential learning: Experience as the source of learning and development*. Englewood Cliffs, New Jersey: Prentice-Hall.

Ladson-Billings, G. (2009). *The dreamkeepers, successful teachers of African American children* (2nd ed.). New York: Jossey-Bass.

Paige, R. M. (Ed.). (1993). *Education for the intercultural experience* (2nd ed.) (pp. 109–135). Yarmouth, Maine: Intercultural Press.

———. (2008, 3–4 October). *Using the IDI to guide personal and organizational development: Challenges and opportunities* (PowerPoint). Presented at the 1st Annual Intercultural Development Inventory Conference, Minneapolis, Minnesota.

Trompenaars, F. & Hampden-Turner, C. (1997). *Riding the waves of culture: Understanding cultural diversity in business* (2nd ed.). Naperville, Illinois: Intercultural Management Publishers NV/Nicholas Brealey.

Section IV

Literature Review Evidence and Considerations

9

Cross-Disability Approach to Inclusion of Children

Amitav Mishra and Mousumi Bhaumik

Early childhood is a crucial phase of growth and development because experiences during this period can influence outcomes across the entire course of an individual's life (UN, 2010; WHO, 2007). As per the 85th Amendment to Article 45 of the Indian Constitution, the government has urged for the state's endeavour to provide early childhood care and education to all children until they complete six years of age. The draft policy of Ministry of Women and Child Development (MoWCD) on early childhood care and education has visualised the promotion of inclusive, equitable and contextualised opportunities for optimal development and active learning capacity of all children. It has urged for the facilitation of an enabling environment through appropriate systems, processes and provisions across the country by ensuring adaptive strategies for inclusion of all children (MoWCD, 2012a, 2012b).

The present chapter highlights some of the Indian experiences and compares them with international development. We know that early childhood provides an important window of opportunity to prepare the foundation for life-long learning and participation for all children, while preventing potential delays in development and disabilities. For children who experience disability, it is a vital time to ensure access to interventions which can help them reach their full potential (Betts & Lata, 2009; UN, 2010). This process is expected to be initiated with early years educational opportunities immediately after or with early intervention services. Inclusion is a process of increasing the presence, participation and achievement of all students in their local schools, with particular reference to those groups of students who are at risk of exclusion, marginalisation or underachievement (Ainscow & Moss, 2002; Mishra & Singh, 2013). The two international legislations, namely, 'United Nations Convention on the Rights of the Child' (UN, 1989) and the 'United Nations Convention on the Rights of Persons with Disabilities' (UN, 2006) summarise that children with disabilities have the same rights as other children—in all aspects related to health care, nutrition, education, social inclusion and protection from violence, abuse and neglect. Ensuring access to appropriate support, such as early childhood intervention and education, can fulfil the rights of children with disabilities, promoting rich and fulfilling childhoods and preparing them for full and meaningful participation in adulthood (Simeonsson, 2000). Therefore, we have to make early years education as inclusive as possible, so that young children with disabilities achieve access and equity in every level of education as they would grow and participate in gainful community life. It is not only important to understand the importance of inclusive early years education, but also necessary to identify the effective strategies for this.

Early Years Crucial for Children Who Are at Risk

At the onset, we must appreciate why early years are crucial for all children including those who are at risk. The early years offer a special opportunity to foster developmental gains in children as 80 per cent of the brain's capacity develops before the age of 3 (Betts & Lata, 2009). The gains are shown to be the highest for those with maximum disadvantage. Equally, early neglect has lasting disabling effects as poor nutrition leads to early childhood stunting, coupled with low stimulation. This contributes to the poor cognitive and educational performance of millions of under-five children who are not fulfilling their developmental potential (Grantham-McGregor, 2007).

Research has also indicated that if these early years are not supported by, or embedded in, a stimulating and enriching physical and psycho-social environment, the chances of the child's brain developing to its full potential are considerably, and often irreversibly, reduced (Biswal, Mistry & Das, 2011; NCERT, 2006). There are three primary reasons for intervening early with an exceptional child: first, to enhance the child's development; second, to provide support and assistance to the family; finally, to maximise the child's and family's benefit to society. Karnes and Lee (1983) have noted that 'only through early identification and appropriate programming can children develop their potential' (p. 10). Early intervention applies to children of school age or younger who are discovered to have or be at risk of developing an impairment or other special need that may affect their development. Early intervention consists of several comprehensive developmental and clinical services for such children and their families for the purpose of lessening the effects of the disabling condition. Early intervention can be remedial or preventive in nature, that is, remediating existing developmental problems or preventing their occurrence (MCWL, 2013).

There is distinct difference between early intervention and early years education. Early intervention is an exclusive service that focuses on intervening the developmental delay and/or disabilities through a multi-disciplinary team; whereas the term early years education is often used to describe non-statutory preschool provision. Early intervention services also have a significant impact on the parents and siblings of an exceptional infant or young child. The family of a young exceptional child often experiences feelings of disappointment, social isolation, added stress, frustration and helplessness. The compounded stress of the presence of an exceptional child may affect the family's well-being and interfere with the child's development (e.g., Hodapp, Ricci, Ly & Fidler, 2003; Johnston et al., 2003).

Through early assessment coupled with intervention, families gain relevant information, especially about what their child can do and about interventions that will optimise his/her learning potential (Betts & Lata, 2009). This also increases the chances that children with disabilities can participate and flourish in inclusive mainstream educational settings. Evidence suggests that one in three infants and toddlers who receive early intervention services do not present later with a disability or require special education in a preschool (UNESCO, 2012a). Even in the most remote and distant rural sections, early years education centres can be operated with minimum resources but without compromising the required commitment. Even such centres can give opportunities mostly through plays along with few systematically planned activities to all young children including children with disabilities. No doubt, it can reduce the developmental gap. Manning-Morton and Thorp (2004) examine the importance of play for children less than 3 years of age and identify a crucial role for adults in supporting and developing such play experiences. Play is seen in relation to all aspects of a child's day, integral to and part of a holistic approach to early education and care for very young children. Bredekamp and Copple's (1997) advocacy of a developmentally appropriate approach to early years curriculum sets out the many principles of child development and learning that inform developmentally appropriate practice in early childhood programmes with disabilities too. Some of these are:

- Domains of children's development—physical, social, emotional and cognitive—are closely related. Development in one domain influences and is influenced by development in other domains.
- Early experiences have both cumulative and delayed effects on individual children's development; optimal periods exist for certain types of development and learning.
- Children are active learners, drawing on direct physical and social experience as well as culturally transmitted knowledge to construct their own understandings of the world around them.
- Play is an important vehicle for children's social, emotional and cognitive development, as well as a reflection of their development.
- Development advances when children have opportunities to practise newly acquired skills as well as when they experience a challenge just beyond the level of their present mastery.
- Children develop and learn best in the context of a community where they are safe and valued, their physical needs are met and they feel psychologically secure.

These principles have significance for early intervention services as intervening early reaps maximum benefits that increases the child's developmental and educational gains and decreases dependence upon social institutions (US Department of Education, 2002). Early childhood intervention focuses on achieving developmental tasks as expected during infancy and early childhood through systematically planned programmes by the team of clinical and developmental professionals.

Neurological development in early childhood is a factor influencing health, learning and well-being. In the early years, safe and supportive learning environments provide opportunities for play, parental involvement, exploration, discovery, rich language development and experimentation. The major developmental domains are given here:

Major Developmental Domains

Area I	*Physical*: Height, weight, general motor coordination, visual and auditory acuity and so on
Area II	*Emotional*: Feelings, self-perception, perception of others related to self, confidence, security and so on
Area III	*Social*: Interactions with peers, elders and youngsters, both one to one and in a group
Area IV	*Cognitive*: Reasoning, problem solving, concept formation, abstraction, imagination, creativity and so on.

Source: Swim and Watson (2011, Chapter 1, p. 6).

Further, Geigert (2013) has discussed various types of developmental tasks that help young children through sensorimotor integration. Some of the developmental tasks are listed here:

- *Sensory–motor development*: Balance, body awareness, coordination, controlled movement, fine motor dexterity, laterality, sensory awareness, self-help skills, visual–motor integration.
- *Perceptual efficiency*: Attention and concentration, directionality, visual discrimination, visual memory, visualisation and spatial relationships. Auditory memory, comprehension, non-verbal expression, verbal facility, vocabulary.
- *Cognition and academic readiness*: Academic readiness, association, classification, creativity, part-to-whole relationships, problem solving, serialisation, quantitative skills.

- *Social and emotional development*: Includes cooperation, imitation, self-control, self-expression, self-esteem, understanding feelings.

Based on the major developmental domains, several developmental tasks can be achieved in early years education through various exploratory activities and play.

Significance of Early Years Education for Children with Disabilities

Universal access to early education must be adapted by all countries. A holistic attention to the very early years of life is critically important for children with disabilities to access formal pre-primary education. Yet, only 56 per cent of all young children worldwide have access to any form of pre-primary services. Although data regarding access for children with disabilities is lacking globally, they are least likely to be included in such programmes. Out of 100 million children with disabilities (age 5 and under) worldwide, 80 per cent of them live in developing countries, where the provision of pre-primary education and other basic services tends to be insufficient (UNESCO, 2012b). In this context, early years education can be the change-maker in strengthening access and participation of young children with disabilities.

The global events have also influenced the early years education and childcare in India. The need for early care and educational services on behalf of children, especially those from economically marginalised communities, has been well recognised. India had crossed a population of 1 billion in 2001. It has the largest child population in the world. This also includes a large number of preschool children with developmental delay and disabilities.

Early years education for children derive their importance from this rationale and from the emerging need arising from various social, economic and demographic changes in the last few decades. These are more specifically changes in the family structure, increase in maternal employment outside the home and a growing demand for education. Good quality early years educational programmes that cater to this age group of 0–6 years are known to produce significant short- and long-term benefits, particularly for children in underprivileged contexts including children with disabilities.

Growth and development is rapid in childhood. During this period, if a child has a problem, and if it is attended immediately, then further damage can be arrested. Parents might lack skills to handle a child who has a problem. Support to them at the right time helps them learn proper handling and prevent the development of negative attitudes towards the child. The whole family can be involved in this. Due to support given at the right time, he/she can become ready for education with other children. If a pattern or practice is set until older age and then professional help is sought, correction becomes very difficult for the child, family and the professional. Therefore, it is ideal to attend early in life if there is a likelihood of childhood disability.

Call for Action

The Early Childhood imperative for the rights of children with disabilities is clear. With almost universal ratification of the Convention on the Rights of the Child and the growing adoption of the Convention of Rights of Persons with Disabilities, duty bearers at all levels must be held accountable to ensure that all girls and boys with disabilities have access to lifelong learning. If the 'Millennium Development Goals' around universal primary education and eradication of poverty are to be met, 'Education for All' initiatives must urgently address the inclusion of children with disabilities from the early years. The 2008 UNESCO International Conference on Education sent a strong message to the international community, calling for greater investment in early assessment and intervention, inclusive early childhood care and education programmes and for equipping teachers with appropriate skills and materials to teach diverse student populations. In essence, promotion of comprehensive, inclusive early years education must become a priority for global development.

An inclusive education will ensure that all children have unimpeded and supportive opportunities to participate in activities, belong to peer groups and still receive the individualised attention that they need in order to acquire developmental skills. From the child rights perspective, India must ensure that no child is rejected because of disability and that the child with disability gets an opportunity to attend programmes in the school or the community. To ensure this goal, the Government of India passed the Persons with Disability Act, 1995. But there is still no clear understanding of how the inclusive early years education can be planned effectively. Through a study, Mishra and Singh (2013) made an effort to answer several questions related to the status of inclusion in early years education in India. The first question to be answered was: How do the early years education centres strive to provide access to a wide range of learning opportunities, activities, settings and environments that support inclusion? It was found that centres are not easily approachable for admission and some preschools have inhibitions in admitting children with disabilities due to the misconception that it would affect the centre's image and relationship that the parents of typical students possess. Negative attitude is not only the biggest obstacle but a significant variable that determines the practice of inclusion for children with special needs (Neilson, 2005; Singh & Mishra, 2012). This is because of some early childhood settings where the staff believe that children with special needs require segregated education facilities (MacArthur, Purdue & Ballard, 2003). These beliefs are grounded in deficit theory (because of deficiencies based on stereotypes); they blame the child for their difference/impairment and compare the child with typical developing children (Moffat, 2011). A study conducted by Mishra and Singh (2013) found that some centres did manage inclusion in a very positive manner even in the absence of special educational orientation, support by an inclusion specialist and the involvement of the government. Moffat (2011) conducted a similar study to find out the factors that promote inclusion in early childhood settings in New Zealand. The study found that (a) positive attitude made inclusive education happen, (b) communication and collaboration helped to build inclusive settings and (c) quality learning experiences enhanced successful inclusion.

Social–emotional development and behaviours that facilitate participation are critical goals of high-quality early years inclusion, along with learning and development in all other domains. In the aforesaid study (Mishra & Singh, 2013), effort was made to find out how the staff/teachers promoted belonging, participation and engagement of children with and without disabilities in his/her setting in a variety of intentional ways. Out of three case studies, one case study of a preschool reported that the entire staff were found to be fully dedicated to promoting belongingness and engaging children with disabilities in a variety of activities along with their typical peers. An important component in the role of an early childhood teacher is the ability to respect children, interact with them and respond to each child's ideas, thoughts and desires (Yael, 2012). In most of the preschools, peers made significant contribution to it. The centres that focused on positive parent–teacher interaction and collaboration contributed significantly to the development of children. Lieber et al. (2002) revealed that when an autistic child was enrolled in a preschool programme in United Kingdom, the child managed well in the mainstream setting because of the positive attitude of the teachers and parents.

Further, it has been observed in India that teachers get cooperation from the parents, but preschools are not supported by the government or other agencies/specialists to improve their role for such children. It is highly desirable for the Indian government to establish a system of services and supports that are not only meant for revising programme and professional standards to incorporate high-quality inclusive programmes, but the system must also succeed in influencing the accountability of the agencies to improve the quality and outcomes of inclusion. At the same time, teacher training needs to be reformed with inputs on how to work effectively with a group of young children, one or more of whom may be significantly challenged in physical, cognitive, language, social or behavioural development. Let us discuss the strategies that promote inclusion in early years education which need to be incorporated into teacher training programmes and framework of early years education in India and similar developing countries.

Promoting Inclusion in Early Years Education

Inclusion is a sound principle and based on knowledge of child development (Christy, 2007). Kids with developmental delays or disabilities of mild to moderate or more extents are placed with typically developing peers to provide them with role models and enhance their self-esteem.

The concept is valid and holds up in application in the right circumstances. In the field of early childhood education, inclusion describes the practice of including children with disabilities in a childcare setting with typically developing children of similar ages, with specialised instruction and support when needed (eXtension, 2013).

For children with special needs, an inclusive childcare programme provides belonging, acceptance and developmentally appropriate practices. They learn typical developing skills from their classmates and when and how to use these skills, and they have an opportunity to develop friendships with typically developing peers (Child Action, Inc., 2013). They are provided opportunities to develop positive attitudes towards themselves and others who are different from themselves. Early years education provides care, stimulation, parental support and access to relevant services and enhances the effects of interventions for children with disabilities (Betts & Lata, 2009). Early intervention services can be delivered within the context of the family. These services aim to improve developmental, social and educational gains, as well as reduce the future costs of special education, rehabilitation and health-care needs. Not only that, it also reduces feelings of isolation, stress and frustration that families may experience. It helps to alleviate and reduce behaviours by using positive behaviour strategies and interventions, and facilitate children with disabilities to grow up to become productive, independent individuals.

When inclusion is done well, it can be a very positive experience for both young children with special needs and their typically developing peers. Childcare providers can play an important role in making inclusive childcare successful. Inclusive childcare can be beneficial, both for the child with a special need and for the other children in the inclusion classroom. Some of the benefits of inclusive childcare for children with special needs include:

- Chances to learn by observing and interacting with other children of similar ages
- Time and support to build relationships with other children
- Chances to practise social skills in real-world situations
- Exposure to a wider variety of challenging activities
- Opportunities to learn at their own pace in a supportive environment
- Chances to build relationships with caring adults other than parents

Typically, developing children can also benefit from interacting with a child with a special need in their childcare programme. Benefits of inclusive childcare for typically developing children include:

- Increased appreciation and acceptance of individual differences
- Increased empathy for others
- Preparation for adult life in an inclusive society
- Opportunities to master activities by practising and teaching others

Real inclusion in the early years benefits everyone. Positive early experiences are essential for later success in school, the workplace and the community. The children and their families benefit in several ways and these are listed here (MoCYS, 2007).

Children benefit by:

- Developing friendships and learning how to play with others
- Learning acceptance, and to be sensitive to individual differences
- Being provided with realistic life experiences that prepare them to live in the community
- Being provided with opportunities to learn from others with differing abilities

And families benefit by:

- Having access to quality childcare
- Watching their children make friends with children from diverse groups
- Sharing hopes, needs and concerns for their children with others
- Choosing a mainstream environment for their child—a positive preschool experience will often encourage parents to choose an inclusive primary school

There is no doubt that including a child with a disability or delay in an early childhood programme can be challenging. But including a child with special needs in a classroom with typically developing children can be extremely worthwhile, not only for the child with a disability or delay, but for all the children in the classroom.

Adaptations in Early Years Education Curriculum

In general, the early years curriculum is based on inclusive principles. Adaptations in early years education curriculum have been widely advocated (Learning and Teaching Scotland, 2006; Siraj-Blatchford, 1998). Practitioners should ensure that all children feel included, secure and valued. Early years experience should build on what children already know and can do. No child should be excluded or disadvantaged because of ethnicity, culture, or religion, home language, family background, special educational needs, disability, gender or ability. The parents and practitioners should work together with an effective curriculum that should be carefully structured. There should be opportunities for children to engage in activities planned by adults and those initiated by them. Practitioners must be able to observe and respond appropriately to children. Well-planned, purposeful activity and appropriate intervention by practitioners will engage children in the learning process. For children to have a rich and stimulating experience, the learning environment should be well planned and organised. Effective learning and development for young children requires high quality care and education by practitioners.

Meeting the Diverse Needs

Early years educational professionals must plan opportunities that build on and extend children's knowledge, experiences, interests and skills and develop their self-esteem and confidence in their ability to learn. Teachers must use a wide range of teaching strategies, based on children's learning needs, and use materials that positively reflect diversity and are free from discrimination and stereotyping. In order to meet the diverse needs, teachers are expected to provide:

- Wide range of opportunities to motivate, support and develop children and help them be involved, concentrate and learn effectively.
- Safe and supportive learning environment, free from harassment, in which the contribution of all children is valued, and where racial, religious, disability and gender stereotypes are challenged.

- Opportunities for children whose ability and understanding are in advance of their language and communication skills.

The curriculum for the foundation stage should underpin all future learning by supporting, fostering, promoting and developing children's personal, social and emotional well-being, in particular by supporting the transition to and between settings, promoting an inclusive ethos and providing opportunities for each child to become a valued member of that group and community so that a strong self-image and self-esteem are promoted. Positive attitudes and dispositions towards their learning need to be built, in particular an enthusiasm for knowledge and learning, and a confidence in their ability to be successful learners. Social skills can be enhanced by providing opportunities that enable them to learn how to cooperate and work harmoniously alongside, and with, each other and to listen to each other.

There are many points that early years educators must consider to meet the diverse needs of the students, such as:

- *Attention skills and persistence*: This facilitates the capacity to concentrate on their own lay or on group tasks.
- *Language and communication*: With opportunities for all children to talk and communicate in a widening range of situations, to respond to adults and to each other, to practise and extend the range of vocabulary and communication skills they use and to listen carefully.
- *Reading and writing*: With opportunities for all children to explore, enjoy, learn about and use words and text in a broad range of contexts and to experience a rich variety of books.
- *Mathematics*: With opportunities for all children to develop their understanding of numbers, measurement, patterns, shapes and space by providing a broad range of contexts in which they can explore, enjoy, learn, practise and talk about them.
- *Knowledge and understanding of the world*: With opportunities for all children to solve problems, make decisions, experiment, predict, plan and question in a varied range of contexts, and to explore and find out about their environment, and people and places that have significance in their lives.

- *Physical development*: With opportunities for all children to develop and practise their fine and gross motor skills, increase their understanding of how their bodies work and what they need to be healthy and safe.
- *Creative development*: With opportunities for all children to explore and share their thoughts, ideas and feelings through a variety of art, design and technology, music, movement, dance and imaginative and role-play activities.

This curriculum recognises how significant high-quality early childhood education programmes can be in children's lives. It is recognised that early childhood programmes encourage active learning, problem solving, effective communication, creativity, social adjustment and participation that benefit children's long-term success in education and citizenship. The curriculum recognises the diversity of experiences and relationships that shape children's lives.

Building Continuity by Valuing Children's Diverse Social and Cultural Understandings

Building continuity means providing an environment that supports children to gradually learn the ways of interacting and behaving in the school setting. These are often particular social and cultural practices that are new to children. Teachers may need to explicitly teach the social and cultural practices that are used in their classroom and school. They must recognise that for some children, the school culture and the home culture may be very different than their existing social and cultural understandings and practices. Further, this may involve:

- Ensuring that there is continuity in the curriculum, and in ways of interacting and learning, as children move from prior care and education into preparatory settings and through school.
- Developing strategies to assist children as they adjust to new settings.
- Assisting children to build relationships with staff and peers in the new setting.

- Clearly explaining the processes for interacting in groups that are particular to their school communities.

Building Continuity by Managing Transition Processes between Settings

A variety of transition processes can be developed to help children and families move effortlessly from home situations into preparatory settings and later into early primary settings. These processes need to be suitably planned and evaluated to ensure they promote continuity. Such transition processes incorporate opportunities for:

- Children and their families to meet teaching staff before the first day.
- Small groups of children to meet, take part in classroom routines and experiences and become familiar with the classroom learning environment.
- Parents and carers to meet, get to know each other and build networks with staff from different settings (such as care and early educational contexts, preparatory and schooling) to meet and visit each other's workplaces, plan transitions, discuss curriculum continuity, including continuity of teaching practice, work together in professional learning experiences and build professional networks.
- Parents and carers to regularly visit the classroom, see their children engaging in contexts and discuss topics of interest.
- Teachers, parents and carers to pass on information about children's learning and development.

Successful transition processes are flexible and responsive to the changing needs and interests of participants—for example, adjusting programmes to allow working or isolated families to visit classrooms when convenient. Transition processes respect individual community differences and are built upon trust. It is important for parents and carers to feel that their ideas, views and needs are valued, respected and taken into account when transition processes are planned. Perceived differences between pre-compulsory and compulsory educational settings often give rise to concerns about whether children will be 'ready' for compulsory schooling. Children and families often construct assumptions and expectations about what school is like. Schools are often viewed as places where children work at desks, interact with larger groups of children, are expected to be in particular places at set times and need to remember different sets of rules for classroom activities, group experiences, lunch breaks and specialist lessons. However, research has shown that, throughout the early phase of schooling, children learn more effectively in an environment that encourages movement, investigation, discussion, outdoor learning and flexible learning contexts (Connell, Shearer, & Tobin, 2006; EQI, 2009). Connell et al. (2006) have reflected that transitions between precompulsory and compulsory schooling settings are more successful when they provide continuity of experiences and offer flexible, child-responsive curriculums that:

- Reflect current understandings about children and how they learn and develop
- Use the information provided by previous teachers about individual children's learning and development
- Build effective partnerships to support learning
- Provide flexible learning environments
- Ensure children learn in a range of learning contexts including play, real-life situations, investigations, transitions and routines and focused learning and teaching

Children's experiences with transitions have an impact on their learning and development as well as their adjustment to new situations in the future. Facilitating successful transitions by building continuities is therefore an important focus for the preparatory year.

Challenges of Diversity within Disability

Cross-disability is an important approach to deal with diversity amongst the learners. Diversity in classrooms may encompass differences in intellectual, communication, sensory abilities; behavioural differences, including children with emotional and behaviour disorders or having severe social maladjustment problems; multiple and severe handicapping conditions, including individuals with mental retardation and physical/ motor or sensory disabilities and physical differences, that include mobility problems and health needs (Rao, 2009). A solution to meet this diversity and a balance between teachers and classrooms can be a cross-categorical approach or cross-disability approach to service delivery adopted by schools. In this approach, students are grouped according to their instructional needs rather than their disability labels. Thus, teachers also can focus on instructionally relevant needs of their students. A cross-disability approach considers students' instructional needs and not disability-specific needs (Haager & Klingner, 2005). The cross-disability movement follows a rainbow approach to include all those who are given a disability label; in fact, some have named it the movement of the 'dis-labled'. It is an approach that does not distinguish between types of disability. In other words, it is an approach which comprehensively takes into account all different kinds of disabilities together and promotes collective planning for classroom instruction.

Drummond (2002) had recommended a number of best practice strategies as given below that Rao (2009) considered relevant in addressing the inclusive classroom teaching based on the cross-disability approach:

- *Interdisciplinary themes and instruction*: It helps motivate students, helps them learn a given topic in great breadth and depth through connections made between different subject areas and prepares students for the real world as they are able to see a connection between real life and school (Rothlein & Fredricks, as cited in Vaughn, Bos & Schumm, 2006).

- *Grouping strategies including pairs, small and large group instruction*: In a classroom with diverse abilities and needs, various grouping structures, such as whole class, small groups and pairs, can be utilised to maximise student engagement and learning. It endorses positive outcomes due to the three important components of cooperative learning groups: positive interdependence, individual accountability and face-to-face interaction.

- *Collaboration and co-teaching*: In a cross-categorical approach, collaboration and co-teaching between early years education teachers and a special education teacher may be a key to success of all students. Friend and Cook (1996) described co-teaching as a process whereby two or more professionals collaborate to share responsibility in three important processes involved in teaching: planning, teaching and evaluating. Co-teaching in inclusive classrooms provides much needed direct support to students with disabilities and support for teachers in terms of co-planning, co-teaching and co-assessing.

- *Theory of multiple intelligences*: Use of multiple intelligences enables teachers to meet individual needs and learning styles of students using the strengths of students in their preferred domain (Rao, 2005).

- *Bloom's taxonomy*: The taxonomy, hierarchical organisation of teaching objectives from the most basic recall level to the highest evaluation level involving critical thinking has widely been acclaimed in literature (Gray, 2002; Kastberg, 2003) as a vehicle to both teach and assess understanding of students with diverse abilities and needs (Rao, 2009).

- *Standards-based planning*: Offers direction as to what students should learn and requires emphasis on three inter-related areas: content standards: subject area skills and knowledge; performance standards: proficiency levels required; and opportunity to learn standards: materials, strategies and structure necessary for successful learning, to successfully teach and adapt a standards-based curriculum for students with learning and behaviour problems (Glatthorn; McLaughlin & Shepard; Quenemoen, Lehr, Thurlow & Massanaair, as cited in Hoover & Patton, 2004).

- *Computer-mediated support and assistive technology*: Focuses on the use of technology to compensate impairment condition and promote learning.

In a very simple way, we may say that good teaching based on universal design for learning (UDL) can effectively address inclusion in most diverse classrooms with the presence of heterogeneous learning abilities.

Conclusion

Education for children with disabilities should focus on inclusion in mainstream settings. While inclusion is consistent with the rights of children with disabilities and is generally more cost-effective than special or separate schools, it cannot happen without appropriate levels of support. The progressive national and local policy, trained staff, accessible facilities, flexible curricula and teaching methods, and educational resources may not be considered as additional investments as these investments are essential and would benefit all children. For all inclusive early childhood education and learning interventions, positive attitudes and responses from and interactions with peers, teachers, school administrators, other school staff, parents and community members are critical (UNICEF, 2007a, 2007b; WHO, 2011). At the same time, teacher training needs to be reformed. The teachers working in early years education centres must know how to work effectively with a group of young children (Allen & Codery, 2012), one or more of whom may be significantly challenged in physical, cognitive, language, social or behavioural development. They must have sound understanding on application of developmental–behavioural approach in order to make classroom management effective and positive, and on how to arrange environment so that every child has developmentally appropriate learning opportunities. The teachers must ensure that every child, with his or her own interests and capabilities, is included with and accepted by other children. As India has a large number of young children with disabilities, in both rural and urban pockets, with limited number of special education professionals, the cross-disability approach in preparing teachers for early years education seems to be the right answer.

Further, teachers must understand how to include parents and caregivers in ways that incorporate and value their first-hand knowledge in planning for their child's learning, and how to facilitate optimum communication development, pre-academics and cognitive learning and adaptive, self-care and independence skills. Deciding what is a deviation from normal development or 'atypical development' raises complex issues and is equally difficult. Therefore, thorough knowledge of normal growth and development is necessary in order to understand and work with all children.

References

Ainscow, M. & Moss, S. (2002). Exploring the use of action research to develop inclusive practices in urban schools. Paper presented at the British Education Research Association Conference, Exeter, UK.

Allen, K. E. & Codery, G. E. (2012). *The exceptional child: Inclusion in early childhood education* (7th ed.). Delhi: Cengage Learning India.

Betts, J. & Lata, D. (2009). Inclusion of children with disability: The early childhood imperative. *UNESCO Policy Brief on Early Childhood*, No. 46.

Biswal, A., Mistry, H. & Das, J. (2011). *Learning achievement and development of cognitive & motor skills: A study on the primary school children with different pre-schooling*. Saarbrucken, Germany: Lambert Academic Publishing.

Bredekamp, S. & Copple, S. (Eds). (1997). *Developmentally appropriate practice in early childhood programs*. Washington, D.C.: National Association for the Education of Young Children.

Child Action, Inc. (2013). *Inclusion of children with disabilities or other special needs (Handout No. 48)*. Retrieved from http://www.childaction.org/families/publications/docs/guidance/Handout48-Caring_For_Children_With_Special_Needs.pdf (accessed 31 January 2013).

Christy, M. (2007). *The facts about special needs inclusion in early childhood programs*. Retrieved from http://voices.yahoo.com/the-facts-special-needs-inclusion-early-childhood-661281.html (accessed 31 January 2013).

Connell, P., Shearer, A. & Tobin, T. (2006). *Early years curriculum guidelines* (p. 3). Brisbane, The State of Queensland: Queensland Studies Authority.

Drummond, T. (2002). *A brief summary of best practices in college teaching intended to challenge professional development of all teachers*. Retrieved from http://www.odec.umd.edu/CD/FACILITI/DRUMMOND.PDF (accessed 12 December 2011).

EQI (Education Queensland International) Australia and Nord Anglia Limited, UK. (2009). *Early years education good practice guide*. Retrieved from http://www.sec.gov.qa/En/SECInstitutes/EducationInstitute/Offices/Documents/GPGEnglish.pdf (accessed 3 January 2013).

eXtension. (2013). *What is inclusive child care?* Retrieved from http://www.extension.org/pages/61602/what-is-inclusive-child-care (accessed 3 January 2013).

Friend, M. & Cook, L. (1996). *Interactions: Collaboration skills for school professionals* (2nd ed.). White Plains, New York: Longman

Geigert, N. (2013). *Pathway to learning: Helping children through sensorimotor integration*. Retrieved from http://caeyc.org/main/caeyc/pdfs/conference/handouts/PathwaytoLearning.pdf (accessed 23 March 2013).

Grantham-McGregor, S. (2007). Developmental potential in the first 5 years for children in developing countries. *Lancet, 369*(9555), 60–70.

Gray, K. C. (2002). Multiple intelligence meet Bloom's taxonomy. *Kappa Delta Pi Record, 38*(4), 184–187.

Haager, D. & Klingner, J. (2005). *Differentiating instruction in inclusive classrooms: The special educator's guide.* Boston, Massachusetts: Pearson Education.

Hodapp, R. M., Ricci, L. A., Ly, T. M. & Fidler, D. J. (2003). The effects of the child with Down syndrome on maternal stress. *British Journal of Developmental Psychology, 21*(1), 137–151.

Hoover, J. & Patton, J. (2004). Differentiating standards-based education for students with diverse needs. *Remedial and Special Education, 25*(3), 74–78.

Johnston, C., Hessl, D., Blasey, C., Eliez, S., Erba, H., Dyer-Friedman, J., Glaser, B. & Reiss, A. L. (2003). Factors associated with parenting stress in mothers of children with fragile X syndrome. *Journal of Developmental and Behavioral Pediatrics, 24*(4), 267–275.

Karnes, M. B. & Lee, R. C. (1983). *Early childhood.* Reston, Virginia: The Council of Exceptional Children.

Kastberg, S. E. (2003). Using Bloom's taxonomy as a framework for assessment. *Mathematics Teacher, 96*(6), 402–405.

Learning and Teaching Scotland. (2006). *Early education support: The Reggio Emilia approach to early years education.* Retrieved from http://www. educationscotland.gov.uk/earlyyears/images/reggioaug06_tcm4-393250.pdf (accessed 3 January 2013).

Lieber, J., Wolery, R. A., Horn, E., Tschantz, J., Beckman, P. J. & Honson, M. J. (2002). Collaborative relationship among adults in inclusive preschool programs. In S. Odom (Ed.), *Widening the circle: Including children with disabilities in preschool programs* (pp. 81–97). New York: Teachers College Press.

MacArthur, J., Purdue, K. & Ballard, K. (2003). Competent and confident children? Te Whariki and the inclusion of children with disabilities in early childhood education. In J. Nuttall (Ed.), *Weaving Te Whariki: Aotearoa New Zealand's early childhood curriculum document in theory and practice* (pp. 131–160). Wellington: New Zealand Council for Educational Research.

Manning-Morton, J. & Thorp, M. (2004). *Key Times for Play.* Buckingham: Open University Press.

MCWL (My Child Without Limits). (2013). *Glossary of terms.* Retrieved from http://www.mychildwithoutlimits.org/resources/glossary-of-terms/ (accessed 16 January 2013).

Mishra, A. & Singh, A. R. (2013). Inclusion of DHH children in early childhood education: Outcomes of selected case studies of preschools. *Journal of National Convention of Educators of the Deaf, 5*(1), 1–17.

MoCYS (Ministry of Children and Youth Services, Ontario). (2007). *Early learning for every child today: A framework for Ontario early childhood settings.* Retrieved from http://www.children.gov.on.ca/htdocs/English/

topics/earlychildhood/early_learning_for_every_child_today.aspx (accessed 31 January 2013).

Moffat, T. K. (2011). *Inclusion in early childhood settings in Aotearoa/New Zealand* (Unpublished Master of Special Education thesis). Massey University, New Zealand.

MoWCD (Ministry of Women & Child Development), Government of India. (2012a). *National early childhood care and education draft policy* (pp. 6–7). New Delhi: MoWCD.

———. (2012b). *Early childhood education curriculum framework (Draft)* (pp. 6–7). New Delhi: MoWCD.

National Council of Education Research & Training (NCERT). (2006). *National focus group on early childhood education.* Position paper No. 3.6. New Delhi: NCERT.

Neilson, W. (2005). Disability: Attitude, history and discourses. In D. Fraser, R. Moltzen & K. Ryba (Eds), *Learner with special needs in Aotearoa New Zealand* (pp. 9–21). Nelsons New Zealand: Cengage Learning.

Rao, S. (2005). Equity pedagogy: Educating exceptional learners with diverse abilities in inclusive setting. In T. Koshmanova (Ed.), *Pedagogy for democratic citizenship* (pp. 73–103). Lviv, Ukraine: University of L'viv Press.

———. (2009). A cross categorical approach to service delivery: Promoting successful inclusion through teacher education. *International Journal of Whole Schooling, 5*(1), 25–40.

Simeonsson, R. J. (2000). *Early childhood development and children with disabilities in developing countries.* Chapel Hill, North Carolina: University of North Carolina.

Singh, A. R. & Mishra, A. (2012). Changing role of special schools in the context of inclusive education: Some evidence based practices. *Journal of NCED, 4*(1), 20–24.

Siraj-Blatchford, I. (1998). *Curriculum development handbook for early education educators.* Stoke-on-Trent, England: Trentham Books.

Swim, T. J. & Watson, L. (2011). *Infants & toddlers: Curriculum and teaching* (7th ed.) (p. 6). Belmont, California: Cengage Learning.

United Nations (UN). (1989). Convention on the rights of the child. New York: UN.

———. (2006). Convention on the rights of persons with disabilities. New York: UN.

———. (2010). Status of the convention on the rights of the child. Report of the Secretary-General in the *65th General Assembly of the United Nations.* New York: UN.

UNESCO. (2012a). *Early childhood care and education: At the occasion of the 2012 EFA Global Action Week.* Retrieved from http://www.unesco.org/ new/fileadmin/MULTIMEDIA/HQ/ED/pdf/ GAW2012-presentation.pdf (accessed 25 December 2012).

———. (2012b). *Review of care, education and child development indicators in early childhood.* Paris: UNESCO.

United Nations International Children's Emergency Fund (UNICEF). (2007a). *Children with disabilities: Ending discrimination and promoting participation, development, and inclusion.* New York: UNICEF.

———. (2007b). *Promoting the rights of children with disabilities (Innocenti Digest No. 13).* Florence: United Nations Children's Fund, Innocenti Research Centre.

US Department of Education. (2002). *No Child Left Behind Act, 2001.* Washington, D.C.: US Department of Education.

Vaughn, S., Bos, C. & Schumm, J. (2006). *Teaching exceptional, diverse, and at risk students in general education classroom.* Boston, Massachusetts: Allyn & Bacon.

World Health Organization (WHO). (2007). *Early childhood development: A powerful equalizer.* Geneva: WHO.

———. (2011). *World report on disability.* Geneva: WHO. Retrieved from http://www.who.int/disabilities/world_report/2011/en/index.html (accessed 25 January 2012).

Yael, D. (2012). Children's perspective research in pre-service early childhood student education. *International Journal of Early Years Education, 20*(3), 280–289.

Young Children with Disabilities in India: Essential Competencies of Early Childhood Educators

Ajay Das, Annamaria Jerome-Raja and Sushama Sharma

Including young children with special needs in early childhood education (ECE) programmes designed for their typically developing peers has
become commonplace in Western developed nations. India, too, responded
to this worldwide reform in the last three decades and implemented a
number of policies, programmes and legislations to appropriately meet
the needs of these children. With the population of 158.7 million children
in the 0–6 years of age however, this task can become enormous for a
government of any size and capacity. India, nonetheless, has been making
continuous efforts in the last three decades to provide appropriate services
to young children with special needs. One of the most recent initiatives in
this endeavour is the draft National Early Childhood Care and Education
(ECCE) Policy. The draft policy was submitted to the Ministry of Women
and Child Development (MoWCD) in June 2012. It affirms the commitment of the Government of India (GOI) to provide integrated services
for holistic development of all children, along the continuum, from the
prenatal period to six years of age. The draft policy underscores that it
is the first time in the country's history that the young child received a
policy focus. Section 5.1.5 of the draft policy clearly outlines that 'Young

children with different abilities would also be reached. Measures would require to be undertaken to ensure early detection and appropriate referrals with linkages for children at risk of developmental delays and disabilities' (MoWCD, 2012a, p. 7).

The roots of the government's commitment, however, can be traced back to the Integrated Child Development Services (ICDS) scheme that it launched in 1975 in selected 33 community developmental blocks of the country. This flagship programme has now been expanded to include 5,659 sanctioned projects and 748,059 *Anganwadi*[1] centres in all 35 states and union territories of India. Such change, however, did not come overnight. It required hard work, perseverance and dedication from all stakeholders, including policy makers, administrators, Anganwadi workers, teachers, parents and researchers. Policy makers in India were challenged by legislative developments in other countries (e.g., the Individuals with Disabilities Education Act, 1990) and the initiatives taken by the United Nations (e.g., UNESCO, 2000) to implement legislation, policies and programmes (e.g., Persons with Disabilities Act, 1995; SSA, 2007) that fostered more equitable educational opportunities for all students. Parental groups became more vocal and asserted their rights by demanding equal opportunities for their children. Administrators, teachers and researchers witnessed the inclusive education models that worked well in other countries and started to adopt those models in their educational settings. Thus, the inclusive education initiative that was being implemented in the rest of the world, particularly in developed nations, also gradually paved its way into Indian schools and ECE centres. Incremental progress has been made towards this endeavour during the last three decades and benefited thousands of students. However, much work still needs to be done to meet the needs of about 30 million children with disabilities in India (Chief Commissioner of Persons with Disabilities, 2007).

The success of inclusion programmes for young children with special needs depends on many different individuals, such as parents, therapists and ECE teachers. In Western countries where these programmes have

---

[1] Anganwadi centres have been established by the Indian government to provide basic health care services to young children living primarily in rural areas. Basic health-care activities include contraceptive counselling and supply of nutrition. Education and supplementation as well as preschool activities are provided to the families of such children.

been successfully implemented, it is the ECE teachers who assume substantial responsibility for the instruction of children with disabilities in
general education classrooms. These teachers are the focus of this chapter.
An examination of their attitude and its importance in the inclusion of such
children will be conducted by way of the review of both Indian and international literature. Then, some recommendations will be made regarding
the skills and competencies that these ECE teachers need to possess to be
successful in working with young children with special needs.

We will, however, begin with providing some background information regarding the policy and programme initiatives of the GOI for the
education of children with disabilities in India.

Government of India Initiatives

During the last three decades, the GOI implemented a number of policies, programmes and legislation that led to the development of inclusive
education for children with disabilities in India. Deep structural changes
in society were occurring simultaneously that affected the programmes
related to the education of students with disabilities. These changes
included the extension of civil liberties to persons from lower castes and
scheduled tribes, and the enhancement of the status of women in society
by means of providing equal educational and employment opportunities.
Some of the initiatives of the GOI that have had profound impact on the
development of educational opportunities for young children with special
disabilities in India include the following.

Integrated Child Development Services Scheme (1975)

Integrated Child Development Services scheme was launched by the
GOI on 2 October 1975. It started on a very small scale in 33 community developmental blocks in the country. It is still under operation and
has been vastly expanded to now become the world's largest outreach

programme serving about 76 million children in India that are between zero and six years of age (MoWCD, 2012b). The objectives of the ICDS scheme have been to:

1. Improve the nutritional and health status of children in the age group of 0–6 years
2. Lay the foundation for proper psychological, physical and social development of the child
3. Reduce the incidences of mortality, morbidity, malnutrition and school dropout
4. Achieve effective coordination of policy and implementation amongst the various departments to promote child development
5. Enhance the capability of the mother to look after the normal health and nutritional needs of the child through proper nutrition and health education

The National Policy on Education (1986)

The National Policy on Education (NPE), 1986, was another major initiative of the GOI towards the promotion of integrated education of students with disabilities. It considered ECCE to be a critical criterion for human development and a feeder and support programme to primary schooling. It emphasised the need for play-based ECCE. The policy outlines specific steps to integrate children with special needs with the general community as equal partners. One of the main aims of the NPE (1986) was the improvement of the teacher training programmes for primary school teachers to work in inclusive education settings. The NPE recognised that the enrolment of special needs students in regular schools could only be meaningful if professional development opportunities were provided to regular school teachers. As a result, a programme for the professional development of teachers was launched in 1987 with support from the central government. During the period 1986–1989, a mass orientation programme for 1.76 million teachers was conducted across the country.

The Programme of Action (1992)

In order to provide further impetus to inclusive education programmes in India, the NPE (1986) was reviewed. The Programme of Action (1992) was developed for the implementation of inclusive education programmes. It envisaged the establishment of District Institutes of Education and Training (DIET) to provide pre-service and in-service education for teachers to enhance their skills to meet the needs of students with disabilities in regular schools. Other proposed initiatives of the Programme of Action included:

1. The training of all regular school teachers, principals and educational administrators in the project area where the Integrated Education for the Disabled Children (IEDC) scheme was being implemented.
2. A proposal for the initiation of credit courses in special education by the Indira Gandhi National Open University (IGNOU) and the National Council of Educational Research and Training (NCERT).

The Persons with Disabilities Act (1995)

In 1995, the GOI passed the Persons with Disabilities (Equal Opportunities, Protection of Rights and Full Participation) Act. The legislation was a major historical milestone in the education of students with disabilities in India. The law underscored the education of students with disabilities in regular schools. It guaranteed non-discrimination and the removal of barriers, both physical and psychological, to facilitate the inclusion of students with disabilities into regular schools.

Sarva Shiksha Abhiyan [Education for All Movement] (2002)

Sarva Shiksha Abhiyan (SSA) is GOI's flagship programme for achievement of universalisation of elementary education (UEE) in a time-bound manner, providing free and compulsory education to the children of the 6–14 years age group. SSA has a special focus on girls' education and children with special needs.

The interventions under SSA for inclusive education are identification, functional and formal assessment, appropriate educational placement, preparation of Individual Educational Plan (IEP), provision of aids and appliances, teacher training, resource support, removal of architectural barriers, research, monitoring and evaluation and a special focus on girls with special needs. SSA ensures that every child with special needs, irrespective of the kind, category and degree of disability, is provided meaningful and quality education. Therefore, SSA has adopted a zero rejection policy. Although the focus of SSA is not directly on ECE, it sets the tone of the government regarding the provisions it has for all children including those with disabilities. As a result, 254,179 schools in the country have established a pre-primary wing for ECCE.

Right of Children to Free and Compulsory Education Act (2010)

This law that came into effect on 1 April 2010 addressed ECCE under Section 11 of the Act which states:

> [W]ith a view to prepare children above the age of three years for elementary education and to provide early childhood care and education for all children until they complete the age of six years the appropriate government may make necessary arrangement for providing free pre-school for such children.

Draft National Early Childhood Care and Education Policy (2012)

As stated in the first paragraph of the chapter, ECCE is the first comprehensive draft policy of its kind for the education and care of young children in India. The draft ECCE policy reaffirms the commitment of the Government of India to provide integrated services for holistic development of all children, along the continuum, from the prenatal period to six years of age. The Policy lays down the way forward for a comprehensive approach towards ensuring a sound foundation, with focus on early learning, for every Indian child. (MoWCD, 2012a, p. 2)

Teacher Perceptions of Inclusion

Teachers are perhaps the most important agents affecting the success of inclusive education programmes. Positive teacher attitudes towards the inclusion of students with disabilities are crucial to successful implementation of these programmes. Examinations of teacher perceptions of inclusion in early childhood settings suggest that many early childhood educators have positive perceptions about the inclusion of young children with special needs (Leatherman, 2007; Mulvihill, Shearer & Van Horn, 2002). Most general education preschool, primary and secondary school teachers believe that inclusion benefits children with and without disabilities. Teachers are likely to support the idea of inclusion, particularly when few instructional adaptations are required, even when they have little self-reported expertise teaching children with disabilities (Scruggs & Mastropieri, 1996). The type of disability also appears to play an important role in teachers' willingness to include a child with a disability in their classroom. Literature has shown that teachers appear more willing to include children with mild disabilities or children who do not inhibit learning in their peers (e.g., those with poor communication skills or the Down syndrome) than children with significant disabilities or children who need teachers' significant involvement.

While perceptions of ECE teachers have been largely positive for the inclusion of young children with special needs, teachers have expressed a number of concerns as well. These concerns mostly relate to their lack of specialised preparation and availability of in-service training (Bricker, 2000). Early childhood teachers need to have training in teaching individualised goals within activities, individualised instruction and progress monitoring. These teachers report an increased level of confidence when additional training is acquired, thus leading to positive outcomes for children in their classrooms. Teachers who had additional training reported fewer needs and perceived barriers to inclusion (Mulvihill et al., 2002; Villines, 2011). It can therefore be inferred that the more education the teacher has, the more successful the programme will be at including a child with a disability.

Regular School Teachers' Competencies for Inclusive Education

Current reform efforts towards school restructuring aimed at implementing effective inclusion programmes present significant challenges for regular school teachers. The success of these efforts depends primarily on the responsiveness and willingness of these teachers to meet the educational and social needs of students with varying abilities. These teachers are now required to have a number of additional skills and competencies, not generally practised in regular education classrooms. The Open File on Inclusive Education (UNESCO, 2001) suggests a number of demands be placed on teachers from the perspective of inclusive curricula, such as regular teachers' involvement in curriculum development at the local level, their skill development for curriculum adaptation, management of a complex range of classroom activities, providing support to students' learning and working outside the traditional subject boundaries and in culturally sensitive ways. A number of authors (Kochhar & West, 1996; Mastropieri & Scruggs, 2010) argue that these teachers are now expected to perform almost all roles as that of a special education teacher. The difference, however, is that they have not received intensive training in those skills that special educators have. This chapter will highlight those additional competencies that regular school teachers need to have in their repertoire to be successful in inclusive classrooms.

According to Mastropieri and Scruggs (2010), regular school teachers need to be knowledgeable about the learning styles and the motivational patterns of students with disabilities. These teachers also must have a clear understanding of the resources and support systems which are available to assist them in working with students with disabilities. They should present information in a manner which enables students to assimilate information more easily. Vaughn and Bos (2012) suggested a number of strategies that regular school teachers would need to accommodate students with disabilities in the regular classroom environment. These include peer tutoring, cooperative learning, mastery learning and applied behaviour analysis. The literature also points out that regular classroom teachers are required to use instructional strategies, such as differentiated instruction (Tomlinson, 2003), activity-based learning (Krisnaswamy & Shankar, 2003), individualised and adaptive instruction (Jangira, Singh & Yadav, 1995) and culture-specific pedagogy and culturally responsive teaching (Valmiki, 2003), to facilitate disabled students' learning outcomes in a regular classroom environment.

The Council for Exceptional Children (CEC, 2010) developed and validated a common core of minimum essential knowledge and skills necessary for entry into professional practice in special education. They included: (a) philosophical, historical and legal foundations of special education; (b) characteristics of learners; (c) assessment, diagnosis and evaluation; (d) instructional content and practice; (e) planning and managing the learning environment; (f) managing student behaviour and social interaction skills; (g) communication and collaborative partnerships and (h) professionalism and ethical practices. Although all of these skills may not be essential for regular classroom teachers, a certain level of proficiency in these competencies, however, is required from these teachers when they are expected to work with special needs children. Of the many competencies that have been identified in this chapter, there are some that are field-tested and advocated as potential methods for delivering effective instruction to students with diverse learning needs. There are many, but some of them, that are widely used, include: class-wide peer tutoring (Stephenson & Warwick, 2002), cooperative learning (Jenkins, Antil, Wayne, & Vadasy, 2003), self-management skills (Snyder & Bambara, 1997), differentiated instruction (Tomlinson, 2003) and use of assistive technology. The school teachers especially need to be proficient in those skills for effective instruction delivery and appropriate management of a classroom that is characterised by diversity.

These essential competencies have been classified under the following seven categories. They will be briefly discussed regarding their relevance to inclusive education followed by a brief review of literature on those competencies. The seven core competencies include:

1. Professional knowledge
2. Classroom management
3. Collaboration
4. Assessment and evaluation
5. Instructional techniques
6. Individualised and adaptive instruction
7. Assistive technology

Professional Knowledge

Professional knowledge in the context of inclusive ECE includes a knowledge and understanding of (a) basic terminology and concepts used in special education; (b) various disabling conditions; (c) a rationale and history of inclusive education; (d) policies, programmes and legislation related to inclusive education particularly at the early childhood level; (e) rights, roles and responsibilities of parents, students, teachers and other professionals and (f) the knowledge of processes and procedures related to Individualised Family Services Plan (IFSP).

Mogharreban and Bruns (2009) reported that one of the factors for successful preschool inclusion programmes is the teacher's knowledge of disabilities and developmentally appropriate skills. Sharma (2002) reported in a survey that Indian teachers required information on the types of disabilities, curriculum adaptation, educational implications, and skills and strategies required for meeting the needs of students with disabilities. Das (2001) reported, after conducting a survey of 223 regular school teachers in Delhi, that 'professional knowledge of special education' was a number two ranked competency among ten others in which the teachers indicated a higher level of need for training to successfully include a child with a disability in mainstream classrooms.

Classroom Management

Classroom management for inclusive education includes the knowledge of (a) basic classroom management theories, methods and techniques for individuals with exceptional learning needs; (b) research-based best practices for effective management of teaching and learning; (c) materials arrangement; (d) organisation of aids and support services and (e) creating a positive atmosphere in the classroom.

The diversity in the classrooms presents a variety of management challenges for regular school teachers. Managing challenging behaviours is of great concern for teachers in the early childhood inclusive settings (Carter, Norman & Tredwell, 2011). For example, students with special needs, particularly those diagnosed with emotional and behaviour disorder (EBD) and autism spectrum disorder (ASD), may present unique behavioural challenges for these teachers. According to Wang, Hartel and Walberg (1993), effective classroom management has been found to contribute more to school learning than curriculum design, classroom instruction, student demographics, home support and school policy. Program-Wide Positive Behavior Support (PWPBS) is a model that is effective in early childhood inclusive settings (Carter et al., 2011) for promoting positive behaviours and decreasing challenging behaviours. Carter and Norman (2010) found that positive behaviour supports (PBS) consultation increased the academic engagement of preschoolers and, also, yielded a higher rate of teacher implementation of PBS in preschool settings.

Collaboration

Collaboration is an interactive process that enables people with diverse expertise to generate creative solutions to mutually defined problems. An ever-increasing diversity in early childhood classrooms has made it necessary for regular classroom teachers to work with special education teachers, parents, teacher assistants and related service providers such as speech and language therapists, physiotherapists and occupational therapists. Their shared expertise and shared ownership of problems make the likelihood of success for the programme greater than if these educators attempted to deal with the problems in isolation.

Regular school teachers could use the following collaborative strategies to provide effective instruction to students with disabilities: peer collaboration, co-teaching and teacher assistance teams. Peer collaboration involves pairs of teachers working together to solve classroom problems. Friend and Cook (2010) defined co-teaching as 'two or more professionals delivering substantive instruction to a diverse or blended group of students in a single space' (p. 109). This is an effective way to utilise each teacher's strengths. Abundant research is available showing the benefits of co-teaching to improve academic achievement of not only students with disabilities but also all students (Friend & Cook, 2010). Teacher assistance teams are also known as support teams, intervention assistance teams or planning teams. In this strategy, a group of teachers meet and brainstorm options for a teacher experiencing problems in the classroom.

The importance of collaboration between teachers and other service providers was emphasised as one of the five major components of a successful early childhood special education (ECSE) programme for children with autism (Schwartz, Sandall, McBride & Boulware, 2004). Wesley (2002) states that sharing the same perspective about the children with disabilities is one of the important aspects of collaboration between the consultant and the teacher in an early childhood inclusive setting.

Assessment and Evaluation

According to a number of writers (McLoughlin & Lewis, 2001), regular school teachers are required to demonstrate competency in assessment to identify the specific needs of students with disabilities. The teachers are required to employ not only basic skills, such as gathering learning and background information of students with disabilities, but also highly specialised skills, such as selecting, administering, scoring and interpreting standardised measurement instruments (ibid.). Friend and Bursuck (1999) suggested that regular school teachers could use assessment information for six instructional and placement decisions for students with disabilities. These include: screening, diagnosis, programme placement, instructional evaluation and programme evaluation.

An evaluation report shows whether or not teaching has been effective. It helps validate successful inclusive education programmes that should be continued and pinpoints problems that should be rectified. Wang, Anderson and Bram (1985) suggested that regular school teachers should be able to evaluate three aspects of student performance while evaluating their success in inclusion programmes: performance, attitudes and process. Performance measures relate to students' achievement in content areas.

Attitudinal measures relate to students' self-concept and their attitudes towards their teachers and non-disabled peers. Process measures encompass the types of interactions students have with their teachers and peers.

Regular school teachers need to be knowledgeable about a variety of evaluation methods to determine the learning outcomes of students with disabilities. They need to demonstrate competency in performance-based assessments, portfolios and curriculum-based assessments (CBA). Performance-based assessments allow teachers to assess students' understanding and proficiency. These assessments allow students to construct a response, create a product or demonstrate what they understand and can do. Friend and Bursuck (1999) argue that these assessments are more likely to reveal student understanding since they call for students to apply knowledge and skills rather than to simply recall and recognise. Alternate assessments, such as portfolio assessments, are also effective ways of evaluating students with disabilities. Portfolios make it possible to capture the learning process over time as well as to assess non-traditional strengths and talents, such as artistic or visual abilities of students. CBA also provides teachers with information on the demands of instructional tasks and allows them to determine the content and pace of an instructional programme. CBA is also more efficient in diagnosis, setting functional goals and programme evaluation for preschoolers in inclusive settings (Macy & Hoyt-Gonzales, 2007). Routine-based assessment and play-based assessment provide better insights and supplement standardised assessment in early childhood inclusive settings (Chamberlin, Buchanan & Vercimak, 2007). Das (2001) reported that regular primary school teachers in Delhi expressed their highest level of training need in 'assessment' among 10 other competencies to successfully include children with disabilities in their classrooms.

Instructional Techniques

Early childhood educators need to be particularly proficient in instructional skills when they have diverse learners in their classrooms. These skills are the ones that they ought to use on a daily basis to provide appropriate instruction to young children with special needs. A number of specific instructional techniques that regular classroom teachers would particularly need to be competent in include: embedded instruction, differentiated instruction and activity-based and experiential learning. Each one of them has been field-tested and validated to demonstrate effectiveness. Other techniques that have also been field-tested with students with special needs include response cards, guided notes, error correction and time trials.

Embedded Instruction

Typically, instruction and intervention for young children with disabilities take place in contrived environments on a one-on-one basis with the teacher. This approach is effective for skill acquisition but lacks the components of generalisation across settings and maintenance over time. With generalisation and maintenance being important components of successful mastery of skills, embedded instruction emerged as a viable option. Sandall, Hemmeter, Smith and McLean (2005) define embedded instruction as identifying times and activities when instructional procedures designed for teaching a child's IEP objectives are implemented in the context of ongoing, naturally occurring activities, routines and transitions in the classroom. An extensive review of literature evaluating the effects of embedded instruction in early childhood inclusive settings revealed that embedded instruction not only aided in better generalisation and maintenance of skills learnt, but it also was found useful in teaching various skills at different developmental levels (Rakap & Parlak-Rakap, 2011). Embedded instruction can be incorporated in all possible settings and times, such as during mealtime, outdoor play time and circle time (Kaderavek, 2009). In a study conducted by Macy and Bricker (2007), embedded instruction was found to be useful in teaching social skills to preschoolers with disabilities by embedding social skills training in daily routines (circle time). Results of this study revealed that the social competency of the targeted children with disabilities improved.

Differentiated Instruction

In the past, regular classroom teachers used ability grouping to deal with variations in student skill levels. Gamoran (1992) reviewed the research on ability grouping and concluded that such an educational practice perpetuated low achievement and widened the gap between high- and low-achieving students. To overcome these difficulties and to successfully accommodate students with disabilities, regular school teachers need to use differentiated instruction. This technique requires the teachers to teach one main lesson for all students with variations for each individual student's needs. It is an instructional approach that allows the regular classroom teacher to plan for all students within one lesson, thereby decreasing the need for separate programmes while permitting the teacher to weave individual goals into classroom content and instructional strategies (Tomlinson, 2003). Thus, a diverse group of learners share an instructional activity in which individually appropriate learning outcomes occur within the same curriculum area. Differentiated instruction allows students to learn from one another in an atmosphere of human diversity. In such classrooms, individual differences are the norm rather than the exception. Differentiated instruction in the context of ECSE includes not only a wide variety of learning opportunities but should also include a variety of assessment options (Kaderavek, 2009). This technique has been well received by regular school teachers who maintain that it is easier than preparing numerous lessons and that classroom instruction has coherence despite individualisation. In a research study, Jangira et al. (1995) found that regular school teachers in India indicated a very high level of training need in 'multi-grade teaching'.

Activity-based and Experiential Learning

According to Bricker and Cripe (1992), activity-based instruction (ABI) is used as an effective approach in early childhood inclusive setting to effectively meet the needs of children with special needs. Activity-based and experiential learning is the highlight of ECE, and it expands its effectiveness even more specifically to inclusive preschool classrooms. In those classrooms that present instruction passively or in isolation and use a lecture format as the dominant form of instruction, many students do not learn, retain and apply knowledge as effectively. Such instructional delivery methods are therefore especially difficult for students with disabilities who are included in regular education classrooms. These students require the teachers to present instruction that is activity-based and allows students to learn through personal experiences. Particularly in early childhood inclusive settings, students, with the use of activity-based and experiential learning, become engaged in discovery, movement, interaction with the environment and manipulation of materials. Also, since such learning uses real-life activities and materials, skill generalisation and transfer are facilitated. Hands-on interactive instructional approaches to a lesson appeal to the senses and make it easier for students with disabilities to learn. Such active learning promotes student attention, increases on-task behaviour and decreases the incidence of negative behaviour. Freiburg and Driscoll (1992) found that students who were actively involved and engaged in lessons learnt better and faster than students who were 'instructionally inactive'. Sadler (2009) describes how preschoolers with and without disabilities learn to count using activity-based teaching strategies.

Individualised and Adaptive Instruction

Individualised and adaptive instruction is an educational approach that recognises, anticipates and programmes for variation according to the student's background knowledge, learning styles, motivation and personal interest. Individualisation or creating an educational programme that is tailored to the unique needs of a child with disability is the hallmark of special education. This is what makes special education different from regular education. However, a well-established system of instruction is needed from ECE teachers if they are to serve all students in their class-rooms, including those with exceptionality. Individualising and adapting instruction is a natural aspect of ECE and lends itself to meet the needs of children with special needs at the preschool level (Hollingsworth, Boone & Crais, 2009).

A conceptual framework for instructional adaptations for students with disabilities was provided by Glaser (1977). He envisaged instructional adaptations as a process of choosing and applying an appropriate teaching action following an assessment-based determination that a previous lesson for a student was unsuccessful. These adaptations, therefore, require teachers to implement alternative teaching actions, such as modifying materials, assignments, testing procedures, grading criteria and varying presentation styles to enhance the success of students with disabilities in regular education classrooms. Regular classroom teachers can also accommodate variations in learning styles by developing each student's educational programme using a range of environmental, physical, social and psychological conditions. For example, necessary adjustment of materials (e.g., highlighting essential content, varying sequence, reducing the length of assignments, alternating assignment presentation formats such as visual, auditory, etc.) and useful learning aids (e.g., visual checklists of steps, story starters, etc.) are part of individualised instruction.

Assistive Technology

Recent advances in technology for special needs students have made it possible for these students to accomplish a number of tasks, while being in a regular education environment, which was not possible earlier. These include the use of iPads, Kurzweil 3000, Read and Write Gold and other communication devices. Therefore, it is imperative that regular classroom teachers have at least some level of knowledge and understanding in the use of such devices and software applications. The use of assistive technology with young children is highly recommended and emphasised by the guidelines provided by the Division of Early Childhood (DEC), a sub-division of the CEC. Research shows that children in their early years are capable of using assistive technology, and that practitioners need additional training in the implementation of assistive technology which can ease some of the barriers of early childhood inclusion (Keramidas & Collins, 2009). However, there is a limited use of assistive technology in early childhood settings due to many different factors (Campbell, Milbourne, Dugan & Wilcox, 2006). Moore and Wilcox (2006) found that more experienced early intervention practitioners were more comfortable with using assistive technology in comparison to practitioners with less experience.

In addition to the 'traditional' knowledge and skill domains discussed thus far in this chapter, regular school teachers are now also expected to demonstrate ability in a number of emerging competencies. The 'new' competencies derive from the social dynamics that are impacting the preschool curriculum. The emerging competencies include maintaining ethical and professional standards (CEC, 2010) and sensitivity towards the cultural background of students with disabilities who are from minority ethnic backgrounds (Mitchell, 2000).

Conclusion

The exemplary and promising practices discussed in this chapter offer a framework within which the aims of inclusive education in India may be realised. These practices also constitute the essential competencies that are needed by regular school teachers for the successful implementation of inclusive education. It is the acceptance, development and implementation of these knowledge, skills and competencies that provides the greatest potential for the success of inclusive education programmes in India. These practices also have the potential to create a unified system of education that would be responsive to the unique learning and psychosocial needs of children with disabilities in India (Das, Gichuru & Singh, 2013). Beginning the inclusion process at the early childhood level will help ease the challenges of inclusion in later years of school. Early inclusion of children with disabilities has the potential to reduce costs at later stages. Research is well documented about the effectiveness of early intervention for children with disabilities in inclusive settings versus early intervention in secluded settings. One of the key factors for the success of inclusion, particularly in the early childhood setting, is the teacher competencies and readiness of regular teachers. All stakeholders, particularly those that are charged with training and with preparing ECE teachers, need to infuse these competencies in their pre-service and in-service training programmes. ECE teachers who are already a part of the workforce should be provided with adequate opportunities for professional development. In this regard, 'one-shot' seminars or workshops would not appear to be the answer. Rather, ongoing professional development opportunities should be made available to these teachers. David and Kuyini (2012) assert that teachers in India have benefited from in-service programmes which form 'part of a long term systemic staff development plan' rather than from 'single-shot' short-term programmes. Also, further research is warranted to determine self-efficacy, current skill levels and training needs of Indian teachers in these skills as this information will help trainers to prioritise areas for training and plan both short- and long-term goals.

References

Bricker, D. (2000). Inclusion: How the scene has changed. *Topics in Early Childhood Special Education, 20*(1), 14–19.

Bricker, D. & Cripe, J. J. (1992). *An activity-based approach to early intervention.* Baltimore, Maryland: Paul Brookes.

Campbell, P. H., Milbourne, S., Dugan, L. M. & Wilcox, M. J. (2006). A review of evidence on practices for teaching young children to use assistive technology devices. *Topics in Early Childhood Special Education, 26*(1), 3–13.

Carter, D. & Norman, R. (2010). Class-wide positive behavior support in preschool: Improving teacher implementation through consultation. *Early Childhood Education Journal, 38*(4), 279–288. doi:10.1007/s10643-010-0409-x

Carter, D., Norman, R. & Tredwell, C. (2011). Program-wide positive behavior support in preschool: Lessons for getting started. *Early Childhood Education Journal, 38*(5), 349–355. doi:10.1007/s10643-010-0406-0

Chamberlin, S. A., Buchanan, M. & Vercimak, D. (2007). Serving twice-exceptional preschoolers: Blending gifted education and early childhood special education practices in assessment and program planning. *Journal for the Education of the Gifted, 30*(3), 372–394.

Chief Commissioner of Persons with Disabilities. (2007). *Disability in India.* New Delhi: Ministry of Social Justice and Empowerment.

Council for Exceptional Children (CEC). (2010). *Core competencies for special educators.* Reston, Virginia: CEC.

Das, A. K. (2001). *Perceived training needs of regular primary and secondary school teachers to implement inclusive education programs in Delhi, India* (Unpublished doctoral dissertation). University of Melbourne, Australia.

Das, A. K., Gichuru, M. & Singh, A. (2013). Implementing inclusive education in Delhi, India: Regular school teachers' preferences for professional development delivery modes. *Professional Development in Education, 39*(5), 698–711. doi:10.1080/19415257.2012.747979

David, R. & Kuyini, A. B. (2012). Social inclusion: Teachers as facilitators in peer acceptance of students with disabilities in regular classrooms in Tamil Nadu, India. *International Journal of Special Education, 27*(2), 1–12.

Freiburg, H. & Driscoll, A. (1992). *Universal teaching strategies.* Boston, Massachusetts: Allyn & Bacon.

Friend, M. & Bursuck, W. D. (1999). *Including students with special needs: A practical guide for classroom teachers* (2nd ed.). Boston, Massachusetts: Allyn & Bacon.

Friend, M. & Cook, L. (2010). *Interactions: Collaboration skills for school professionals* (6th ed.). Upper Saddle River, New Jersey: Pearson.

Gamoran, A. (1992). Is ability grouping equitable? *Educational Leadership, 50,* 11–17.

Glaser, R. (1977). *Adaptive education: Individual diversity and learning.* New York: Holt, Rinehart & Winston.

Government of India. (1995). *Persons with Disabilities (Equal Opportunities, Protection of Rights, and Full Participation) Act, 1995.* New Delhi: Government of India.

Hollingsworth, H. L., Boone, H. & Crais, E. R. (2009). Individualized inclusion plans at work in early childhood classrooms. *Young Exceptional Children, 13*(1), 19–35. doi:10.1177/1096250609347259

Jangira, N. K., Singh, A. & Yadav, S. K. (1995). Teacher policy, training needs and perceived status of teachers. *Indian Educational Review, 30*(1), 113–122.

Jenkins, J. R., Antil, L. R., Wayne, S. K. & Vadasy, P. F. (2003). How cooperative learning works for special education and remedial studies. *Exceptional Children, 69*(3), 279–292.

Kaderavek, J. N. (2009). Perspectives from the field of early childhood special education. *Language, Speech & Hearing Services in Schools, 40*(4), 403–405. doi:10.1044/0161-1461(2008/08-0019)

Keramidas, C. & Collins, B. C. (2009). Assistive technology use with the birth to three population: A rural perspective. *Rural Special Education Quarterly, 28*(1), 38–48.

Kochhar, C. A. & West, L. L. (1996). *Handbook for successful inclusion.* Gaithersburg, Maryland: Aspen.

Krisnaswamy, K. & Shankar, J. (2003). Integration and Inclusion—How are they different? Paper presented at the National Seminar on Inclusive Education Practices in Schools, NCERT, Delhi.

Leatherman, J. (2007). 'I just see all children as children': Teachers' perceptions about inclusion. *The Quarterly Report, 12*(4), 594–611.

Macy, M. & Hoyt-Gonzales, K. (2007). A linked system approach to early childhood special education eligibility assessment. *Teaching Exceptional Children, 39*(3), 40–44.

Macy, M. G. & Bricker, D. D. (2007). Embedding individualized social goals into routine activities in inclusive early childhood classrooms. *Early Child Development & Care, 177*(2), 107–120. doi:10.1080/03004430500337265

Mastropieri, M. A. & Scruggs, T. E. (2010). *The inclusive classroom: Strategies for effective instruction* (4th ed.). Upper Saddle River, New Jersey: Prentice-Hall.

McLoughlin, J. A. & Lewis, R. B. (2001). *Assessing students with special needs* (5th ed.). Upper Saddle River, New Jersey: Merrill/Prentice-Hall.

Ministry of Women and Child Development (MoWCD). (2012a). *Draft national early childhood care and education (ECCE) policy*. New Delhi: Government of India.

————. (2012b). *Integrated Child Development Services (ICDS) scheme*. Retrieved from http://wcd.nic.in/ (accessed 16 December 2012).

Mitchell, D. (2000, December). Criteria of effective teaching in inclusive classrooms. Paper presented at the Annual Conference of New Zealand Association for Research in Education, Hamilton, New Zealand.

Mogharreban, C. & Bruns, D. (2009). Moving to inclusive pre-kindergarten classrooms: Lessons from the field. *Early Childhood Education Journal*, *36*(5), 407–414. doi:10.1007/s10643-008-0301-0

Moore, H. W. & Wilcox, M. J. (2006). Characteristics of early intervention practitioners and their confidence in the use of assistive technology. *Topics in Early Childhood Special Education*, *26*(1), 15–23.

Mulvihill, B., Shearer, M. & Van Horn, M. (2002). Training, experience and childcare providers' perceptions of inclusion. *Early Childhood Research Quarterly*, *17*, 197–215.

Rakap, S. & Parlak-Rakap, A. (2011). Effectiveness of embedded instruction in early childhood special education: A literature review. *European Early Childhood Education Research Journal*, *19*(1), 79–96. doi:10.1080/13502 93X.2011.548946

Sadler, F. H. (2009). Help! They still don't understand counting. *Teaching Exceptional Children Plus*, *6*(1), 1–12.

Sandall, S., Hemmeter, M. L., Smith, B. J. & McLean, M. E. (2005). *DEC recommended practices: A comprehensive guide*. Longmont, Colarado: Sopris West.

Schwartz, I. S., Sandall, S. R., McBride, B. J. & Boulware, G. (2004). Project DATA (developmentally appropriate treatment for Autism): An inclusive school-based approach to educating young children with autism. *Topics in Early Childhood Special Education*, *24*(3), 156–168.

Scruggs, T. E. & Mastropieri, M. A. (1996). Teacher perception of mainstreaming/inclusion. *Exceptional Children*, *63*(1), 59–74.

Sharma, K. (2002). Attitudinal changes—Breaking the psycho-social barriers. *Journal of Indian Education*, *27*(4), 85–89.

Snyder, M. & Bambara, L. (1997). Teaching secondary students with learning disabilities to self-manage classroom survival skills. *Journal of Learning Disabilities*, *30*, 534–543.

Stephenson, P. & Warwick, P. (2002). Peer tutoring in the primary science classroom. *Investigating: Australian Primary & Junior Science Journal*, *17*, 11–14.

Tomlinson, C. (2003). *Fulfilling the promise of the differentiated classroom: Strategies and tools for responsive teaching*. Alexandria, Virginia: Association for Supervision and Curriculum.

United Nations Educational Scientific and Cultural Organisation (UNESCO). (2000). *The United Nations Millennium Development Goals*. Paris: UNESCO.

————. (2001). *Open file on inclusive education: Support materials for managers and administrators*. Paris: UNESCO.

Valmiki, A. (2003). Towards culturally inclusive education: Preparing culturally responsible teachers to engage in culturally specific pedagogy. Paper presented at the National Seminar on Inclusive Education Practices in School, NCERT, Delhi.

Vaughn, S. & Bos, C. (2012). *Strategies for teaching students with learning and behavior problems* (8th ed.). Upper Saddle River, New Jersey: Pearson.

Villines, M. (2011). *Early childhood inclusion: Teacher perception of supports needed to fully include children with special needs* (Unpublished doctoral dissertation). Portland State University, Oregon.

Wang, M. C., Anderson, K. A. & Bram, P. J. (1985). *Toward an empirical database on mainstreaming: A research synthesis of program implementation and effects*. Pittsburgh, Pennsylvania: Learning Research and Development Center, University of Pittsburgh.

Wang, M. C., Hartel, G. D. & Walberg, H. J. (1993). Toward a knowledge base for school learning. *Review of Educational Research, 63*, 249–294.

Wesley, P. W. (2002). Early intervention consultants in the classroom: Simple steps for building strong collaboration. *Young Children, 57*(4), 30–34.

Conclusion

Sophia Dimitriadi

Not everything that is faced can be changed,
but nothing can be changed until it is faced

James Baldwin
Writer

Diversity is the reflection of the multi-identity that is found in all people across all continents. In education, diversity refers to the creation of a learning environment that enables inclusion of as many identities of children as possible within its programme, in a sensitive and equitable manner. It is highly important to value diversity and foster inclusion in the early years education; during this period, young children form their ideas about self and others which will eventually establish their attitudes as future citizens.

In this book, diversity and inclusion in early years education have both been regarded in a broad range of theory and practice. Much has been written over the last decades on equality, diversity and inclusion in education, and numerous research papers and textbooks can be found there to confirm this. However, the pursuit for a more inclusive educational system continues even today, although one would say that our present seems to provide the right timing for a fully inclusive educational environment.

The present edited volume has provided some new perspectives for a better understanding of diversity and inclusion issues, with clear emphasis on the early years of education. We believe that the heterogeneous collection of chapters that composes the book has offered the reader the advantage of acquiring knowledge which derives from the research works and practices of people with multiple academic and working backgrounds. Even more importantly, the fact that all chapters indicatively reflect philosophies, theories, issues and practices from different corners of the earth has been evaluated as the originality of this endeavour.

We know that it is not feasible to change all things; on the other hand, for those that can be changed, we know that this cannot just happen overnight. The joint effort of the people involved in this edited volume has resulted in a sincere and thoughtful attempt to face the things that need to be changed or improved for inclusionary education in the early years. As such, we feel and hope that it can contribute a little something to the social building for better future citizenship.

About the Editor and Contributors

Editor

Sophia Dimitriadi has been a Lecturer in Early Years Education at the Department of Early Childhood Education, Technological Educational Institute of Athens, Greece, since 1999, after completing her postgraduate studies in Education at the University of Hull, UK. She has also worked as an early years teacher. Sophia has conducted research projects that have been published in indexed international journals, and has presented her research findings in conferences. She has also edited the book *Μαθαίνω τον κόσμο παίζοντας: Από τη γέννηση έως τριών ετών* [*Learning through play: From birth to age 3*]. Sophia is the proud mother of two children.

Contributors

Gülçin Alpöge, born in Istanbul, is working as a Professor in the Faculty of Education at Boğaziçi University. She graduated from the American College in Turkey. She has an MA in Education from New York University and a PhD in Psycholinguistics. She worked with preschool children in two different countries as a teacher and as a director and in the foundation of two nursery schools. Alpöge writes academic books and designs curriculum programmes. She also writes for children and has published 30 books, and she has a CD where she reads her own stories for children.

Mousumi Bhaumik has been working at NIMH Model Special Education Centre, New Delhi, for the last 15 years. She has a Bachelor's degree in Mental Retardation from National Institute for the Mentally Handicapped

(NIMH), and Master's degrees in Education and Special Education (Visual Impairment and Mental Retardation) from Kurukshetra University and Ramakrishna Mission Vivekananda University respectively. She has a postgraduate Professional Certificate in Special Education (Hearing Impairment) from Indira Gandhi National Open University (IGNOU), New Delhi, and a PhD from Mahatma Jyotiba Phule Rohilkhand University to her credit. She has published research papers and chapters in several journals and books. For her contribution, she has received the Best Teacher Award from Lions Club, New Delhi.

Ajay Das teaches undergraduate and graduate courses in special education at Murray State University in Kentucky. He has extensive international experience working with students with disabilities, parents and classroom teachers in Australia, Japan, India and the United States. His research interests include inclusion, teacher education and special education in developing countries.

Dorothy R. Howie is a New Zealander currently based in the School of Psychology, at the University of Auckland, New Zealand. She has had a career of teaching and research in Inclusion and the teaching of thinking, both in New Zealand and in the United Kingdom. In 2011, she published the UK commissioned book *Teaching students thinking skills and strategies: A framework for cognitive education in inclusive settings*. She has worked for a number of years with Feuerstein's *Theory of mediated learning experience*, and her chapter discusses the use of this theory in international early childhood interventions, particularly by Professor Pnina Klein and colleagues.

Annamaria Jerome-Raja (EdD) is an Assistant Professor of Exceptional Student Education at Florida Memorial University, Miami. Her experiences include working with children with mental retardation, autism and cerebral palsy, ranging from early intervention to post-secondary programmes at both the clinical and classroom levels. Jerome-Raja's research interests include early childhood special education, computer-assisted instruction, evidence-based instructional strategies, inclusion and personnel preparation in special education.

Mary Wangechi Kamunyu is a Lecturer at the School of Arts and Social Sciences, Maasai Mara University, Kenya. Currently, she is pursuing her PhD in Linguistics from Egerton University. She holds an MPhil in Linguistics (2001) and BEd (Arts) in English and Literature (1996), both from Moi University, Eldoret, Kenya. She has 16 years of teaching experience. She specialises in Early Childhood Development (ECD), language education and linguistics. She is a member of All Third World Studies (ATWS), Kenya Institute of Management (KIM) and Global Education Research Association (GERA). She has published more than 10 research papers in different international journals and has participated in more than 20 international conferences.

Hayal Köksal is a teacher trainer, researcher and author. Köksal has been promoting total quality in education (TQE) since the 1990s. She has been the Director General of Turkey within the 'World Council for Total Quality and Excellence in Education (WCTQEE) of India' since 2003. She has written 14 books. She localised and coordinated the 'Innovative Teachers' programme of Microsoft Turkey. Köksal is conducting some elective and compulsory pedagogic formation courses at the Educational faculty of Boğaziçi University, such as 'Introduction to the Teaching Profession', 'Innovative Teaching', 'Nonviolence in Education' and 'Conflict Resolution'.

Eucharia McCarthy is a Senior Lecturer in Special Education and Director of the Curriculum Development Unit, Mary Immaculate College, Limerick, Ireland. Her publications include *PASSPORT—Parents and students specialised programme of reading together* (2001), *What difference?—Working effectively with children who have special educational needs in early years settings* (2007, with Una Quigley and Mary Moloney) and she is the co-author of *STRANDS—Strategies for teachers to respond actively to the needs of pupils with Down Syndrome* (Doherty, U., Daly, P., Egan, M., Coady, M., Holland, M., Long, S., Kelleher, D., McCarthy, E. and O'Sullivan, S. [2011]).

Amitav Mishra, BMR (Bachelor Degree in Mental Retardation) (Gold Medal), MA (Psychology), MSEd, PhD, is involved in the training of teachers in Special Education as a professor at School of Education,

IGNOU, New Delhi. He has experience of 23 years in pre-service and in-service teacher training and of experimenting with instructional strategies in inclusive classrooms involving cross-disability situations. With 40 scholarly publications, he serves as editor to the *Journal of National Convention of Educators of the Deaf.* He has been honoured with the 'Eunice Shriver Kennedy Award' from Special Olympics, the 'Derozio Award' from Indian Council of Secondary Education and the Governor's Award for Excellence in Services to Persons with Disabilities.

Mary Moloney lectures in Early Childhood Studies at Mary Immaculate College, Limerick, Ireland. Her PhD research, for which she received the Mary Immaculate College Doctoral Award, 2009, examines the impact of national and international early education policies in preschool and primary contexts in Ireland. She has published in *Irish Educational Studies*, the *European Early Childhood Research Journal*, *NZ Research in Early Childhood Education Journal* and *3–13 Education*. She is currently a member of a research team, comprising Mary Immaculate College and Dublin Institute of Technology, funded by the Irish Research Council, to undertake a national study on school readiness in Ireland.

Jean-Baptiste Quillien is a PhD student in Educational Psychology at the University of Minnesota, in Cognition and Learning track. He has worked in both France and the United States as a physical education, Latin and French teacher in early childhood and in K-12 multicultural settings. His main research interests are agile thinking, learning and cognition, second language acquisition, bilingualism, multiculturalism and creativity in the classroom.

Veronica R. Quillien is the founder of 'The Metamorphosis Project®', an after-school programme geared towards promoting early college readiness among students from disadvantaged backgrounds. She holds a Bachelor's degree in Speech Communication and a Master's degree in Intercultural Relations. She works with Minneapolis Parks and Recreation Board as a Community Engagement Coordinator. Her current work is focused on coordinating and leading extensive community engagement strategies for collaborative impact, which results in the delivery of high-level programmes and services. Her research interests are focused on culture, teaching and language, and immigration issues as they relate to education and adaptation.

Sushama Sharma is a Professor of Special Education at Kurukshetra University in India. She has been the Chairperson of the Department of Special Education and also Dean of the Faculty of Education, Kurukshetra University, India. Her research interests include inclusive practices, societal and teachers' attitudes towards persons with disabilities, creating awareness regarding disabilities from prevention to rehabilitation, procrastination and conscientiousness across students with disabilities.

Gabriela M. Theis works as an Associate Student Services Specialist for The University of Wisconsin Superior, United States. In this position, she assists and supports students from multicultural backgrounds with issues that are hindering their success in education as well as developing and implementing programmes to retain and graduate multicultural students. Theis holds a Master's degree in Educational Leadership, a Bachelor's degree in Computer Science and a BA degree in Language (Spanish). One of her accomplishments is implementing an after-school programme, 'The Metamorphosis Project®'.

Agnes N. Toth is an Associate Professor at Institute of Education and Psychology, University of West Hungary, having 15 years' teaching experience in Special Education and 20 years in Teacher Education. Her PhD degree deals with inclusive education of students with special needs, but she deals with teacher education and training as well. She is a member of several different professional bodies, such as Doctorate School of the University of Salerno (UNISA, Italy), Editorial Board of Alfredo Guide (Naples, Italy), Public Body of Hungarian Scientific Academy, Editorial Advisory Board of Research Journal of Manohari Devi Kanoi Girls College (MDKG, India) and Association of Hungarian Public Education Experts.